GW00994872

Eric Novotny
Editor

A .... R.

A.
be
N

Pre
CC

"
L   :e
                                                                             ıt
LIT]   )F
In a   S,
cluc   ıe
erer   at
Buf   ıls
pert   r-
McС   ıy
enc   of
is e   at
cial!   ⁊e
that
a Vi
19 ı
chaı
surv
obs   ʒy
sity

Assessing Reference and User Services in a Digital Age

Assessing Reference and User Services in a Digital Age has been co-published simultaneously as *The Reference Librarian*, Numbers 95/96 2006.

Monographic Separates from *The Reference Librarian*™

For additional information on these and other Haworth Press titles, including descriptions, tables of contents, reviews, and prices, use the QuickSearch catalog at http://www.HaworthPress.com.

Author: See *MANUSCRIPTS*, copyright page.

Assessing Reference and User Services in a Digital Age, edited by Eric Novotny, MS (No. 95/96, 2006). *Explores the impact of the Internet on the field of evaluation, focusing on electronic reference and instruction; presents research results and offers expert advice on assessing online reference and instruction.*

The Changing Face of Government Information: Providing Access in the Twenty-First Century, edited by Suhasini L. Kumar, MA, MLS (No. 94, 2006). *An examination of all aspects of providing current and future electronic access to government information.*

New Directions in Reference, edited by Byron Anderson, MA, MLIS, and Paul T. Webb, MA, MLIS (No. 93, 2006). *"An interesting collection. . . . I was especially intrigued by Harry Meserve's insider's evaluation of San José's merger of public and university library services, and Anderson's activist call for librarians to fight aspects of the Digital Millennium Copyright Act." (Andrew B. Werthheimer, PhD, Assistant Professor, Library & Information Science Program, University of Hawaii at Manoa)*

The Reference Collection: From the Shelf to the Web, edited by William J. Frost (No. 91/92, 2005). *An essential guide to collection development for electronic materials in academic and public libraries.*

Relationships Between Teaching Faculty and Teaching Librarians, edited by Susan B. Kraat (No. 89/90, 2005). *Documents the efforts of teaching librarians to establish effective communication with teaching faculty.*

Research, Reference Service, and Resources for the Study of Africa, edited by Deborah M. LaFond and Gretchen Walsh (No. 87/88, 2004). *Examines reference services in terms of Africa and libraries in both the United States and Africa.*

Animals Are the Issue: Library Resources on Animal Issues, edited by John M. Kistler, MLS, MDiv (No. 86, 2004). *Contains listings of written and electronic resources that focus on the ethics of animal treatment and use.*

Digital versus Non-Digital Reference: Ask a Librarian Online and Offline, edited by Jessamyn West, MLib (No. 85, 2004). *A librarian's guide to commercial Ask A Librarian (AskA) and tutorial services and how they compare to traditional library services.*

Cooperative Reference: Social Interaction in the Workplace, edited by Celia Hales Mabry, PhD (No. 83/84, 2003). *This informative volume focuses on effective social interactions between library co-workers, presenting perspectives, firsthand accounts, and advice from experienced and successful reference librarians.*

Outreach Services in Academic and Special Libraries, edited by Paul Kelsey, MLIS, and Sigrid Kelsey, MLIS (No. 82, 2003). *Presents an array of models and case studies for creating and implementing outreach services in academic and special library settings.*

Managing the Twenty-First Century Reference Department: Challenges and Prospects, edited by Kwasi Sarkodie-Mensah, PhD (No. 81, 2003). *An up-to-date guide on managing and maintaining a reference department in the twenty-first century.*

Digital Reference Services, edited by Bill Katz, PhD (No. 79/80, 2002/2003). *A clear and concise book explaining developments in electronic technology for reference services and their implications for reference librarians.*

The Image and Role of the Librarian, edited by Wendi Arant, MLS, and Candace R. Benefiel, MA, MLIS (No. 78, 2002). *A unique and insightful examination of how librarians are perceived–and how they perceive themselves.*

Distance Learning: Information Access and Services for Virtual Users, edited by Hemalata Iyer, PhD (No. 77, 2002). *Addresses the challenge of providing Web-based library instructional materials in a time of ever-changing technologies.*

Helping the Difficult Library Patron: New Approaches to Examining and Resolving a Long-Standing and Ongoing Problem, edited by Kwasi Sarkodie-Mensah, PhD (No. 75/76, 2002). *"Finally! A book that fills in the information cracks not covered in library school about the ubiquitous problem patron. Required reading for public service librarians." (Cheryl LaGuardia, MLS, Head of Instructional Services for the Harvard College Library, Cambridge, Massachusetts)*

Evolution in Reference and Information Services: The Impact of the Internet, edited by Di Su, MLS (No. 74, 2001). *Helps you make the most of the changes brought to the profession by the Internet.*

Doing the Work of Reference: Practical Tips for Excelling as a Reference Librarian, edited by Celia Hales Mabry, PhD (No. 72 and 73, 2001). *"An excellent handbook for reference librarians who wish to move from novice to expert. Topical coverage is extensive and is presented by the best guides possible: practicing reference librarians." (Rebecca Watson-Boone, PhD, President, Center for the Study of Information Professionals, Inc.)*

New Technologies and Reference Services, edited by Bill Katz, PhD (No. 71, 2000). *This important book explores developing trends in publishing, information literacy in the reference environment, reference provision in adult basic and community education, searching sessions, outreach programs, locating moving image materials for multimedia development, and much more.*

Reference Services for the Adult Learner: Challenging Issues for the Traditional and Technological Era, edited by Kwasi Sarkodie-Mensah, PhD (No. 69/70, 2000). *Containing research from librarians and adult learners from the United States, Canada, and Australia, this comprehensive guide offers you strategies for teaching adult patrons that will enable them to properly use and easily locate all of the materials in your library.*

Library Outreach, Partnerships, and Distance Education: Reference Librarians at the Gateway, edited by Wendi Arant and Pixey Anne Mosley (No. 67/68, 1999). *Focuses on community outreach in libraries toward a broader public by extending services based on recent developments in information technology.*

From Past-Present to Future-Perfect: A Tribute to Charles A. Bunge and the Challenges of Contemporary Reference Service, edited by Chris D. Ferguson, PhD (No. 66, 1999). *Explore reprints of selected articles by Charles Bunge, bibliographies of his published work, and original articles that draw on Bunge's values and ideas in assessing the present and shaping the future of reference service.*

Reference Services and Media, edited by Martha Merrill, PhD (No. 65, 1999). *Gives you valuable information about various aspects of reference services and media, including changes, planning issues, and the use and impact of new technologies.*

Coming of Age in Reference Services: A Case History of the Washington State University Libraries, edited by Christy Zlatos, MSLS (No. 64, 1999). *A celebration of the perseverance, ingenuity, and talent of the librarians who have served, past and present, at the Holland Library reference desk.*

Document Delivery Services: Contrasting Views, edited by Robin Kinder, MLS (No. 63, 1999). *Reviews the planning and process of implementing document delivery in four university libraries–Miami University, University of Colorado at Denver, University of Montana at Missoula, and Purdue University Libraries.*

The Holocaust: Memories, Research, Reference, edited by Robert Hauptman, PhD, and Susan Hubbs Motin (No. 61/62, 1998). *"A wonderful resource for reference librarians, students, and teachers . . . on how to present this painful, historical event." (Ephraim Kaye, PhD, The International School for Holocaust Studies, Yad Vashem, Jerusalem)*

Electronic Resources: Use and User Behavior, edited by Hemalata Iyer, PhD (No. 60, 1998). *Covers electronic resources and their use in libraries, with emphasis on the Internet and the Geographic Information Systems (GIS).*

Assessing Reference and User Services in a Digital Age

Eric Novotny, MS
Editor

Assessing Reference and User Services in a Digital Age has been co-published simultaneously as *The Reference Librarian*, Numbers 95/96 2006.

The Haworth Information Press®
An Imprint of The Haworth Press, Inc.

New York • London • Victoria (AU)
www.HaworthPress.com

Published by

The Haworth Information Press®, 10 Alice Street, Binghamton, NY 13904-1580 USA

The Haworth Information Press® is an imprint of The Haworth Press, Inc., 10 Alice Street, Binghamton, NY 13904-1580 USA.

Assessing Reference and User Services in a Digital Age has been co-published simultaneously as *The Reference Librarian*, Volume 46, Number 95/96 2006.

Cover design by Wendy Arakawa.

Library of Congress Cataloging-in-Publication Data

Assessing reference and user services in a digital age / Eric Novotny, editor.
     p. cm.
    Published also as v. 46, no. 95/96, 2006 of the Reference librarian.
    Includes bibliographical references and index.
    ISBN-13: 978-0-7890-3349-9 (alk. paper)
    ISBN-10: 0-7890-3349-6 (alk. paper)
    ISBN-13: 978-0-7890-3350-5 (pbk. : alk. paper)
    ISBN-10: 0-7890-3350-X (pbk. : alk. paper)
    1. Electronic reference services (Libraries)–Evaluation. 2. Electronic reference services (Libraries)–United States–Case studies. I. Novotny, Eric. II. Reference librarian.
Z711.45 .A77 2006
025.5'2–dc22
                                    2006002640

Indexing, Abstracting & Website/Internet Coverage

This section provides you with a list of major indexing & abstracting services and other tools for bibliographic access. That is to say, each service began covering this periodical during the year noted in the right column. Most Websites which are listed below have indicated that they will either post, disseminate, compile, archive, cite or alert their own Website users with research-based content from this work. (This list is as current as the copyright date of this publication.)

Abstracting, Website/Indexing Coverage . . . . Year When Coverage Began

- *Academic Search Premier (EBSCO)*
  <http://www.epnet.com/academic/acasearchprem.asp> **1995**

- *Advanced Polymers Abstracts (Cambridge Scientific Abstracts) <http://csa.com>* **2006**

- *Aluminum Industry Abstracts (Cambridge Scientific Abstracts)*
  <http://www.csa.com> **2006**

- *Biomeditaties (Biomedical Information of the Dutch Library Association)*
  <http://www.nvb-online.nl> **2006**

- *Cabell's Directory of Publishing Opportunities in Educational*
  Technology & Library Science <http://www.cabells.com> **2006**

- *Cambridge Scientific Abstracts (a leading publisher of scientific information*
  in print journals, online databases, CD-ROM, and via the Internet)
  <http://www.csa.com> **2006**

- *Ceramic Abstracts (Cambridge Scientific Abstracts) <http://www.csa.com>* **2006**

- *Composites Industry Abstracts (Cambridge Scientific Abstracts) <http://csa.com>* **2006**

- *Computer and Information Systems Abstracts (Cambridge Scientific Abstracts)*
  <http://www.csa.com> **2004**

- *Corrosion Abstracts (Cambridge Scientific Abstracts) <http://www.csa.com>* **2006**

- *CSA Engineering Research Database (Cambridge Scientific Abstracts)*
  <http://csa.com> **2006**

(continued)

(continued)

(continued)

*Special bibliographic notes related to special journal issues
(separates) and indexing/abstracting:*

- indexing/abstracting services in this list will also cover material in any "separate" that is co-published simultaneously with Haworth's special thematic journal issue or DocuSerial. Indexing/abstracting usually covers material at the article/chapter level.
- monographic co-editions are intended for either non-subscribers or libraries which intend to purchase a second copy for their circulating collections.
- monographic co-editions are reported to all jobbers/wholesalers/approval plans. The source journal is listed as the "series" to assist the prevention of duplicate purchasing in the same manner utilized for books-in-series.
- to facilitate user/access services all indexing/abstracting services are encouraged to utilize the co-indexing entry note indicated at the bottom of the first page of each article/chapter/contribution.
- this is intended to assist a library user of any reference tool (whether print, electronic, online, or CD-ROM) to locate the monographic version if the library has purchased this version but not a subscription to the source journal.
- individual articles/chapters in any Haworth publication are also available through the Haworth Document Delivery Service (HDDS).

Assessing Reference and User Services in a Digital Age

CONTENTS

ABOUT THE EDITOR

Eric Novotny, MS, has served as Humanities Librarian for History at Pennsylvania State University since 2001. He previously worked at the University of Illinois-Chicago as Reference Librarian, at the University of Texas at Austin as History Librarian, and at the University of Illinois as Librarian and Academic Resident. He has been an ALA committee member and committee chair and has been a presenter at ALA and SIRSI conferences. His work has appeared in the journal *College & Research Libraries*, in the Association of Research Libraries' SPEC Kit #268: Reference Service Statistics and Assessment, in the book *Evaluating References Services: A Practical Guide*, and in the Proceedings of the 4th Northumbria International Conference on Performance Measurement in Libraries and Information Services: Meaningful Measures for Emerging Realities.

IN MEMORIAM

William Katz

Dr. William (Bill) Katz passed away on September 12, 2004. Dr. Katz was Editor of the Haworth journals *The Acquisitions Librarian* and *The Reference Librarian* as well as *Magazines for Libraries*, *RQ* (the journal of the Reference and Adult Services Division of the American Library Association), and the "Magazines" column in *Library Journal*. In addition to his contributions to library science as an author and editor, he was a much-beloved professor in the School of Information Science and Policy at the State University of New York at Albany and a mentor to many of his former students in their professional lives. His association with The Haworth Press began in 1980 and lasted more than two decades. His steady hand, friendly guidance, and steadfast leadership will be missed by all of us at *The Acquisitions Librarian*, *The Reference Librarian*, and The Haworth Press.

Preface

This book explores evaluation of reference services from a variety of perspectives. The scope of reference services is broadly defined to include traditional reference as well as instructional activities provided online.

The chapters are as rich and varied as the backgrounds of the authors. Experienced researchers provide results of studies conducted to determine the nature and effectiveness of online reference services offered by libraries. Practitioners and administrators from different institutional settings (academic libraries, public libraries, consortiums, etc. . . .) provide their perspectives on the issues facing librarians seeking to assess their electronic services. Approaches vary from case studies of individual libraries to discussions of the best methods and approaches. A major theme that emerges is the need to develop standards by which libraries can assess their individual performances in a larger context. The articles contained in this work make significant contributions to this ongoing discussion.

Eric Novotny

[Haworth co-indexing entry note]: "Preface." Novotny, Eric. Co-published simultaneously in *The Reference Librarian* (The Haworth Information Press, an imprint of The Haworth Press, Inc.) No. 95/96, 2006, p. xxi; and: *Assessing Reference and User Services in a Digital Age* (ed: Eric Novotny) The Haworth Information Press, an imprint of The Haworth Press, Inc., 2006, p. xvii. Single or multiple copies of this article are available for a fee from The Haworth Document Delivery Service [1-800-HAWORTH, 9:00 a.m. - 5:00 p.m. (EST). E-mail address: docdelivery@haworthpress.com].

Available online at http://ref.haworthpress.com
xvii

Introduction

Eric Novotny

In 2001 I published an article on evaluating electronic reference[1] in which I noted the scarcity of research devoted to electronic reference, and the subsequent lack of standards for evaluating such services. As libraries scrambled to establish new virtual reference points, no consensus had emerged regarding how to evaluate these new services, either from a methodological, efficiency, or a quality perspective. If at that time the evaluation of e-reference was in its infancy, it would be fair to characterize the current environment as the "adolescent phase." Like a gawky teenager, the field is growing in unexpected ways, and is finding its voice, albeit not yet a fully mature one.

The essays contained here reflect the multiplicity of approaches that characterize our evaluative efforts today. Reflecting their diverse backgrounds, the authors explore evaluation of reference services from a variety of perspectives. Andrew Briedenbaugh discusses the planning process used at a public library in Florida for implementing a new chat service. He offers advice on how public libraries can build a case for the new service, and suggests which data should be collected. Buff Hirko reports on efforts to create a Virtual Evaluation Toolkit for use by Washington's statewide Virtual Reference Project, a multi-type library consortium, while Ruth Vondracek shares the experiences of a university library when entering a state-wide e-reference consortium. She offers advice and issues to consider before committing to such a partnership while concluding that OSU has benefited from the cooperative arrange-

[Haworth co-indexing entry note]: "Introduction." Novotny, Eric. Co-published simultaneously in *The Reference Librarian* (The Haworth Information Press, an imprint of The Haworth Press, Inc.) No. 95/96, 2006, pp. 1-3; and: *Assessing Reference and User Services in a Digital Age* (ed: Eric Novotny) The Haworth Information Press, an imprint of The Haworth Press, Inc., 2006, pp. 1-3. Single or multiple copies of this article are available for a fee from The Haworth Document Delivery Service [1-800-HAWORTH, 9:00 a.m. - 5:00 p.m. (EST). E-mail address: docdelivery@haworthpress.com].

Available online at http://ref.haworthpress.com
doi:10.1300/J120v46n95_01

ment. The librarians from San Jose State University (Lauren Miranda Gilbert, Mengxiong Liu, Toby Matoush, and Jo Bell Whitlatch), a unique combined public and academic library, discuss the criteria they plan to use to assess their joint services. They offer a model for evaluating electronic reference services that can be used in either public or academic library settings.

As noted by M. Kathleen Kern in her article on wholistic evaluation, the growth in evaluation is fueled in part by the ready availability of transcripts. The automatic capturing of the entire reference transaction has generated a mini-Renaissance in reference evaluation. The analysis of chat transcripts is a key component of many of the studies in this collection, including Joseph Fennewald's comparisons of question categories for in-person and online reference transactions, and Lesley M. Moyo's analysis of the use of instruction in the virtual environment. Chat transcript analysis helped Caleb Tucker-Raymond and Loree Hyde develop a set of quality measures for chat reference. Their analysis offers data on which aspects of chat reference library staff are performing well at, and which areas we need to improve upon. This data will be especially useful for ongoing training conversations with staff providing reference services online.

In addition to chat transcript analysis, libraries continue to employ a creative mix of strategies to explore their services. Laurie Probst and Michael Pelikan report on the use of a "Tell Us What You Think" button to gather user feedback during a time of system migration. In a valuable research study Kirsti Nilsen and Catherine Sheldrick Ross asked library school students to submit a reference question online and report on their experiences. The students' comments and perspectives provide a useful look from the "other side" of the e-reference transaction. Based on their analysis of the student's reports, the authors are able to recommend specific "Do's" and "Dont's" for virtual and e-mail reference service providers.

For those seeking additional techniques there is no shortage of advice on how to approach an evaluation of your library's e-mail or chat service. M. Kathleen Kern advocates taking a wholistic approach to evaluation. This involves integrating evaluation of your virtual and traditional reference services. Librarians from San Jose State offer a detailed description of their plans to evaluate their combined public/academic library environment, while Melissa Gross, Charles R. McClure, and R. David Lankes suggest measures to determine the cost/benefits of your virtual reference service and offer direction toward developing a general cost model for information services.

As is the case in many reference departments, the scope of reference services for this issue is broadly defined to include reference as well as instructional activities provided online. The librarians at Utah State University describe how they developed an online instructional module based on user needs. Their conclusion is that students want fast, easy information–they think they are good searchers, and they confuse speed and convenience with accuracy or ease of use. The implications of these findings for public service and Web designers are discussed. Lesley M. Moyo provides an analysis of the amount and type of instruction provided in online reference encounters. She compares this to in-person reference to determine whether the rate and nature of library instruction varies by the medium in which the reference interaction takes place.

While the essays in this volume are impressive in the breadth and depth of topics they explore, there are still many unresolved issues in the field of evaluating electronic reference services. As yet there is no consensus on standards. This makes it difficult to truly compare an individual library's performance. This is changing slowly. To help readers act on the models offered here, contributors were asked to include the instruments they used in their studies. Buff Hirko provides a Virtual Evaluation Toolkit, while Caleb Tucker-Raymond has developed nineteen quality measures based on an analysis of chat transcripts from the Oregon statewide reference service. Other authors provide sample surveys or other instruments they have used or recommend. It is hoped that the publication of these studies, and the inclusion of the instruments that have been developed, will encourage replication so that the profession can build on the insights from these papers.

NOTE

1. Novotny, Eric. "Evaluating electronic reference services: Issues, approaches and criteria." *The Reference Librarian* no. 74 (2001) pp. 103-20.

doi:10.1300/J120v46n95_01

LIBRARY CASE STUDIES
AND RESEARCH RESULTS

Benchmarking Librarian Performance
in Chat Reference

Loree Hyde
Caleb Tucker-Raymond

SUMMARY. Librarians participating in Oregon's collaborative statewide virtual reference project used an analysis of chat reference transcripts to evaluate librarian performance. doi:10.1300/J120v46n95_02 *[Article copies available for a fee from The Haworth Document Delivery Service: 1-800-HAWORTH. E-mail address: <docdelivery@haworthpress.com> Website: <http://www.HaworthPress.com> © 2006 by The Haworth Press, Inc. All rights reserved.]*

KEYWORDS. Virtual reference, chat reference, evaluation, assessment, transcripts

Loree Hyde is affiliated with the Oregon Institute of Technology. Caleb Tucker-Raymond is affiliated with the Multnomah County Library.

[Haworth co-indexing entry note]: "Benchmarking Librarian Performance in Chat Reference." Hyde, Loree, and Caleb Tucker-Raymond. Co-published simultaneously in *The Reference Librarian* (The Haworth Information Press, an imprint of The Haworth Press, Inc.) No. 95/96, 2006, pp. 5-19; and: *Assessing Reference and User Services in a Digital Age* (ed: Eric Novotny) The Haworth Information Press, an imprint of The Haworth Press, Inc., 2006, pp. 5-19. Single or multiple copies of this article are available for a fee from The Haworth Document Delivery Service [1-800-HAWORTH, 9:00 a.m. - 5:00 p.m. (EST). E-mail address: docdelivery@haworthpress.com].

Two of the hallmarks of librarianship are that we believe we are better searchers than most patrons and that we have rigorous tests for the authority of the information we find. The first is part of the impetus for providing a chat reference service at all, but when our digital reference exit surveys tell us our patrons are satisfied 85 percent of the time, the second forces us to question our data and to make sure we have an accurate way of measuring our performance. This article describes our efforts to measure librarian performance in chat reference by using use transcript analysis.

BACKGROUND

Oregon's statewide digital reference service, L-net, is a collaborative service provided by 23 library systems in the state and available to all of its citizens. We provide a live chat service, offered 48 hours a week, and an e-mail reference service, offered all the time. Demand for the service has not been overwhelming; we have had an average of 228 chat reference sessions (our software does not give us an easy way to count the actual number of questions asked in each chat reference session) and 159 e-mail reference questions per month over the 12-month period between October 2003 and September 2004.

Partner libraries include large academic institutions, community colleges, school libraries, and public libraries of all sizes. Our partner libraries also represent our geographic diversity, which has been important because we aim to serve people living in every corner of the state, and having local expertise and enthusiasts has made that possible.

L-net staff are mostly MLS-or-equivalent-holding librarians, with the exceptions being individuals from our largest (Multnomah County Library, Portland) and smallest (Malheur County Library, Ontario) participating public libraries. We do not consider holding an MLS or equivalent to be a requirement for providing the service, but do expect that staff perform reference service on a regular basis.

Our service was launched in April 2003 as a pilot project called Answerland. The pilot project had pressure to launch the service before the end of the school year, and as a result we put off developing some important policies until August, 2003. Representative teams of librarians from our partner libraries created a privacy policy, developed service guidelines, re-named the service, decided what to do about reimbursing librarians, reviewed our choice of vendor, and assessed the service. The assessment team that worked on evaluating chat transcripts consisted of the authors of this article.

The service's original evaluation tool consisted of a survey which popped up on each patron's screen at the end of a chat reference session. Based on this exit survey, we found that our patrons have been overwhelmingly satisfied with our chat reference service. Eighty-five percent of respondents say they were satisfied with the answer they received, and only four percent said they would not use the service again. This seemed too good to be true, so we investigated.

We looked at the results of the survey, and found that only one in five patrons were filling it out. Several reasons could account for this lack of response: patron browsers could be blocking the pop-up window from appearing, technical difficulties could prevent some patrons from reaching the end of their session, and some patrons probably just refused to fill out the survey. Data from questions such as "How easy was it to understand the librarian's responses?" which asked the patron to rate the service on a scale of one to seven, showed that very few respondents (seven percent) gave us a rating of three, four, or five. In general, the patrons who filled out the survey rated us either highly or lowly. We were missing almost everyone in between who might have had a mediocre experience.

We decided that a better way to measure our service would be to compare librarian performance with the service guidelines our services team had created in August 2003 (http://www.oregonlibraries.net/staff/docs/service_guidelines.shtml). A sticky problem was that the guidelines had not been very well promoted. They weren't announced until the following spring, around the same time we conducted this study. Could we really expect librarians to follow a set of standards they might not know about? No, but we could create a benchmark for our performance and use it as a standard to measure our success in the future.

As evaluators, we found that our guidelines were not written with assessment in mind. Some were so straightforward we could use a computer program to measure them ("The librarian should send the welcome message when they connect to the patron"), while others seemed nearly impossible to measure ("The librarian should strive for a hybrid of instruction and giving answers"). Many guidelines could be measured with a good look at the chat transcript, but how can we accurately determine what a librarian was striving for?

We went over our guidelines and placed them in three categories: those that could be measured with an automatic process, those that could not be measured, and those that could be measured with transcript evaluation.

Some of the guidelines posed a difficulty because they relied on information that was not recorded in the transcript. For example, one guideline asks that librarians do preliminary searching in another window, but we had no way of knowing if the librarian did this or not, unless the librarian stated it explicitly in the transcript. Since these facets of the transaction were not recorded in our transcripts, we did not try to hold librarians to these guidelines.

To evaluate librarian performance based on our guidelines, we decided on a checklist of measures, based on example checklists from New Jersey's Q and A NJ service (http://www.qandanj.org/manual/ checklist.htm) and the now-defunct LSSI Green Awards, which rewarded librarians who performed exceptionally well in chat reference. Our checklist (http://www.oregonlibraries.net/staff/docs/evaluate.shtml) asked if each measure was met (yes), not met (no), or not applicable (n/a) for this transcript.

Table 1 lists each of our service guidelines, which category we placed it in (can be measured with an automatic process, cannot be measured, and can be measured with transcript evaluation), and which measure on our checklist the guideline is related to. Our checklist of measures is in the Appendix to this article.

One of our guidelines ambiguously states that librarians should follow the RUSA Guidelines for Behavioral Performance of Reference and Information Service Providers (http://www.ala.org/ala/rusa/ rusaprotools/referenceguide/guidelinesbehavioral.htm), but these guidelines are so robust, it would be cumbersome to try to measure each facet. From RUSA's document, we identified seven specific guidelines which applied to chat reference and were important to our service, making up measures three to nine on our checklist.

Other service guidelines were combined into single measures, so in the process we ended up modifying some wording to help the guidelines fit into our checklist model.

There were also two guidelines which could only be measured with transcript evaluation that we chose to ignore:

> *Librarians should seek to answer questions with quality Web sources.* We used paper worksheets and face-to-face conversation to conduct our evaluations. Evaluating online sources would take extra time and the use of a computer. It is important to use high quality and authoritative sources to answer any reference question,

but we felt a rigorous focus on sources would distract from comparing librarian performance to our service guidelines.

Librarians should expect appropriate behavior from the patron and respond with the pre-written script provided for dealing with inappropriate behavior. The librarian should then disconnect if the patron's behavior continues not to meet appropriate standards. We chose to acknowledge that prank calls happen by making a category for them on our evaluation worksheet, but decided that responding to prank calls was not a core component of our service.

Based on our sample checklists, we also added a measure that had not been included in our guidelines, *The patron expressed satisfaction* (measure 15). This is the only measure we used that examines patron behavior, and we thought it was important to look at in relation to librarian behavior.

Our final transcript evaluation form had 19 measures to be considered for assessment, with the subheadings *Behavior Guidelines*, *RUSA Guidelines for Behavioral Performance*, *Digital Reference Guidelines*, and *Conditional Situations*.

At first, we worried that we had included too many guidelines and that the process would become too time consuming. After a dry run, we found reading transcripts to be the time-consuming part, and in the end kept all 19 measures, as we felt that they were all equally important.

Holding on to a mission and a method, we had no idea how to determine success. We had nine months of questions to work with, but a scarce few of them were answered by a librarian with an awareness of our service guidelines. We decided that the best way to proceed was to perform our process on a sample of transcripts taken after the guidelines were published and to use the result as a benchmark for future evaluations.

It was also apparent from the dry run that we would want to categorize the transcripts themselves to help us analyze the resulting data. We chose to divide the questions as follows: *reference, local library question, obscene/harassment* (later re-labeled *prank*), *technical problem,* and *follow-up* (for instances of when a patron connects more than once asking the same question). We were definitely interested in exactly how many questions were "reference" and how many were local library policy questions. Creating a few more categories helped us get a more accurate picture of librarian behavior. For example, a librarian dealing with a patron who had disconnected and later re-connected should not be expected to start with a fresh reference interview.

TABLE 1. L-Net Service Guidelines, Evaluation Category and Related Checklist Measure.

Guideline	Category	Checklist Measure
Calls should be answered as quickly as possible.	Can be measured with an automatic process.	
Librarians should send a welcome message immediately to the patron.	Whether or not the welcome message is sent can be measured with an automatic process. Immediacy can not be measured.	
Librarians should quickly review the patron's question and location.	Cannot be measured.	
If the patron's question indicates that they believe they have contacted a local library, briefly explain that the service is staffed by librarians from all over Oregon.	Cannot be measured.	
Librarians should engage in a brief reference interview if the question is not clear.	Can be measured by transcript evaluation.	1
Librarians should use interpersonal communication practices that promote effective provision of reference service (RUSA Guidelines for Behavioral Performance of Reference and Information Services).	Can be measured by transcript evaluation, but more specific measures may be helpful.	3, 4, 5, 6, 7, 8, 9
The librarian should frequently let the user know what she is doing. If the search takes time, keep the patron informed.	Cannot be measured.	
Answers for most quick factual information should be provided in approximately 15 minutes at the time of service.	Cannot be measured.	
Librarians should chat in a friendly and professional manner designed to make the patron feel at ease.	Can be measured by transcript evaluation.	2
Librarians should strive for a hybrid combination of instruction and "giving answers."	Cannot be measured.	13
Librarian should encourage the development of the patron's information seeking behavior by providing some instructional guidance.	Can be measured by transcript evaluation.	13
Librarians should use chat communication techniques to keep the patron engaged.	Can be measured by transcript evaluation.	
Information should be sent in small pieces, not large paragraphs.	Can be measured by transcript evaluation.	12
Librarians should be familiar with and use the bookmarked sites and pre-written scripts available to them whenever possible to facilitate an efficient transaction.	Can be measured with an automatic process.	11

Guideline	Category	Checklist Measure
Appropriate use of spelling and grammar is expected while striking a balance between speed and professionalism.	Speed cannot be measured. Professionalism and appropriate use of spelling and grammar can be measured by transcript evaluation.	2
Librarian should explain what they are planning to do before they execute a search or visit a link.	Can be measured by transcript evaluation.	10
Responses should include an explanation of the librarian's search process or strategy for finding the information.	Can be measured by transcript evaluation.	13
Librarian should conduct searches in a separate browser window in order to limit patron confusion.	Cannot be measured.	
Librarians should seek to answer questions with quality Web sources.	Can be measured by transcript evaluation.	
Librarian should use the patron's "home" library to answer library-specific questions or to acquaint the patron with local resources.	Cannot be measured.	
Resources quoted or used should be fully cited.	Can be measured by transcript evaluation.	14
Legal, medical, and statistical information should not be interpreted. Librarians should indicate that they are unable to provide an interpretation.	Can be measured by transcript evaluation.	16
Questions about local library services that are unable to be answered using the library's Web site should be referred to that library using the RefTracker system.	Can be measured by transcript evaluation.	17
Questions requiring specialized knowledge or resources that are not available to the librarian should be referred to a specialist using the RefTracker system.	Can be measured by transcript evaluation.	18
Librarians should keep the user informed about any technical problems.	Cannot be measured.	
During busy service times, librarians should indicate that there may be a delay in response and offer to respond to the question later.	Cannot be measured.	19
During busy service times, librarians should seek help from other librarians in Oregon through instant messaging software.	Cannot be measured.	
Librarians should expect appropriate behavior from the patron and respond with the pre-written script provided for dealing with inappropriate behavior. The Librarian should then disconnect if the patron's behavior continues not to meet appropriate standards.	Can be measured by transcript evaluation.	

It was important to us to include as many librarians in the evaluation process as possible. We needed librarians as a labor source for reading and evaluating transcripts and also felt that the exercise would be a good way to familiarize librarians with our service guidelines. It could also help librarians to begin thinking about what worked well in the chat environment and, for those who had answered only a few or no questions, expose them to a broader range of chat reference interactions. Finally, as a statewide project, it made sense to make the exercise as participatory as possible. We took the show on the road and involved staff from eight libraries around the state (Multnomah County Library, Portland State University, Oregon State University, University of Oregon, Eugene Public Library, Jackson County Library Services, Oregon Institute of Technology, and Corvallis-Benton County Library).

Evaluators were given consistent instructions for the assessment process, but because of the number of evaluators involved, we expected analysis of transcripts to be highly subjective and encouraged librarians to work together on the process. Most transcripts were read, discussed by groups of two people, and given a single evaluation. Other transcripts were read and evaluated by an individual.

In retrospect, it would have been more accurate to have each transcript evaluated two or three times by different evaluators, for consistency in interpretation of the service guidelines.

The service is usually staffed by a single librarian, with each library taking up to two two-hour shifts each week. For this reason, there can be as many as 48 different librarians staffing the service in a two-week period. We took a sample of a full two weeks of chat reference transcripts (143 transcripts) to cover this breadth.

To assure anonymity, we stripped personal information about each librarian and patron from the transcript, and removed any e-mail addresses in the transcript. To make the process more manageable, we printed them out. It was one of the few digital reference activities we have done that does not involve working at a computer.

RESULTS

After the evaluation sheets were marked for each transcript, we entered the data into a spreadsheet and counted how often each guideline was met, how often it was not met when it could have been, and how often the guideline was not applicable. We scored each measure by counting the percentage of times a guideline was met in an applicable situation. Excluding transcripts where a guideline was not applicable in our overall score gives us a more accurate picture of how well librarians are performing. For example, with measure 9, *The librarian encouraged the patron to contribute ideas while searching*, we are only interested in knowing if the librarian met this measure when a search was performed.

Table 2 represents the tabulated results of our analysis, showing the text and number of the measure, the number of times (of 143) that the librarian met the measure, the number of times they did not, the number of times the measure was not applicable, what percentage of the time the measure was met when it was applicable, and how often it was applicable overall. For measures 3 to 9, the number in parentheses indicates which specific RUSA guideline that the measure relates to.

It turned out that the applicability of each guideline was highly variable, with measures being applicable in anywhere from 8.4 percent to 90.2 percent of chat reference transcripts. Many participants asked, "When is a reference interview *not* applicable?" and later found themselves checking Not Applicable for measure 2 when they came across a straightforward question such as "What time does the Philomath Library close today?" Our overall analysis includes technical problems and prank calls, which are also situations where a reference interview may not be necessary.

ANALYSIS

Counting all measures equally, L-net librarians met service guidelines in 62.4 percent of applicable situations. Librarians met the guidelines more often when applying chat techniques to the reference interview, such as alerting the patron that a Web page is being sent, keeping messages brief, and citing print sources (measures 10 to 12). Librarians scored generally met the guidelines less often than the overall average when applying RUSA guidelines to the digital reference interview.

Of the seven measures we identified (measures 3 to 9), librarians met our guidelines more often than the overall average for only measure 3, *The librarian signaled an initial understanding of the patron's needs*. Other guidelines were met less often, with measure 8, *The librarian identified and stated search qualifiers that may limit results such as date, language, comprehensiveness, etc.*, being met only 37.5 percent of the time. A simple explanation for this bizarrely low score is that, as we

TABLE 2. Tabulated Results of Transcript Evaluation Measures.

Measure	Yes	No	n/a	% yes of applicable	% applicable
1. The librarian engaged in a reference interview.	77	42	24	64.7%	83.2%
2. The librarian chatted in a friendly and professional manner, e.g., avoided jargon and refrained from interjecting value judgements about the nature of the question.	108	21	14	83.7%	90.2%
3. The librarian signaled an initial understanding of the patron's needs. (2.4)	86	41	16	67.7%	88.8%
4. The librarian rephrased the patron's question or request and asks for confirmation to ensure that it is understood. (3.4)	47	69	27	40.5%	81.1%
5. The librarian asked open-ended questions to encourage the patron to expand the request or present additional information. (3.5)	52	51	40	50.5%	72.0%
6. The librarian used closed and/or clarifying questions to refine the search query or to clarify confusing terminology. (3.6)	53	43	47	55.2%	67.1%
7. The librarian broke the search query into specific facets. (4.0)	41	37	65	52.6%	54.5%
8. The librarian identified and stated search qualifiers that may limit results such as date, language, comprehensiveness, etc. (4.3)	21	35	87	37.5%	39.2%
9. The librarian encouraged the patron to contribute ideas while searching. (4.10)	44	39	60	53.0%	58.0%
10. The librarian sent messages to the patron between sending Web pages.	69	18	56	79.3%	60.8%
11. The librarian and patron maintained a two-sided conversation.	101	23	19	81.5%	86.7%
12. The librarian sent information in small pieces.	97	14	32	87.4%	77.6%
13. The librarian offered or provided some instructional guidance, including the search process or strategy.	33	71	39	31.7%	72.7%
14. The librarian fully cited resources, unless authorship was otherwise indicated. (Web pages pushed do not need to be cited.)	21	12	110	63.6%	23.1%

Measure	Yes	No	n/a	% yes of applicable	% applicable
15. The patron indicated satisfaction before the librarian ended the call.	72	44	27	62.1%	81.1%
16. Legal, medical and statistical information was not interpreted.	12	0	131	100.0%	8.4%
17. Questions requiring detailed information from the patron's "home" library were referred.	13	9	121	59.1%	15.4%
18. Questions requiring detailed information from an in-depth resource unavailable to the librarian were referred.	13	4	126	76.5%	11.9%
19. If the librarian was too busy to take the call right away, the question was referred.	6	9	128	40.0%	10.5%
Total	966	582	1,169	62.4%	57.0%

said above, we did not promote the service guidelines or the RUSA guidelines to librarian staff.

Librarians also scored well when there was little room to ignore or misinterpret a guideline. Measure 16, *Legal, Medical and Statistical information was not interpreted*, scored the highest with librarians meeting it 100 percent of the time it was applicable.

Because of the collaborative nature of our service, librarians staffing the service will most likely work with patrons familiar with libraries other than the librarian's own. Librarians scored poorly in guidelines that applied to these situations, including referring questions when appropriate (measures 17 and 19) and providing some instructional guidance (measure 13).

We also summarized the data by question type, as identified by the transcript analyzers. Table 3 shows the percentage of time each measure was met in applicable situations, broken down for our seven categories. Except for "reference," most categories have too little data to take too seriously. We found that librarians scored consistently better when the question was categorized as a "local library question" as opposed to all questions.

ADDITIONAL FINDINGS

Besides benchmarking for progress and future use, we found that the study gave us some insights into the study that we may not have otherwise thought of.

TABLE 3. Percentage of Time Librarians Met Each Measure, When Applicable, by Category. Some Chat Transcripts Were Placed in More Than One Category.

	Category						
Measure	Reference n = 116	Local n = 16	Librarian Busy n = 7	Dropped n = 17	Follow-up n = 10	Technical Problem n = 16	Prank n = 6
1	65.7%	64.3%	33.3%	41.7%	62.5%	66.7%	83.3%
2	85.2%	93.3%	100.0%	75.0%	80.0%	54.5%	80.0%
3	69.4%	73.3%	50.0%	50.0%	70.0%	70.0%	100.0%
4	43.4%	41.7%	0.0%	27.3%	50.0%	55.6%	25.0%
5	52.8%	57.1%	33.3%	11.1%	62.5%	42.9%	75.0%
6	54.3%	90.0%	66.7%	37.5%	28.6%	28.6%	40.0%
7	52.3%	100.0%	66.7%	28.6%	62.5%	37.5%	0.0%
8	37.0%	80.0%	0.0%	0.0%	0.0%	0.0%	50.0%
9	52.8%	80.0%	50.0%	12.5%	33.3%	42.9%	50.0%
10	80.6%	81.8%	100.0%	85.7%	60.0%	62.5%	50.0%
11	80.2%	100.0%	100.0%	41.7%	66.7%	77.8%	66.7%
12	88.5%	100.0%	100.0%	81.8%	80.0%	77.8%	66.7%
13	33.0%	45.5%	66.7%	0.0%	42.9%	28.6%	33.3%
14	65.5%	66.7%	0.0%	66.7%	50.0%	66.7%	n/a
15	62.2%	93.3%	100.0%	11.1%	0.0%	14.3%	25.0%
16	100.0%	100.0%	n/a	n/a	100.0%	100.0%	n/a
17	71.4%	33.3%	0.0%	n/a	n/a	100.0%	n/a
18	75.0%	n/a	50.0%	50.0%	50.0%	50.0%	n/a
19	40.0%	0.0%	33.3%	n/a	100.0%	n/a	n/a
Average	63.3%	75.8%	65.5%	39.1%	54.9%	52.5%	58.0%

A cross tabulation of measures 1 (*The librarian engaged in a reference interview*) and 15 (*The patron indicated satisfaction before the librarian ended the call*) revealed that patrons expressed satisfaction 65 percent of the time when a reference interview was done but only 53 percent when one was not done. When a reference interview was not necessary, 75 percent of the patrons expressed satisfaction. Table 4 shows the number of times the patron expressed satisfaction when a ref-

TABLE 4. Patron Satisfaction vs. Reference Interview.

Patron Expresses Satisfaction

		Yes	No	n/a	% yes of app.
Reference Interview?	**Yes** (n = 77)	45	24	8	65.2%
	No (n = 42)	21	18	3	53.8%
	N/a (n = 24)	6	2	16	75.0%

erence interview was done, when it was not, and when it was not applicable.

Similarly, a cross-tabulation of measure 1 and an overall score revealed that librarians who conduct reference interviews tend to follow other service guidelines as well, while librarians who do not conduct reference interviews did not follow the service guidelines. Table 5 compares measure 1 in a given transcript to the overall score for that transcript.

We were interested in how many calls were reference (81.1 percent) and how many were local policy questions (10.5 percent), and also found out how many were pranks (4.2 percent) and how many were dropped calls (14.7 percent). Some questions fit more than one category.

ASSESSING THE EVALUATION PROCESS

The transcript evaluation exercise turned out to be a valuable learning experience for librarians who participated. They left the exercise understanding the service guidelines better, with firsthand examples of what worked and what did not.

At the close of each evaluation session, we asked the transcript evaluators to fill out a brief survey. Ninety-one percent of evaluation participants said that the exercise would help to provide better digital reference service. This is a figure we *can* believe because we made sure each participant filled out the survey.

In regard to the evaluative process, the majority felt that the instructions were clear, but that some of the guidelines were not. As a result, the measure called into question most frequently (measure 8, *The librarian identified and stated search qualifiers that may limit results such as date, language, comprehensiveness, etc.*) will be eliminated

TABLE 5. Reference Interview vs. Overall Score.

| | | Overall compliance with service guidelines | | | |
		Yes	No	n/a	% yes of app.
Reference Interview?	Yes (n = 77)	636	231	519	73.3%
	No (n = 42)	173	281	297	38.1%
	n/a (n = 24)	80	23	330	77.7%

from future evaluations. Evaluators also expressed interest in seeing the patron's demographic information that was available to the librarian during the transaction, such as their library affiliation and whether the patron indicated that she was a student.

It was apparent in our evaluation sessions that librarians enjoyed reading the transcripts and that they learned from them. Staff gained insight into the range of possible virtual reference interactions, how to handle different situations, techniques for meeting our chat reference guidelines, and some learned a few new online sources. They might be better virtual reference librarians already, but our immediate need is to set actual goals for improvement and talk about what we can do to achieve them. Our benchmarking process is only useful if we perform more evaluations to compare our performance as we grow as a service and as professionals.

APPENDIX

For measures 3 to 9, the number in parentheses indicates which specific RUSA guideline the measure relates to.

Transcript no.   **Categories:** Reference Question/Local Service Question/ Dropped/Follow-up/Librarian Busy/Technical Problem/Prank

1. The librarian engaged in a reference interview.
2. The librarian chatted in a friendly and professional manner, e.g., avoided jargon and refrained from interjecting value judgements about the nature of the question.
3. The librarian signaled an initial understanding of the patron's needs. (2.4)
4. The librarian rephrased the patron's question or request and asked for confirmation to ensure that it was understood. (3.4)
5. The librarian asked open-ended questions to encourage the patron to expand the request or present additional information. (3.5)
6. The librarian used closed and/or clarifying questions to refine the search query or to clarify confusing terminology. (3.6)
7. The librarian broke the search query into specific facets. (4.0)
8. The librarian identified and stated search qualifiers that might limit results such as date, language, comprehensiveness, etc. (4.3)
9. The librarian encouraged the patron to contribute ideas while searching. (4.10)

DIGITAL REFERENCE GUIDELINES

10. The librarian sent messages to the patron between sending Web pages.
11. The librarian and patron maintained a two-sided conversation.
12. The librarian sent information in small pieces.
13. The librarian offered or provided some instructional guidance, including the search process or strategy.
14. The librarian fully cited resources, unless authorship was otherwise indicated. (Web pages pushed do not need to be cited.)
15. The patron indicated satisfaction before the librarian ended the call.

CONDITIONAL SITUATIONS

16. Legal, medical and statistical information were not interpreted.
17. Questions requiring detailed information from the patron's "home" library were referred.
18. Questions requiring detailed information from an in-depth resource unavailable to the librarian were referred.
19. If the librarian was too busy to take the call right away, the question was referred.

Same Questions, Different Venue:
An Analysis of In-Person
and Online Questions

Joseph Fennewald

SUMMARY. This study applied traditional categories used for classifying questions presented at reference desks to online reference services. Questions presented at Penn State's subject libraries were classified as 'Where Is,' 'Troubleshooting,' 'Policy and Service,' and 'Reference.' Definitions and examples were provided to the librarians and staff covering thirteen reference desks. These categories were then applied to Penn State's e-mail and chat reference transactions for the Fall 2002 semester. Although the types of questions were similar across the three services, there were differences in the proportion of questions by categories. This suggests that services have similar, yet distinct, functions and that the type of questions submitted differ between in-person and online and also between e-mail and chat. doi:10.1300/J120v46n95_03 *[Article copies available for a fee from The Haworth Document Delivery Service: 1-800-HAWORTH. E-mail address: <docdelivery@haworthpress.com> Website: <http://www.HaworthPress.com> © 2006 by The Haworth Press, Inc. All rights reserved.]*

KEYWORDS. Question analysis, classification schemes, reference services, e-mail reference, virtual reference

Joseph Fennewald is Head Librarian, Penn State University–Hazleton Campus.

[Haworth co-indexing entry note]: "Same Questions, Different Venue: An Analysis of In-Person and Online Questions." Fennewald, Joseph. Co-published simultaneously in *The Reference Librarian* (The Haworth Information Press, an imprint of The Haworth Press, Inc.) No. 95/96, 2006, pp. 21-35; and: *Assessing Reference and User Services in a Digital Age* (ed: Eric Novotny) The Haworth Information Press, an imprint of The Haworth Press, Inc., 2006, pp. 21-35. Single or multiple copies of this article are available for a fee from The Haworth Document Delivery Service [1-800-HAWORTH, 9:00 a.m. - 5:00 p.m. (EST). E-mail address: docdelivery@haworthpress.com].

INTRODUCTION

Communication by e-mail and chat has become common place. Libraries have responded by developing online reference services–ways for users to communicate their information needs by e-mail or through chat. Initially, they offered e-mail reference services to respond to questions needing short, factual responses. These services have expanded, however, and users are no longer restricted in the types of questions they can submit. Likewise, chat reference services have developed from simple 'instant messaging' to include Web site co-browsing. Librarians have been enthusiastic about these new developments. Reports in the literature and conferences on online reference services are frequent.[1] Libraries are now evaluating the effectiveness of these services.

This article explores the differences between transactions at reference desks and online reference sessions, examining the questions submitted in-person with those posed in e-mail and through chat online sessions. It tests how well traditional categories used to classify questions presented at reference desks apply to questions submitted online. Question analysis provides valuable information which can be used to measure workload, set staffing levels, monitor use patterns, and submit aggregate numbers to the Association of Research Libraries.[2] Analyses of the transcripts recording questions and answers provide richer data. By reviewing transcripts, it is possible to identify the difficulties library users encountered, the skills and knowledge needed by librarians covering these services, the databases used, and the subject areas being researched. Fortunately, electronic transactions typically preserve full transcripts of the interaction between patron and librarian.

LITERATURE REVIEW

Several studies of online services have found the questions presented at reference desks to be similar to those submitted online. In their study of e-mail transactions at California State University-Chico, Diamond and Pease note that "users ask similar questions whether in person or via an e-mail reference service."[3] Foley also found that the questions "posed during chat reference were very similar to those received at the reference desks"[4] in her study of the University of Buffalo's instant messaging reference service.

Surprisingly, few studies have compared in-person with both e-mail and chat online reference questions. One exception is that of M. Kathleen

Kern reported at the Annual Reference Research Forum. In her study at the University of Illinois at Urbana-Champaign, she found that, although there were similarities in the types of questions, there were differences in the frequency in which certain types of questions were submitted online rather than in-person.[5] She developed categories inductively from the reference questions. My study also compared questions submitted in-person, e-mail, and chat but used a different methodology. I classified questions using pre-existing categories.

It is important to have well defined categories to compare services. In separate studies of chat reference services, Desai[6] and Sears[7] both classified questions using William Katz's typology of ready reference, specific search, and extended reference questions.[8] In addition to reference questions, Sears identified questions that were either library policy or directional.[9] Hodges also used traditional categories to classify e-mail questions submitted at a "large university in the Southeast." She found that "questions received by digital reference simulate those received by traditional reference services (i.e., ready reference, service/policy, information literacy, technological problems, etc.)."[10] Using traditional categories to classify online reference sessions, we can compare online with reference desk transactions.

METHODOLOGY

The reference desk data used in this study was collected from thirteen subject libraries at Penn State's University Park campus from November 3-9, 2002. During this week, the library was open 105 hours. Librarians, library staff, or student assistants provided coverage at the thirteen subject libraries whenever the library is open. The data on digital transactions were taken from the transcripts of 751 e-mail sessions and 405 chat sessions from August 27 to December 20, 2002. Penn State's online reference services can be accessed from the library's home page under the heading 'Get Help!' The online services also appear in the library's catalog as 'Ask.' Users can submit an e-mail question at any time. The chat service, known as the Virtual Reference Service (VRS), is available thirty-nine hours per week (Sunday, 6-9 p.m.; Monday-Thursday, 3 p.m.-12 a.m.). A reference librarian reviews all e-mail questions and answers them directly or refers them to a subject specialist or technical assistant. The VRS is covered only by reference librarians who do so from a computer in the library or their home, at the main campus or one of the 23 other campus locations.

Categories used to classify questions presented in-person were applied to those submitted to the e-mail and chat reference services also. The University Libraries at Penn State classify such questions into four categories. They are 'Where Is,' 'Policy and Service,' 'Troubleshooting,' and 'Reference.' Each category is defined and examples of typical questions have been supplied to the library staff responding to in-person queries. The definition of a reference question adheres to the Association of Research Libraries' reference transaction definition. (See Appendix A. Penn State University Library's Category Definitions with Sample Questions.) I added a fifth category, 'Other,' to the online transactions because questions emerged that did not easily fit into the existing categories.

Transcripts of in-person questions were not available. Therefore, comparisons between in-person and online reference services are limited. However, it is possible to draw conclusions about how the services differ based on the five categories employed in this study. As in other studies, transcript analyses were used to identify frequent questions submitted online. Transcripts offer important advantages. They are automatically recorded and thus not labor intensive. They capture the actual transaction without interfering with the process. Bias is less of a concern as the transcripts allow us to examine the questions as presented.

RESULTS

Asking a question in-person is much more common in these data than is submitting a request online. To take only one week, that of November 3-9, 2002, there were 4,406 in-person questions presented to the thirteen subject libraries. During the same period, the e-mail reference service received 55 questions and VRS received 29 questions. The libraries at the main campus serve a student population of approximately 40,000. Thus, there were approximately 1,100 questions per 10,000 students during this week. In contrast, the online reference services are available to all of Penn State's 80,000 students. Proportionately, the online services generated far fewer questions. There were 6.8 e-mail questions and 3.6 chat sessions per 10,000 students. A check of a full year revealed similar disproportions. There were 162,841 in-person, 12,352 e-mail, and 802 chat reference transactions. That is 20,355 in-person questions compared to 1,544 e-mail and 100 chat transactions per 10,000 students. Of course, these are relatively new services that may increase in popularity over time.

Where Is . . .

The most significant difference between in-person and online questions was found in the proportion of 'Where Is' or directional questions (Table 1). Questions are classified as 'Where Is' if they involve "assistance with the location of a service, facility, person, or resource within the Libraries. May require consulting a print or electronic resource." Forty-two percent of the questions presented in-person were classified as directional. This was a considerably higher percentage than either online reference service: e-mail (5%) and VRS (13%). Most of the directional questions the online services received were location of library online databases or e-reserves. There were very few (7 e-mail and 4 chat) questions that asked the location of call numbers, microfilm collections, book drops, and copiers. These questions occurred much more frequently at the reference desks.

Policy and Services

There were equal proportions of policy and service questions submitted in-person (14%) and by e-mail (12%). There were fewer policy-related questions submitted to VRS (6%). Policy and service questions request information about library policies, procedures, collections, or resources. Again, the questions submitted to the online services appeared similar to those submitted in-person. For example, patrons asked, "How many items can I check out?" or "As an alumnus, can I borrow books from the library?" There were also a number of questions from non-PSU users asking about access to subscription services. Requests for hours, FAX machines for student use, coin changers, and reserving study carrels also occurred.

TABLE 1. Comparison of All In-Person, E-Mail, and VRS Questions

	In-person	E-mail	VRS
Where Is . . .	42%	5%	13%
Policy and Services	14%	12%	6%
Troubleshooting	6%	16%	5%
Reference	38%	60%	72%
Other	NA	7%	4%
(N) = 100%	(4406)	(751)	(405)

A high proportion of e-mail policy and service questions were referred to library departments. Forty-one requests were referred to Access Services, Interlibrary Loan, and other departments. In addition, there were frequent suggestions for purchases as well as requests to place items on reserve. Both purchase suggestions and reserve requests have links on the same page as the online reference services suggesting that users do not distinguish between the different e-mail request options. There were no requests submitted to VRS to purchase an item or place an item on reserve.

Troubleshooting

Users' expectations may account for the differences in the technical questions submitted across services. Of the three services, e-mail reference service had the highest percentage of technical questions. Sixteen percent of e-mail questions were technical as opposed to 6 percent in-person and 5 percent via VRS. This category includes "questions about access to online databases, OPAC, proxy server, network connection or logon."[11] The most frequent problem was authentication. As with purchase suggestions, there is a 'Get help with a technical problem' link on the same page as the online reference services. One explanation for the higher number of reports of technical problems to e-mail than VRS is the possibility that the user was simply reporting a technical problem.

Other

'Other' was used for online questions to indicate non-library questions, compliments or complaints, and unclear questions. (Data sheets used at the reference desks did not include an 'Other' category.) Twelve e-mail questions and 13 chat questions asked for information on campus events and concerts, help in finding non-library faculty or staff, or assistance in navigating the University's Web pages. These questions could be classified as 'Reference' when presented at reference desks or they are not counted. Yet, they are indicative of the library's role as an information center for its institution.

The immediacy of e-mail, and its presumed anonymity, generated more complaints than VRS–and, possibly the reference desks. There were no complaints in the VRS transcripts. The changes in the library's Web pages generated most of the e-mail complaints. The library introduced its new Web design prior to this study and users complained about the difficulty they had finding something, "It took me 30 minutes to find ProQuest. I hate the new pages." The second category that generated the most complaints was frustration with accessing databases due to authentication or network errors. Only two of the 25 complaints dealt with personnel issues.

This category also includes vague requests. These were mostly e-mail questions which required clarification. For example, "I need two articles" without specifying either source or the topic.

Reference

Whereas the majority of questions at reference desks were 'Directional,' the majority of questions submitted to Penn State's online reference services were 'Reference' questions. Only 38 percent of the in-person questions were classified as reference. On the other hand, 60 percent of the e-mail questions and 72 percent of the VRS questions were reference queries.

In-person reference questions were also recorded by length of time, 'less than 5 minutes,' '5-10 minutes,' and 'more than 10 minutes.' The time spent per online question was not available. Instead, modifying Katz's categories, online reference questions were classified as either ready reference, strategy-based, or extended reference (Table 2). These categories suggest the level of difficulty and the presumed time needed to answer the question. Of the three services compared, ready reference questions were more frequent in-person than online. The majority of reference questions presented to the reference desks, 66 percent, took less than 5 minutes. Although there are flaws with comparing the time for in-person reference questions to the type of online reference ques-

TABLE 2. Comparison of All In-Person, E-Mail, and VRS Reference Questions

	In-person*	E-mail	VRS
Ready Reference	66%	4%	13%
Strategy-Based	25%	85%	84%
Extended Reference	9%	10%	3%
(N) = 100%	(1682)	(447)	(291)

*Categories for in-person reference questions were based on time. Ready reference were less than 5 minutes, strategy-based were 5-10 minutes, extended were more than 10 minutes. Categories for online reference questions were based on the complexity of the question.

tions, the data suggests that reference questions presented in-person are not as extensive as those presented online. However, this may also be due to the high number of questions presented in-person does not allow more time. This should be further studied.

As indicated, the lack of transcripts for in-person reference transactions limits the comparison between services. Because the majority of online questions were identified as reference, transcripts were analyzed to determine the types of reference questions being asked and the differences between the two online services (Table 3).

Ready Reference

For online services, questions that can be quickly answered using 'information sources' were classified as ready reference. There were three subtypes of ready reference questions:

1. Requests for factual information that could be quickly answered, "What is the latitude and longitude of Pittsburgh?"
2. Requests to clarify terminology, "I recently put a 'hold' on a book using the Web browser, but I don't know exactly what this means."
3. Requests for information that was answered with a canned message or a Web site prepared by library instruction, "What is the difference between scholarly and popular publications?"

Of the types of ready reference, the questions that received factual information was small in both the e-mail and chat reference services. Only eight of the 68 ready reference e-mail questions (12%) and only three of the 46 ready reference chat questions (6%) were responded with short, factual responses. Although users may submit questions that they thought would have been quickly answered, such as "What is the per-

TABLE 3. Comparison of E-Mail and VRS Ready Reference Questions

	E-mail	VRS
Quick, factual responses	12%	6%
Pre-formatted response	16%	74%
Terminology	72%	20%
(N) = 100%	(68)	(46)

centage of alcohol abuse by elementary students?" these questions were often answered by providing them with a list of possible references.

Eleven (16%) of the e-mail ready reference questions received referrals to online information sites or 'canned messages' answering frequently asked questions. The number of referrals to prepared Web sites or canned messages was three times greater in the chat reference service. Thirty-four (74%) of the VRS ready reference questions were answered using a prepared site. The reason, in part, is that students were given a library assignment in which they needed to ask the VRS librarian for sources of book reviews and a canned message was created to respond to these questions.

The difficulty users have understanding library terminology was clear in the transcripts. These questions were more often submitted to e-mail (72% of the ready reference e-mail questions) than VRS (20% of the ready reference chat questions). Several terms from the library's catalog generated such questions. There were frequent questions about the 'Hold' function. Users were also confused by call numbers beginning in X (the designation for books ordered but not received) and items identified 'Never Due' (books charged to interlibrary loan or bindery). Tracking questions specific to terminology would be valuable for improving Web page design and other patron interfaces.

Strategy-Based

The majority of research questions submitted online was categorized as 'Strategy-Based.' Warner writes such questions "require the formulation of a strategy to locate an answer and require selection of resources."[12] Warner's concept was adopted rather than Katz's specific search category for several reasons. Katz does not clearly define specific search questions. Instead, he writes that the answers "almost always take the form of giving the user a document, a list of citations, a book, a report, an Internet site, etc. . . . This query often is called a bibliographical inquiry, because the questioner is referred to a bibliographical aid such as the catalog, an index, or a bibliography."[13] In academic libraries emphasis is given to instruction. The end result may be a document, a list of citations, or a book, but the process involves showing the user the best strategy to solve the problem presented. Answers providing strategies were evident in the transcripts of both online reference services. E-mail responses often provided the user with several resources that could be consulted to answer the question posed. The VRS transactions also revealed that the librarian had often recommended several resources that could be consulted. It seems likely that 'Information Literacy' has been adopted as a category in several studies[14] to capture the frequency in which librarians offer strategies rather than specific sources to their academic patrons.

The strategy-based category was further subdivided into 'Catalog,' 'Database,' 'Starting point for papers,' and 'Other' (Table 4). Questions classified as either 'Catalog' or 'Database' included instruction in their use, understanding search results, or refining a search. A typical catalog question was "How do I find videos held in the library?" Questions were also classified as 'Catalog' if the book requested was not found in Penn State's catalog and the librarian referred the user to one of the virtual union catalogs.

The e-mail and chat transcripts revealed that many Penn State users do not know whether they may request materials from other Penn State locations or how to do so. There were a number of e-mail questions asking for help obtaining items from other campus locations. Others would seek reassurance that they followed the procedure correctly.

A number of 'strategy-based' questions were specific requests on searching a database. ProQuest was the most frequently used of the databases available to Penn State faculty and students. Requests for database assistance were more common in VRS (39%) than e-mail reference services (21%).

The prevalence of questions generated by students' research assignment led to its own category. Typically, students indicated that they have been given a library assignment and needed a number of articles and/or books on an assigned topic. Again, there was a higher proportion of these questions in VRS (43%) than e-mail reference service (23%). In VRS the librarian would often escort the user into several databases to locate books and articles on their topic.

TABLE 4. Comparison of E-Mail and VRS Strategy-Based Reference Questions

	E-mail	VRS
Catalog	35%	16%
Database	21%	39%
Starting points for paper, etc.	23%	43%
Other	21%	2%
(N) = 100%	(333)	(235)

Questions that were not specific to the catalog or databases and were not clearly assignment-related were treated as 'Other.' Initially, I attempted to create a category for 'Instruction' or 'Information Literacy' as done in earlier studies. However, the prevalence of instruction throughout the responses made this difficult. Questions that could be instructional were classified as 'Other.' A good example of an instructional question is the e-mail request, "I'm trying to find an article that was written using primary research but when I use the search engine it only gives me articles that contain the words primary and research."

Extended Reference

'Extended Reference' questions involved more complicated research questions and took longer to answer than ready-reference or strategy-based questions. In-person questions identified as taking more than 10 minutes were classified as 'extended reference.' E-mail questions were considered in this category if they could not be answered by the librarian and were referred to a subject specialist. In VRS a question was classified here if it required an e-mail follow-up. There were fewer 'extended reference' questions in VRS (3%) than in-person (9%) or e-mail (10%). As Desai wrote, "It seems that patrons regard [instant messaging] reference as a medium suited to quick exchanges only."[15]

CONCLUSION

Libraries are likely to continue to pursue online reference services as electronic means of communication continue to develop. At this time, Penn State users continue to patronize in-person services most frequently. There were 1,100 in-person questions compared to only 10.4 online transactions per 10,000 students. With marketing and increased visibility, it is anticipated that online reference transactions will increase. The data reported here provide a benchmark with which to monitor future growth.

This study found that the traditional categories used to classify questions presented at reference desks can be fruitfully applied to online reference services. There are benefits to using the traditional categories. They allow for longitudinal studies to examine the pattern of questions over time. They also comply with the data gathering efforts of national organizations, such as the Association of Research Libraries. However, the four categories used in this study have limitations. They do not describe the problems users encounter with the library. Transcripts of on-line reference sessions, however, do provide such information. These transcripts revealed that users often have difficulty understanding library terminology. They also document the problems users have navigating the library's Web pages. Transcripts also demonstrated the library's import-ance as an information center for its campus.

The lack of in-person transcripts limited comparisons of the types of reference questions between the three services. Analyzing the online transcripts identified differences between the two online services. E-mail requests were more specific. E-mail questions reflect an immediacy that wasn't apparent in VRS. E-mail users questioned terminology and pol-icy, suggested purchases, reported technical problems, and complained. In contrast, the VRS users were more likely to request assistance in se-lecting the appropriate database, determining the best terms, and evalu-ating the results. Future comparisons of in-person to online reference transactions should include transcripts of in-person interactions. To avoid bias in librarians' reporting these transactions, the use of record-ing devices should be considered.

This study also found that 62 percent of the e-mail questions and 43 percent of the chat questions were specific to Penn State University and its libraries. These included questions about Penn State University Li-braries' policies and services, the location of their facilities, and PSU campus events. They also included reference questions that were spe-cific to the library's collections, either the terms of agreement for using a subscription service or referrals to subject specialists or archivists. This raises questions about the feasibility of using consortia or contract services to provide online reference services.[16] It is clear in these data that librarians who staff chat reference services need to be familiar with the library's databases as well as its specific policies and services. In ad-dition to answering questions on courses, campus events, and material location, a librarian must know the campus the patron attends. Although the numbers of directional and policy-related questions are fewer than reference questions, they also require that librarians be familiar with the patron's institution. What implications this has for staff training for li-braries joining consortia to offer online services needs to be further ex-plored. For e-mail reference services these questions can be forwarded to the respective institution.

As previous studies suggest, in-person questions were similar to those posed online. However, the frequencies of different types of questions varied. There were a higher proportion of 'Directional' questions pre-sented at the reference desks than online. When patrons used the online services, they used them primarily for 'Reference' questions. Previous studies have argued that it is not necessary to staff reference desks with librarians when most of the questions are directional or policy-related.[17] It would seem, however, that the prevalence of reference questions submitted online necessitates that reference librarians staff these services.

Although this study focused on the type of questions presented in-person and online, we need to also consider the person presenting the question. What types of patrons are more likely to use an online reference service than a personal encounter? Does the age of the patron or their involvement in distance education affect their preference? Can we profile the users who come to reference desks and compare their characteristics with those who use online services? The types of questions patrons submit are similar. It is likely that their profiles would be too. We offer library users a growing variety of information sources; we are now able to offer a variety of information services. We continue to do what libraries have been doing for years–be responsive to our patrons' needs and wants.

NOTES

1. A search in *Library Literature Index* identified 146 articles in the past five years on online reference services. Another indication of the popularity of this topic is the establishment of the Virtual Reference Desk Conference that has been held annually since 1999.

2. Penn State University Libraries, "Why Keep Statistics At All?" (handout).

3. Wendy Diamond and Barbara Pease, "Digital Reference: A Case Study of Question Types in an Academic Library," *Reference Services Review* 29, no. 3 (2001): 217.

4. Marianne Foley, "Instant Messaging Reference in an Academic Library: A Case Study," *College & Research Libraries* 63, no. 1 (January 2002): 44-45.

5. M. Kathleen Kern, "What Are They Asking? An Analysis of Questions Asked at In-person and Virtual Service Points" (Paper presented at RUSA MOUSS 9th Annual Reference Research Forum, Toronto, Canada, June 21, 2003).

6. Christina M. Desai, "Instant Messaging Reference: How Does It Compare?" *The Electronic Library* 21, no. 1 (2003): 23.

7. JoAnn Sears, "Chat Reference Service: An Analysis of One Semester's Data," *Issues in Science and Technology Librarianship*. Fall 2001 [Online] Available: http://www.istl.org/istl/01-fall/article2.html [July 25, 2003].

8. William A. Katz, *Introduction to Reference Works* (Boston: McGraw-Hill, 2002), 15-19.

9. Sears (2001).

10. Ruth A. Hodges, "Assessing Digital Reference," *Libri* 52, no. 3 (September 2002): 167.

11. Hodges 2002, 162.

12. Debra G. Warner, "A New Classification for Reference Statistics," *Reference & User Services Quarterly* 41, no. 1 (Fall 2001): 53.

13. Katz 2002, 17.

14. Studies by Diamond and Pease 2001 and Foley 2002 use 'Information literacy' to classify reference questions.

15. Desai 2003, 23.

16. Sears (2001) raised this issue in her study of chat reference services at Auburn University.

17. Jeffrey St. Clair and Rao Aluri, "Staffing the Reference Desk: Professionals or Nonprofessionals?" *The Journal of Academic Librarianship* 3, no. 3 (July 1977): 153.

BIBLIOGRAPHY

Bushallow-Wilbur, Lara, Gemma DeVinney, and Fritz Whitcomb. "Electronic Mail Reference Service: A Study," *RQ* 35, no. 3 (Spring 1996): 359-71.

Desai, Christina M. "Instant Messaging Reference: How Does It Compare?" *The Electronic Library* 21, no. 1 (2003): 21-30.

Diamond, Wendy, and Barbara Pease. "Digital Reference: A Case Study of Question Types in an Academic Library," *Reference Services Review* 29, no. 3 (2001): 210-18.

Foley, Marianne. "Instant Messaging Reference in an Academic Library: A Case Study," *College & Research Libraries* 63, no. 1 (January 2002): 36-45.

Garnsey, Beth A., and Ronald R. Powell. "Electronic Mail Reference Services in Public Library," *Reference & User Services Quarterly* 39, no. 3 (Spring 2000): 245-54.

Hodges, Ruth A. "Assessing Digital Reference," *Libri: International Journal of Libraries and Information Services* 52, no. 3 (Sept. 2002): 157-168.

Katz, William A. *Introduction to Reference Work.* 8th ed. Boston: McGraw-Hill, 2002.

Kern, M. Kathleen. "What Are They Asking? An Analysis of Questions Asked at In-person and Virtual Service Points" (Presentation at RUSA MOUSS 9th Annual Reference Research Forum, Toronto, ON, June 21, 2003).

Lederer, Naomi. "E-Mail Reference: Who, When, Where, and What is Asked," *The Reference Librarian* 74 (2001): 55-73.

National Information Standards Organization. *Library Statistics: An American National Standard.* Betheseda, MD: NISO Press, 1997.

Sears, JoAnn. "Chat Reference Service: An Analysis of One Semester's Data," *Issues in Science and Technology Librarianship* (Fall 2001), http://www.istl.org/istl/01-fall/article2.html (accessed July 25, 2002).

Sloan, Bernie. "Asking Questions in the Digital Library" (Presentation at the 2002 Virtual Reference Desk Conference, Chicago, IL, November 15, 2002) http://www.lis.uiuc.edu/~b-sloan/vrd_files/frame.htm (accessed July 29, 2003).

St. Clair, Jeffrey, and Rao Aluri. "Staffing the Reference Desk: Professionals or Nonprofessionals?" *The Journal of Academic Librarianship* 3, no. 3 (July 1977): 149-153.

Warner, Debra G. "A New Classification for Reference Statistics," *Reference & User Services Quarterly* 41, no. 1 (Fall 2001): 51-55.

doi:10.1300/J120v46n95_03

APPENDIX A

Penn State University Library's Category Definitions with Sample Questions

Category	Definition	Examples
Where Is . . .	Assistance with the location of a service, facility, person, or resource within the Libraries. May require consulting a print or electronic resource.	• Do you have a stapler I can borrow? • Where's the nearest restroom? • I'm supposed to see***. Where will I find her? • This notice says to pick up my hold at the Pattee Lending Services Desk. Where is that?
Policy and Service	Requires knowledge of library or university policies and procedures. Requires knowledge of services available in the libraries.	• How do I check out a book? • I graduated from Penn State ten years ago. Can I borrow books from the library? • I graduated from Penn State ten years ago. Can I get access to your article databases? • I got an overdue notice, but I returned the book last week. • How do I put this article on reserve for my class?
Trouble-shooting and other equipment	Request for assistance in using or resolving a problem with a piece of equipment or a network resource.	• The printer is jammed. Can you fix it? • I'm trying to scan these images and copy them onto a CD, but I keep getting an error message. What am I doing wrong? • Can I print double-sided copies?
Reference	A question requiring knowledge of library collections or services, subject expertise, or other specialized knowledge. The range of questions may extend from a basic search of The CAT to a complex need involving selecting resources or developing a search strategy.	• How can I access The CAT from home? • How do I find a video in The CAT? • Do you have any books written by Stephen Ambrose? • I need to write a research paper on the theory of evolution and I'm supposed to use five articles and five books. Where do I start? • I'm drafting my dissertation proposal and I need to gather some preliminary information on governmental organizations that support cultural development projects.

Listening to Our Users:
System Migration and the Evaluation
of Web-Based Library Services

Laurie Probst
Michael Pelikan

SUMMARY. At Penn State, a "Tell Us What You Think" user feedback button on the Libraries home page provided a convenient mechanism for users to respond to our system migration and the changes they saw in The CAT, our library catalog. The immediate impact of the new system on our users was dramatic, and included strong criticism from a small, but vocal, minority. Within a few months, however, the complaints and comments about the new catalog moderated and the majority of the e-mail traffic coming into the library switched into questions about library services and requests for assistance. doi:10.1300/J120v46n95_04 *[Article copies available for a fee from The Haworth Document Delivery Service: 1-800-HAWORTH. E-mail address: <docdelivery@haworthpress.com> Website: <http://www.HaworthPress.com> © 2006 by The Haworth Press, Inc. All rights reserved.]*

KEYWORDS. Descriptors, system migration, evolution of user services, user studies, use studies, assessment and evaluation, MIS in libraries

Laurie Probst is Head of Public Services (E-mail: lkp5@psu.edu); and Michael Pelikan is Technology Initiatives Librarian (E-mail: mpp10@psu.edu), both at University Libraries, The Pennsylvania State University, University Park, PA 16802.

[Haworth co-indexing entry note]: "Listening to Our Users: System Migration and the Evaluation of Web-Based Library Services." Probst, Laurie, and Michael Pelikan. Co-published simultaneously in *The Reference Librarian* (The Haworth Information Press, an imprint of The Haworth Press, Inc.) No. 95/96, 2006, pp. 37-51; and: *Assessing Reference and User Services in a Digital Age* (ed: Eric Novotny) The Haworth Information Press, an imprint of The Haworth Press, Inc., 2006, pp. 37-51. Single or multiple copies of this article are available for a fee from The Haworth Document Delivery Service [1-800-HAWORTH, 9:00 a.m. - 5:00 p.m. (EST). E-mail address: docdelivery@haworthpress.com].

INTRODUCTION

In May 2001, after several years of planning and development, The Pennsylvania State University Libraries implemented a new integrated library system. The move from a twenty-year-old locally developed system to SIRSI Unicorn led to many changes in library operations and in the work of the library faculty and staff. It also affected our users in ways that we did not expect. A "Tell Us What You Think" button on the Libraries home page provided a convenient mechanism for users to respond to our system migration and the changes they saw in The CAT, our library catalog. Analysis of the questions and comments we received during the four months after the system migration has provided insight into user search behavior and problems with functionality and design of the catalog interface. Perhaps more importantly, the migration also provided us with an unexpected opportunity to evaluate and expand our Web-based user services.

In many respects, the story of this button is a story about "our needs" versus "theirs." When we hit upon the idea for the "Tell Us What You Think" button, we were focused upon our own need for user feedback. Our users, however, seized upon the button as a way to have their own needs for service and assistance met, and they did so as if this had been our intended purpose for the button all along. The popularity of this button was a clear indication that our existing "contact us" services were not meeting user needs and that we had an opportunity to build a new service that would meet this growing need.

"TELL US WHAT YOU THINK"–AND WHAT YOU NEED

In the nineteen weeks covered in this analysis (May-September 2001), we received 667 "Tell Us What You Think" messages. In the early stages of analyzing these messages, we observed two distinct types of messages and began to assign them to two categories: "About the CAT" (complaints, comments, or questions about the new catalog) and "Service Requests" (questions about or requests for library services). While most messages fell clearly into one or the other category, 24 were assigned to both. When compiled into weekly totals and plotted, a clear pattern was revealed, confirming our early perceptions. (See Diagram 1.) During the first eleven weeks (May-August 2001), 80% of the 395 messages received were about the catalog. From that moment forward, even as weekly totals fluctuated, the proportion of "About the CAT" messages continued to decline as the proportion of "Service Requests" messages steadily increased. Of the 272 messages received in

DIAGRAM 1

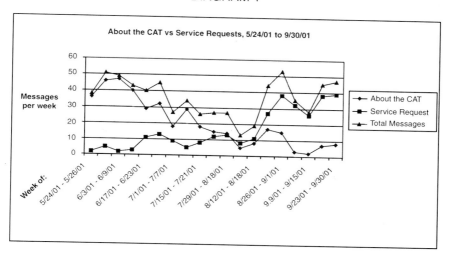

About the CAT vs Service Requests, 5/24/01 to 9/30/01

the second eight weeks (August-September 2001), only 23% were about the catalog. The remaining 77% during this second period were requests for help with some aspect of the new system or with some aspect of existing library services. The total number of inquiries per week varied in relation to the academic calendar, with, for example, a significant decrease in August when campus populations are lowest, but the trend in proportions persisted. It is interesting to note that many of the services that we received comment upon had been in place before the new OPAC appeared, and represented policies and practices that had not been changed in any significant way by its unveiling.

We analyzed these 667 messages to learn which groups within our user population had responded over the period under examination. For example, because the student population was relatively low during the period of summer classes, we expected that most comments would come from faculty and staff. This expectation was confirmed, with 41% of the comments coming from faculty and staff, 37% from students, 8% from library staff, and 13% from other user categories across the entire period of study. Faculty and staff comments decreased considerably in the second part of the test period. Student comments increased, in part because of the increase in the undergraduate student population with the start of the fall semester. Comments from library staff decreased dramatically in the second part of the test period.

The patterns we observed raised several questions. Our users identified problems in functionality that clearly needed to be addressed, but the causes of those problems were not always clear. In some cases, there were technical problems with the migration. In other cases we suspected that users had difficulty in adjusting to the new interface, or that the reported problems were indications of users' imperfect search skills and knowledge, brought to our attention with the interface change. For our user population, the long-term impact of interface changes was less of an issue than improving the delivery of critical library services. The relatively rapid decline in complaints about the catalog seemed to indicate that our users adapted fairly quickly to the interface changes. However, their continued frustration in using The CAT raised questions about whether, as a service point, it supports the independence and self-sufficiency that surveys such as LibQUAL indicate are important to our users.[1]

Similarly, the variations among the user populations prompted related questions. The decline in questions from faculty and staff suggested that these users were surprised, and inconvenienced, by the interface change, but that they quickly adjusted to the new interface. After that point, their need for communication with the library slowed. In contrast, the use of the button by graduate students remained steady throughout the test period and use by undergraduates increased. Were the students more likely to take the "Tell Us What You Think" instruction less literally and adapt it to their purposes? The graduate students, like the faculty, were unhappy with the disruption of the interface change but, unlike the faculty, they continued to use the button to ask about library services. We suspect that undergraduates were even more likely to ask about library services, but since the last few weeks of the test period coincided with return of students for fall classes, the data are inconclusive. Use of the button by library staff was almost exclusively about the catalog, primarily reports of problems and concerns about the interface.

User Reaction to the New ILS–Weeks 1-11

To identify the specific problem areas our users encountered, we assigned each of the "About the CAT" messages to one or more of nineteen sub-categories covering The CAT interface, functionality, and services as well as other Web site resources, such as interlibrary loan or other databases. We realized that it made sense to examine user comments in these categories as clues revealing service expectations of our users. Of the 395 messages received in the first eleven weeks, over half (59%) fell into five categories that mirror users experience moving through stages of the information-seeking process. We received broad general comments, questions about authentication (perceived as an impediment to service), difficulties in constructing searches and interpreting results, and requesting materials.

General Comments

While many comments were too vague to identify specific problems or difficulties, in the aggregate, they provided an important insight into user expectations. Given the constantly changing nature of resources on the Internet, we expected that most users would adapt easily to the new "look and feel" of the catalog: that the changes in functionality would be more problematic than changes in design and screen layout. We were struck by the number of people who were clearly frustrated by changes in the catalog. Further we were concerned to learn that the design and layout changes were perceived in some cases as changes in functionality, to the extent that users were unable to identify those functions that remained unchanged. These users were quite comfortable with the old catalog and resented having to relearn everything–or even anything–in the new system. Our suspicion that some of our users adapted less easily to changes in the library Web than they might in other areas of the Internet was strengthened when we received similar complaints after the library home page was revised in Fall 2002.

Examples of User Comments

I think it stinks. It's much harder to use than the old one. I've typed in the names of authors of books I know you have. Nothing. The boolian searching is way off. Tear the whole thing out and go back to the old one.

I like the colorful pages and different functions in the new version. Thanks for your efforts to make it better. I found it more complicated in the search function. I think there could be a page that is a just for simple search, which is like the one we have now. It might be easier to find where to input the query.

This is a classic case of fixing something that wasn't broken . . . The old one had a very simple screen with one line where I typed in what I was looking for, and then I clicked on a nice big green "GO" icon. The new one has too many pull-down menus, and too many lines to type things. Plus, I had to scan the screen for several seconds before I found the button that actually initiated the search. Why did it take me so long? Because it's a small, gray button like everything else on the screen.

Authentication

In the first months after implementation, users were required to authenticate several times: to get into the catalog, and later to access some of the do-it-yourself functions, such as the "I Want It" button and renewing books. Complaints about redundancy and inefficiency came swiftly: our users saw this as an impediment to service. While most of this redundancy has been addressed, the issue of multiple authentications as users moved across the Web site still persists in certain situations, especially for users working remotely. Since many users prefer remote access, such issues are a primary component of service quality and user satisfaction. As Anne Lipow has reminded us, "It is not the user who is becoming remote from the library; it is the library that is becoming remote from the user."[2]

Example of User Comment

Hello, Can you clarify what the purpose of authenticating is now, or will be if changed? I have used staff, public and remote computers, accessing the CAT and databases with and without authenticating first, and I find that no matter what I do, such as "I want it," "Vel," some databases, I have to re-authenticate anyways. So, is it really necessary to authenticate if one wants to do anything besides search the Cat? Thanks.

Constructing Searches and Interpreting Results

Some users reported difficulty in determining how to search for the information they desired and in interpreting results screens. Faced with a multi-line keyword search screen, with alternative browse and call number search screens, many users sought assistance in searching for known items, for items by subject and by call number. Searches for known journal titles presented the greatest problems. They reported difficulty in identifying information about locations and item availability. While we were able to attribute some of these difficulties to users' unfamiliarity with the new system, we were also able to identify problem areas in the system itself including navigating through long lists, locating relevant information on the display screens, and interpreting the display order of search results.

Examples of User Comments

> *The new LIAS catalog is easier to read–I like that the brief titles list provides call numbers and location. However, if I type in an exact title, the brief titles list gives me twenty or more records, many of which have only the vaguest similarity to what I typed. This would not be a problem were it not for the fact that the title which exactly matches what I typed is buried in the middle of the list. If titles could be organized by closest match first, the CAT would be much, much easier to use.*

> *Hi. I am a grad student. I do not like the new version of the CAT. I find it much harder to use and I often get too many responses to simple inquiries. When looking for a specific journal, the browse function works much, much better than the search function even when the search function is narrowed only to journals in a certain library. If I type in the exact name of a journal, I get a thousand responses that have all or even none of the words I typed in. It took me 30 minutes to figure out that the browse function was more direct when looking for something that I know the title of.*

> *My experience of the new results screen is that there is too much information to sort through quickly. It seems as though you've gotten rid of a level where there was a simplified list that one could select the most likely candidate from. Now there is no visual difference between titles, and extraneous information (publisher, etc.). Is there a way to at least underline titles, or better, to put that simpler layer back in?*

Requesting Materials

In the old catalog, the "I Want It" button was a popular service. Originally designed to facilitate recalls and requests for materials from one of the twenty-four Penn State campus libraries, it was also used to request retrieval of on-campus materials to be picked up at a circulation desk. While the service was retained in the new catalog, users had difficulty finding it on the new screens and were concerned that it had been discontinued. Here, the changes in design and screen layout clearly had an adverse effect on users' ability to adapt to the new system, and to locate and use this existing service.

Examples of User Comments

> *I am enrolled in****** *and I need a book from the PSU library in order to complete an assignment. However, I am not at University Park and the book is not at the nearest branch campus. Is it possible to have a book from one branch campus library be sent to another branch campus (either Lancaster or Delaware County)? And if so, how long would it take for it to arrive? And would it be possible to return it to the library at University Park since I will be there in month?*

> *After a search how do you request that a book be delivered to your campus? On the old system it was intuitive, and directly on the web page that the book was found. With the new system browsing is required and I still have not found the answer.*

Requests for Services–Weeks 12-19

In contrast to the first eleven weeks when messages were primarily about the catalog, the messages received in the second eight weeks (August-September) were primarily services requests and they fell into a different distribution pattern. Over half (53%) of these messages were distributed across only four sub-categories: requesting materials, electronic reserves and other Web-based licensed and unlicensed resources, circulation, and interlibrary loan. Of these, only the first, requesting materials, constituted a significant proportion of each group of questions. The other four sub-categories that were predominant in the first period constituted only 18% of this second period.

The high incidence of queries about requesting materials during both periods was a strong indication that users had problems with both the interface change and the functionality of this popular service. While the messages in the first period tended to be complaints about "where did the 'I Want It' button go?" the messages in the second period either asked if it was possible to request materials or reported problems in using the service. To these users, the function of the "I Want It" button was not intuitive. Experienced users were thrown by the design change and inexperienced users were not able to identify that the service existed. Clearly, we needed further investigation into these problems. Messages in the other four categories were fairly straightforward reports of problems or requests for instruction in using electronic reserves, using the other databases on the library Web site, as well as interlibrary loan and other circulation functions, such as renewing books.

LISTENING TO OUR USERS

In their review of the literature on OPAC searching, Large and Beheshti concluded that analysis of user behavior is one of the most difficult components to study, commenting that "most of the cognitive work involved in searching continues to rest with the searcher rather than the system."[3] In her studies, Christine Borgman has argued that, while "research in information seeking indicates that users formulate questions in stages," system design still "assumes that users formulate a query that represents a fixed goal for the search and that each search session is independent."[4] More recent studies, such as those by Slone and Bilal, have investigated the search behaviors of various populations using both library catalogs and the Internet. While their work has increased our knowledge of user behavior, their conclusions confirm that more research and development is needed to design systems that incorporate this growing body of knowledge.[5] Similarly, Kibbee and Ward argue that greater attention should also be given to users during system migrations when there is both an opportunity to examine user behavior and a need to provide additional support to users during the transition to a new system.[6]

Our experience at Penn State confirms these findings, and adds further support to the call for more research into user behavior in order to build more effective Web-based services. Taken in the aggregate, the messages we received raise questions about the search behaviors of users, specifically their knowledge of the library catalog and search techniques, their thought processes in constructing search strategies, and their perceived success rates. For example, was the high incidence of perceived changes in functionality that were merely design changes an indication that users are easily, if only temporarily, confused by design changes, or are there more fundamental problems in their understanding of library catalogs? If the OPAC is a service point whose utility becomes the basis for users' evaluation of the quality of services we offer, we must be prepared to distinguish between the services our OPAC provides and our users' capabilities to exploit it fully. Not only do we need to design these services based on empirical evidence of user behavior, we must also design instructional resources to educate users to take advantage of the services. Both of these are critical to building better library services.

Pent Up Demand for E-Reference/Help Desk Services

What began as a simple mechanism to encourage feedback evolved, from our users' point of view, into a new point of service, especially to those for whom the computer was already their primary means of access to the library and its services. We expected to receive general questions relating to library services, but we were surprised by how quickly the traffic on this prominently placed button surpassed the traffic from the many long-standing "contact us" e-mail links dotted throughout the library Web site. This rapid, user-initiated transformation of the "Tell Us What You Think" button from a feedback mechanism into a Web-based service point was a clear indication of pent up demand for better, more prominent e-reference and user support services. Indeed, it serves as a clear indication that our users, without prompting or redirection, simply expected that this was the way to access library services. Our assessment of this situation has given us some insights into the evolving world of library services. The Web environment has allowed us to push library services, such as interlibrary loan, course reserves, and some circulation functions to the user. The resulting reduction in the need for staff mediation of these services has created efficiencies for both the library and the user. At the same time, the loss of that point of interaction has broadened the gap between our users' understanding of the complex processes that underlie these transactions and our ability to build an intuitive Web-based system in which such understanding is unnecessary.

A significant number of the questions received were in the broad category of technical support: problems with network access, authentication, or access to specific databases or electronic course reserves. Responding to these queries presented challenges in training librarians to troubleshoot or refer these problems, underscoring the need to compile documentation in a knowledge base and to build relationships with other campus and IT help desks to address problems that extended beyond the control of the library. It also became clear that these questions provide us with information useful in monitoring the status of library systems and network access and in identifying and responding to system failures.

Evolution from "Tell Us What You Think" to Ask!

In almost two years since the new SIRSI system was implemented, the Penn State University Park e-services environment has evolved from a decentralized system of approximately 40 e-mail or Web form links managed by approximately 25 library units (including fourteen subject libraries, Special Collections, and five access services units) to a new central service that is increasingly integrated with existing unit-level service points. This complex Web environment reflects the traditional, location-based organization of the library, its collections, and its services. Unfortunately, this organization is opaque and even irrelevant to most of our users, appearing mostly to create confusion as they attempt to navigate through our Web environment. Perhaps more significantly, by the nature of their approach to the feedback system, our users are telling us that they regard the electronic environment as the library's natural element, to an extent that surpasses our own efforts to evolve in that direction.

As we embark on an extensive project to rethink and reconfigure the delivery of library resources via our Web pages, it seems clear that, in concept, we should be building a help desk service that facilitates access to the library and provides assistance across functions and library units. The concept would require training and support to develop staff competencies across functions, from reference to circulation to interlibrary loan to troubleshooting network and technical problems. It is also especially critical to integrate staff participation across diverse units. Without a general reference unit to serve as an administrative home, the ownership or responsibility for this service function is less clear.

In January 2002, an E-Reference Services Task Force was formed to survey existing services and to propose a model for a centralized, Web-based reference service. After conducting a literature review, performing benchmarking within the Penn State Libraries and with peer institutions, and evaluating available software and management systems, including the SIRSI/Unicorn Requests module, the group moved quickly to launch the new service in Fall 2002 as part of a redesign of the library home page. The new button and logo, "Ask!" is prominent on all upper level pages and in The CAT and collocates related services, from chat to e-mail to directories for phone and in-person contacts. In bringing this suite of services together, we allow our users to select the contact level appropriate to their needs and expectations.

The infrastructure supporting this new service is designed to manage questions, collect use data, build a knowledge base, and provide a centralized infrastructure to support a decentralized service. We will continue development of this management system to support further expansion of this service into other areas of the library Web site. In building this transparent system we are seeking to mediate between the library's complex, decentralized structure and the user who has information need, but may not know where to direct his or her question. We are also seeking to incorporate predictability into our Web design, recognizing that the common look and feel of the button, regardless of where it appears on the Web site, will better support our users' information-seeking behavior.

The integration of reference service points has also created opportunities for the integration of FAQs and related services. In designing Web-based library services, providing "self-help" resources is critical to building a successful user interface. Just as we are moving from an environment of multiple, independent service points to a unified system of linked service points (seamless access), we are working toward an environment of a single, dynamically generated FAQ resource, supported by the central knowledge base. The efficiencies to be gained in such an environment, both for library staff and library users, are as important as improvements in delivery of timely and effective access to information. Success in this endeavor depends heavily upon the appropriate application of emerging technologies as well as the cooperation of libraries, ILS providers, and commercial content providers.

Learning from Our Users (Can I C U 2 Day?)

The invitation to our users to talk to us provided valuable information that we must now apply to the improvement of library services. User needs and expectations take on greater importance in the current higher education environment where assessment and accountability factor directly into the budget and planning process. Through the "Tell Us What You Think" button our users gave us the opportunity to view our library services through the lens of their experience. For many of them, it was perfectly natural to push the button and start asking for service, "right here, right now"–in effect, to seize control the transaction and make it theirs. Without having made a collective decision to do so, our users' collective behavior gave us vitally important clues to questions we weren't even asking, through their spontaneous approach to our offerings.

Examples of User Comments

> *hello, my friend is going to a football camp at this college. he said it would start on the 2 of july. i am writing to you to verify if this is true and if so, what dorm would he be in and when would he be there*

> *I would think that on the desktops of all University computers there should be a shortcut to LIAS webpage, rather than having to fish it out from the PSU webpage itself. This would seem a very natural addition since the library catalog is the most viewed academic website at a university.*

Our analysis of user comments leads us to suspect that a number of Penn State library users are generally unaware both of the search capabilities in the new system as well as the depth of resources available. Many users construct searches at a very basic level and do not explore the advanced capabilities of the system. As a research library, we catalog and organize information at a level that supports the highly specialized research of our faculty and other advanced users who knowingly require access to the depth and breadth of our collections. At the same time, by sheer numbers of users much, if not most, of the searching directed at our catalog does not demand that level of access. From the standpoint of designing services, this raises important questions. Should we be doing more to facilitate access at that basic search level? Should we strive to improve the system's ability to provide smart answers to bad queries: not just relevance but depth and breadth—even if that is beyond what the users demand? Should we increase our efforts to bring the users' abilities up to the level of the system's abilities?

Another common theme in user comments was the criticism of network infrastructure, a kind of "zero tolerance" for anything less than reliable and consistent access to library resources over the Internet. From their perspective, this is service at its most basic level: our users expect constant, ubiquitous access, and anything less is perceived as a breakdown in essential service.

It also became clear that to many of our users the library as a discrete entity is much becoming more difficult to define. The library's home page is no longer a monolithic entrance. Personal bookmarks, personal portals, course management systems, and a growing multiplicity of access devices give library users the ability to select relevant entrance points and to identify resources pertinent to their needs. They can define the library they need for their purposes "on the fly." The library that they build will likely bear only coincidental resemblance to the physical library's floor plan, let alone its organizational chart. The challenge for us is to build in optimum navigability and functionality to lead those users to additional resources beyond those they have already identified. Clearly, such boundaries seem irrelevant to many users who regard them, it seems, as impediments to taking full advantage of the continuum of information resources. In the recent user study sponsored by the Digital Library Federation and the Council on Library and Information Resources, Amy Friedlander observed that "faculty and graduate students, in particular, seem to be omnivorous in their appetite for information, creative in their strategies for seeking and acquiring information in all forms, and very independent. They appear to seek tools, services, and facilities that they can use where and when the need them."[7] Among the recent studies looking at student use of the Internet, findings about students' use of library resources and students' use of Internet resources have raised questions about their ability to distinguish among them. Two other studies, the *OCLC White Paper on the Information Habits of College Students*, and the Pew Internet & American Life report, *The Internet Goes to College*, suggest that students prefer using the Internet for their information needs, although the OCLC report indicates that 70% do use the library Web site for "at least some of their assignments."[8] What isn't clear in this data is how users move between library Web sites and external Internet resources such as Web portals, course Web pages, or search engines. Given that they do move between them, it is critical that we have some understanding of the user's point of origin and path into the library Web site.

CONCLUSION

The implementation of our new integrated library system provided unexpected opportunities to investigate user searching behavior, assess existing library services, and initiate an expansion of Web-based services. Through the information collected from the "Tell Us What You Think" button we have identified areas for further research in our ongoing effort to improve the functionality of our catalog. We will continue to explore system functionality and usability, focusing on library services, such as course reserves and interlibrary loan; user behavior in searching and navigating the library Web site; and user satisfaction.

NOTES

1. Colleen Cook and Fred M. Heath, "Users' Perceptions of Library Service Quality: A LibQUAL + Qualitative Study. " *Library Trends* 49n4 (2001): 548-584. See also the comprehensive bibliography available at http://www.libqual.org/documents/admin/LQ+biblio.pdf.

2. Anne Grodzins Lipow, "Reference Services in a Digital Age." *Reference & User Services Quarterly* 38n1 (1998): 47.

3. Andrew Large and Jamshid Beheshti, "OPACS: A Research Review. " *Library & Information Science Research* 19n2 (1997), p. 128.

4. Christine L. Borgman, "Why Are Online Catalogs *Still* Hard to Use?" *Journal of the American Society for Information Science* 47n7 (1996): 493.

5. Debra J. Slone, "Encounters with the OPAC: On-Line Searching in Public Libraries." *Journal of the American Society for Information Science* 51n8 (2000): 757-73. Debra J. Slone, "The Influence of Mental Models and Goals on Search Patterns During Web Interaction." *Journal of the American Society for Information Science and Technology* 53n13 (2002): 1152-69. Dania Bilal, "Children's Use of the Yahooligans! Web Search Engine: 1. Cognitive, Physical, and Affective Behaviors on Fact-Based Search Tasks." *Journal of the American Society for Information Science* 51n7 (2000): 646-65.

6. Jo Kibbee and Jennifer Ward, "The Impact of System Migration on Users: Assessing and Addressing Reactions to a New Public Access Catalogue. " In Proceedings of the 3rd Northumbria International Conference on Performance Measurement in Libraries and Information Services, Northumberland, England, August 27-31, 1999. Newcastle upon Tyne: Information North for the School of Information Studies, University of Northumbria at Newcastle, 2000, p. 87.

7. Amy Friedlander, *Dimensions and Use of the Scholarly Information Environment: Introduction to a Data Set.* Washington, D.C.: Digital Library Federation and Council on Library and Information Resources, October 2002, p. 18. Available at http://www.clir.org/pubs/reports/pub110/contents.html.

8. OCLC White Paper on the Information Habits of College Students, June 2002, p. 6. Available at http://www2.oclc.org/oclc/pdf/printondemand/informationhabits.pdf, and Steven Jones, The Internet Goes to College: How Students are Living in the Future with Today's Technology. Washington, DC: Pew Internet & American Life Project, September 15, 2002, pp. 12-13. Available at http://www.pewinternet.org/reports/pdfs/PIP_College_Report.pdf.

doi:10.1300/J120v46n95_04

Evaluating Virtual Reference
from the Users' Perspective

Kirsti Nilsen
Catherine Sheldrick Ross

SUMMARY. This article discusses the evaluation of virtual reference services from the user perspective. It is one outcome of a long-term research project, The Library Visit Study, which has been conducted in three phases at the University of Western Ontario for more than a decade. These studies have identified the need for, and essential components of, reference interviews and good reference behaviors. The third phase of this research focuses on the factors that make a difference to the users' satisfaction with their virtual reference experience and whether these are the same or different from the ones we identified as important in face-to-face reference. An examination of user accounts of virtual reference transactions indicates that the reference interview has almost disappeared. Among the reasons identified for staff failure to conduct reference interviews in the virtual environment are: the nature of written vs. spoken interaction; the librarian's perceived need to respond quickly in this environment; and the rudimentary nature of the forms used in e-mail ref-

Kirsti Nilsen is Adjunct Professor (E-mail: knilsen@uwo.ca); and Catherine Sheldrick Ross is Professor and Dean (E-mail: ross@uwo.ca), both in the Faculty of Information and Media Studies, The University of Western Ontario, London, Ontario N6A 5B7, Canada.

[Haworth co-indexing entry note]: "Evaluating Virtual Reference from the Users' Perspective." Nilsen, Kirsti, and Catherine Sheldrick Ross. Co-published simultaneously in *The Reference Librarian* (The Haworth Information Press, an imprint of The Haworth Press, Inc.) No. 95/96, 2006, pp. 53-79; and: *Assessing Reference and User Services in a Digital Age* (ed: Eric Novotny) The Haworth Information Press, an imprint of The Haworth Press, Inc., 2006, pp. 53-79. Single or multiple copies of this article are available for a fee from The Haworth Document Delivery Service [1-800-HAWORTH, 9:00 a.m. - 5:00 p.m. (EST). E-mail address: docdelivery@haworthpress.com].

erence. The article includes a list of behaviors that users identified as either helpful or unhelpful and concludes with some implications of the research for good virtual reference service. doi:10.1300/J120v46n95_05 *[Article copies available for a fee from The Haworth Document Delivery Service: 1-800-HAWORTH. E-mail address: <docdelivery@haworthpress.com> Website: <http://www.HaworthPress.com> © 2006 by The Haworth Press, Inc. All rights reserved.]*

KEYWORDS. Virtual reference, evaluation, reference interview, library user studies, field research

INTRODUCTION

Since 1991, a group of researchers at the University of Western Ontario has been engaged in a long-term research project, the Library Visit Study, which examines what happens when users ask reference questions in libraries. This empirical study takes a user-centered, rather than a system- or staff-centered perspective, in order to examine user perceptions of their experiences with the reference transaction. In the first two phases of the Library Visit Study, we examined the reference transaction as it occurs face-to-face in the physical space of a public or academic library. Findings have been published in a number of articles[1] and a book entitled *Conducting the Reference Interview*.[2] In this previous work, we identified some commonly occurring problems in the face-to-face reference transaction and suggest some remedies. In the present paper, we report on some initial findings from phase 3 of the Library Visit Study, in which we focus on users' perceptions of the interview transaction in the virtual environment. In this latest phase, we are interested in identifying the key factors in the virtual reference transaction that make a difference to users and to their evaluation of the success of the transaction. We are especially interested in the role of technology and the changes that may have been introduced when the users' contacts with the library reference services are mediated through e-mail or chat services.

The library literature uses a variety of terms to refer to technologically-mediated reference, including virtual reference, digital reference, electronic reference, remote reference, and real-time reference, each one with its own definition. In using the term "virtual reference" here, we have used the definition provided in the guidelines for implementing and maintaining virtual reference services developed by the ALA's Machine Assisted Reference Section (MARS) Committee:

> Virtual Reference is reference service initiated electronically often in real-time, where patrons employ computers or other Internet technology to communicate with reference staff, without being physically present. Communication channels used frequently in virtual reference include chat, videoconferencing, Voice over IP, e-mail and instant messaging. While online sources are often utilized in provision of virtual reference, use of electronic sources in seeking answers is not of itself virtual reference. Virtual reference queries are often followed-up by telephone, fax, and regular e-mail, even though these modes of communication are not considered virtual.[3]

Throughout this paper, we use the term "virtual reference" as defined above. The term "chat" is used to refer to all real time, synchronous services, including instant messaging. The term "e-mail" refers to e-mail used for virtual reference purposes (i.e., to ask and answer reference questions). Other e-mail messages are identified as "regular e-mail."

METHOD USED FOR THE STUDY

The data analyzed in this paper were produced by students in consecutive offerings of an advanced course in reference and information services in the MLIS program at The University of Western Ontario and in one course of reference management at the University of Toronto. As an assignment for the course, students were asked to approach a virtual reference desk provided by a Canadian library and ask a question that interested them personally. They could choose to ask their question at either a university or a public library and were given the choice of using either e-mail or chat services. Students were required to choose different libraries. The completed assignments that students submitted included the following elements:

1. detailed step-by-step accounts of exactly what happened in the reference transaction after they asked their question.
2. reflections on their experience which summarized which aspects of the transaction they found helpful and which aspects they found unhelpful.

3. completed questionnaires asking for an evaluation of their experience as users of the reference service, including a question that asked about their "willingness to return."
4. transcripts of the chat sessions or copies of the e-mail exchanged.

The written reports (elements 1 and 2) provide qualitative data on individual users' perceptions, while the questionnaires provide quantitative data that can be summarized. In addition, the copies of e-mails exchanged or transcripts of chat sessions provide an additional source of evidence not readily available for face-to-face transactions. Virtual reference has an innate advantage over face-to-face reference for researchers interested in a fine-grained and accurate record of what happens, step-by-step, during the transaction. With traditional reference, researchers must first laboriously tape-record and transcribe the exchange between user and librarian. In the case of virtual reference, an electronic record of the transaction is automatically generated and provides independent evidence of how well questions are negotiated and answered.

The findings reported in this paper are based on accounts, questionnaires, and transcripts submitted as the result of 85 visits undertaken between February and May 2005 to virtual reference desks at public and university libraries in Canada. Given the choice of visiting a chat service or of using an e-mail service, some students who had never used chat services and did not want to try it for a course assignment chose to visit reference services that offered the more familiar e-mail environment. Others who tried to use chat services were sometimes faced with university library restrictions on types of users; in many cases the libraries' Web sites noted that users needed to have some affiliation with the institution concerned. As it happened, unaffiliated users who tried to use these services were usually not questioned and did, in fact (in most cases) receive responses. However, some reported feeling uneasy in their role, such as one person who noted, "I was very uncomfortable with misleading the reference librarian; however, I continued the reference interview," and another who worried that s/he would be challenged and "would be in some kind of trouble" for using the system. When restrictions were noted on the Web site, some users felt sufficiently discouraged that they veered off to another service. Of the 85 accounts of visits to virtual reference desk sites, 25 (29.4%) used chat services, while 60 (70.6%) used e-mail services. The types of libraries and services visited by the 85 users are identified in Table 1.

TABLE 1. Type of Library and Service Visited

	University	Public	Total
Chat	16	9	25
E-mail	29	31	60
Total	45	40	85

REVIEW OF THE LITERATURE

Bernie Sloan's online "Digital Reference Service Bibliography"[4] demonstrates the recent rapid growth in the literature on virtual reference. In this respect, the literature mirrors what is happening in libraries as virtual reference moves from being the province of a handful of early adopters to being a commonly-offered service, especially in academic libraries. As with the literature reporting any new phenomena, initially the published work on virtual reference focussed on describing the nature of the service, its prevalence, and its inflections in particular local settings. Most of the studies have been case studies of virtual reference services offered at individual libraries, usually academic libraries. Typically librarians who have pioneered a new service in their library setting report what challenges they faced and what they learned in the process of introducing the pilot service. Often data are provided on the nature of the technology used, the staff training required to mount the service, the promotion of the new service, the frequency of use of the virtual reference service, typical questions asked, and some preliminary indications of who the users are and their evaluation of the service they received. Data types that are easy to gather routinely have been the most frequently reported, e.g., the IP addresses of the users (in-library vs. off campus), peak periods of use, the duration of the sessions, or the numbers of sessions per week.

Although the evaluation of reference service in general has a long and rich literature, the evaluation of virtual reference is just beginning. In particular, there has been very little research that focuses explicitly on the evaluation of virtual reference from the users' perspective. The published literature has largely depended on in-house data captured in user logs and on surveys of users within a single library. Predictably the bulk of the attention has been paid to academic libraries, since, with some notable exceptions, public libraries have been somewhat slower to introduce virtual reference service.[5] Various easy-to-obtain surrogates for user satisfaction have been reported, such as response time as a measure of delays in getting service or the duration of the interaction as an indicator of the amount of service provided. Response times for e-mail services are usually described in terms of how long the patron must wait to hear back from an e-mailed question. With a chat service that is open and sufficiently staffed, the response time is synchronous, but chat transactions can be analyzed in terms of how long the user waits in a holding queue and how long the reference transaction lasts. In one collaborative consortium, Sloan found that "63% of users waited fewer than 30 seconds before being contacted by a librarian, and 73.5% were contacted in one minute or less."[6] Most authors note that using chat is more time-consuming for librarians than are in-person transactions. Time spent using chat services can vary widely. Kibbee, Ward, and Ma report an average of 9.8 minutes, but the time ranged from 40 seconds to 58.5 minutes,[7] and in a pilot study of chat reference quality, White, Abels, and Kaske reported that chat transactions ranged from 3 minutes to 29 minutes, with an average of 12 minutes.[8] Joanne Smyth reported that sessions averaged 13 minutes.[9] Sloan found that the median was 13 minutes, 11 seconds, and that only 12% of transactions lasted less than five minutes.[10] The type of questions asked can affect transaction time. When they classified questions as university-oriented vs. library-oriented, Curtis and Greene found that the former averaged 9.37 minutes, while the latter averaged 12.08 minutes.[11]

Apart from the analysis of transaction logs, most of the evaluative literature has been based on surveys of users. Case studies describing and evaluating the virtual reference service offered by a particular academic library often include a section on users' perceptions of services provided, sometime in comparison with face-to-face reference service or with telephone service. Most of what has been reported has come from Web-based surveys of a particular system that typically ask such questions as: Who are you? How did you find out about our service? How easy did you find the software to use? How satisfied were you with the service provided? What other kinds of our Library reference services have you used recently or ever? Typically the data come from responses to online questionnaires that pop up at the end of a chat session. The perhaps predictable result is that people who go to the trouble of answering the survey indicate high levels of user satisfaction. For example, Ruppel and Fagan report the data derived from a short survey and also a long survey on an instant messaging (IM) service offered at the Southern Illinois University Carbondale academic library. The short survey appeared immediately after users disconnected from the IM service and produced 340 completed surveys from an undisclosed number of transactions. Ruppel and Fagan note that users were "overwhelmingly positive": "Of [the 340 respondents] 82% said IM reference is a 'very' good method of getting help, while 7% said it was a fairly good method of getting help." Answers received were judged to be "very" helpful by 82% and 12% said the answers were "somewhat" helpful.[12] Similarly Marianne Foley reported that 45% of the 262 respondents to an online questionnaire on the IM reference service at the University of Buffalo reported being "very satisfied," while 79% were "satisfied" or better. Summarizing a list of verbatim comments from users such as "easy, fast and cool," she noted that the comments were "unexpectedly positive and very rewarding."[13]

Other case studies of particular library services have produced similarly gratifying results, although quite possibly surveys that result in negative results are less likely to be reported by the library system offering the service. Reporting on chat reference at Carnegie Mellon University, Marsteller and Neuhaus noted that of almost 75% of respondents (58 out of 78) indicated that they had received the information they needed and almost 90% (69 out of 78 respondents) said that they would use the service again.[14] Likewise Kibbee, Ward, and Ma reported high satisfaction rates with the real-time reference service at the University of Illinois at Urbana Champaign, noting that the results were "gratifying": "[n]early 90 per cent of the respondents reported the completeness of the answer to their question was very good or excellent. Nearly 85 per cent found the service easy to use and would use it again."[15]

Rather than using pop-up questionnaires to evaluate chat reference, Corey Johnson sent e-mail questionnaires to students and faculty at two universities. He found that only one in ten were aware of the chat reference service, and only nine of the 276 respondents (of 976 randomly surveyed) had actually used the service. Using willingness to return as a satisfaction measure (see below), he found that only 1 of the 9 was willing to use the service again.[16] Johnson's findings suggest that the method of disseminating the survey instrument can make a difference in findings. The typically high satisfaction rates recorded for pop-up surveys need to be taken with many grains of salt.

A number of investigators have been interested in teasing out the differences that users experience between using traditional reference and using virtual reference service. In order to compare users' perceptions of their experience with the physical reference desk and the virtual reference desk, Ruppel and Fagan distributed a 15-question survey to students enrolled in six sections of a library skills course that enrols from

30-40 students per section. The 52 respondents who returned the survey evaluated both the virtual reference and the physical reference services in terms of their perceived advantages and disadvantages. Respondents for the most part were very positive about the chat (IM) service, claiming that they liked its speed, convenience, and anonymity. Advantages of the traditional reference desk singled out by users were the "personal touch" received and the direct help provided–e.g., "it's always nice to talk and see a real person" and "[librarians] could actually help you locate a specific book on the shelf." When asked why they usually do not ask for help at traditional library help desks, the responses were similar to those long reported in the literature: 29% noted that staff "did not look like they want to help or they look too busy," 23% said they felt stupid for not knowing already, 17% did not want to bother going to the library building, and 10% did not think the person at the desk would know the answer. An interesting reason for not using the physical reference desk that was identified by 23% of respondents is that they did not want to get up from the computer, presumably for fear of losing their place.[17] Other studies show that many of the questions come from on-campus locations and even from patrons who are sitting at workstations near the physical reference desk.[18]

Surveys, though useful in some respects, nevertheless have familiar limitations. The data from pop-up surveys do not reflect users who have disappeared during the electronic transaction or who couldn't connect to it in the first place. Most users in fact do not fill out the surveys. Of 600 sessions analyzed by Kibbee, Ward, and Ma, only 130 provided completed questionnaires.[19] Only 20% of data logs examined by Marsteller and Neuhaus contained completed questionnaires.[20] The satisfaction information in the Saskatchewan Libraries 2003 evaluation of its virtual reference project notes that the 39 feedback messages received account for only 6% of users.[21] It is impossible to know whether or not there is some systematic difference between those who answer the survey and those who do not. Quite possibly unhappy or disgruntled users might be too irritated to fill in the questionnaires.

So far the literature evaluating virtual reference service mirrors the early phase of evaluation studies of traditional reference service. Typically libraries initially conducted studies with their own reference users and found them willing to report high levels of satisfaction on questionnaires. Then came studies based on unobtrusive observation, from which was derived the famous 55% rule.[22] Hernon and McClure measured the accuracy of answers provided by libraries when surrogate users posed questions to which the right answer was known in advance.

This research indicated that reference librarians on average provide correct answers to only 55% of the questions they get. But what about digital reference? Does the 55% rule apply here as well?

While unobtrusive observation is often recommended as a method for evaluating virtual reference services in libraries, there have not yet been many studies published. Neil Kaske and Julie Arnold used unobtrusive observations to evaluate responses from a number of libraries.[23] Here students in a graduate course on reference asked test questions and measured success by the correctness of the answer provided and the inclusion of citations for the sources. Unlike the studies previously mentioned that evaluated virtual reference service in a single library setting where the investigators themselves worked, the study by Kaske and Arnold looks at multiple sites. It provides data on what happened when the test questions were asked in 36 libraries offering real-time reference services (six public libraries and thirty academic libraries). Twelve test questions were used such as "What was the population of Afghanistan in 2000 and what is their official language?" and "How many people died in automobile accidents each year in the past five years?" Each student tried to ask his or her assigned test question in chat sessions in 15 different libraries and also sent their question to the e-mail reference service of 15 libraries. In total, 180 chat sessions were attempted, including 47 cases where the session was not completed, usually because the service wasn't available. Of the 133 completed chat transactions, correct answers were provided almost 55% of the time. Correspondingly, 180 e-mail sessions were attempted. Of the 107 completed e-mail sessions, correct answers were provided 60% of the time. This left 73 e-mail reference questions that were not answered for various reasons, including ineligibility of the user for service and "no e-mail reference available." Once we eliminate from calculation those queries sent to libraries that don't purport to offer virtual reference service, it seems that the 55% rule still holds, where success is measured by correctness of answer provided.

Another unobtrusive research method involves using records of transactions. Chat transcripts provide an easily accessible research resource for a single library or a consortium wishing to evaluate its virtual reference service. Other researchers use transcripts kept by Tutor.com or other chat software providers. For example, White, Abels, and Agresta reported at the 2004 Virtual Reference Desk conference on a study in which 400 chat transcripts provided by Tutor.com were evaluated using content analysis and then compared with 179 chat sessions conducted by students using questions derived from the 400 transcripts.[24] Using questionnaires, the students reported on their search experiences, judging questions, answers and interviews. On the basis of these evaluations, White, Abels, and Agresta found that "the better the chat interview, the better the response to the question."[25] Just as chat transcripts can be used for evaluation, copies of e-mails can also be evaluated, though there have been even fewer studies of e-mail transactions.

The use of chat transcripts does raise privacy concerns. Confidentiality needs to be ensured, a requirement made more difficult by the USA Patriot Act. In David Lankes' 2004 work, *The Virtual Reference Experience*, lawyer Glen Bencivengo urges librarians to keep records for only a short time, evaluate them quickly, and destroy all transcripts.[26] Librarians should also ensure that chat software providers, such as LSSI (Tutor.com), are not keeping transcripts unless they are fully anonymized.

In evaluation of face-to-face reference service, the next step after unobtrusive observation and success measured by correctness of the answer was a series of studies that focussed on the experiences of real users. These studies investigated what happens when users ask questions that matter to them personally and evaluate the answers provided in terms of their own needs. Joan Durrance pointed out that there is more to providing an adequate answer than can be measured by the simple test of correctness or accuracy. She therefore proposed and tested a new indicator: the user's willingness to return to the same staff member at a later time. In her study of 266 reference interviews in academic, special, and public libraries, Durrance found that a user's willingness (or unwillingness) to return was significantly related to eleven interpersonal and search skill variables. She found that users were "far more forgiving when library staff members had weak interviewing skills or gave inaccurate answers than they were if the staff member made them feel uncomfortable, showed no interest, or appeared to be judgmental about the question."[27] Durrance's research together with that of Marie Radford[28] and the reports of the first two phases of the Library Visit Study[29] provide some evidence about the factors that influence the user's willingness to return in the traditional face-to-face setting.

But what about the factors important to users in the virtual reference environment? Phase 3 of the Library Visit Study is an attempt to begin to address this question. To study vitural reference from the users' perspective, we have adapted the research method previously used in the Library Visit Study to investigate the face-to-face reference transaction.

WILLINGNESS TO RETURN

Throughout the Library Visit research project we have used Joan Durrance's "willingness to return" indicator as a user-centered measure for evaluating reference service. After completing their virtual library visit, students filled out a questionnaire which included the question: "Given the nature of this interaction, if you had the option, would you return to this digital reference site again with another question?" They were given the option of saying, "Yes," "No," or "Not Sure." Transactions were counted as successful where the users said "Yes" and were counted as unsuccessful where the users said "No" or "Not Sure." Table 2 compares the success rates of phases 1 and 2 with those reported in the 85 questionnaires submitted to date for phase 3, success being defined as a "Yes" response to the question on willingness to return to the same service in the future.

The numbers of virtual library visits reported here are too low to be able to make any generalizable claims about differences in success rates between public and academic libraries. These preliminary findings do suggest, however, that the success rate for virtual reference as a whole is similar to the success rate for face-to-face reference, which has consistently been in the area of 55% to 65% in almost every study that has used unobtrusive observational methods. We had anticipated that the users in phase 3 might be harder to please than the novice users in phases 1 and 2, who had not yet been introduced to reference interviewing skills and in some cases had no idea of what to expect from a reference transaction. Familiar as they were with traditional reference, however, many phase 3 users were novices in the area of virtual reference and were using the service for the first time. Many were pleasantly surprised at the

TABLE 2. Success Rates, Phases 1, 2 and 3: *Would You Be Willing to Return?*

Phase/Type of Library	No. of Library Visits	% Reporting Yes
Phases 1 & 2 face-to-face visits combined:		
Public libraries	182	61%
University libraries	79	75%
Total: Public & university libraries	261	65%
Phase 3 virtual visits		
Public libraries	40	62.5%
University libraries	45	55.5%
Total: Public & university libraries	85	59%

service they received such as this user of e-mail reference: "I could not believe the amount of authoritative sources that the e-mail contained. I was floored. I thought to myself, now that is the kind of information provider that I want to be."

Of the 25 virtual library visits to chat reference services, 17 users (68%) declared themselves willing to return. In comparison, 33 of the 60 users who used e-mail service (55%) declared themselves willing to return. The numbers of users are too low for us to claim any significant differences in satisfaction rate between chat and e-mail in this report. However, it does seem, from the student-users' accounts, that they found the chat experience more intense, possibly because of the novelty of the technology involved. Unless they had had previous experience with chat or instant messaging, users tended to find the chat process quite intimidating. One user commented, "I had butterflies in my stomach when a reference librarian was available . . . I felt relief when the session was over." Some users became enthusiastic about chat reference, as one said, "Ultimately I found the experience to be very positive and easily accessible; I did not find that the reference interview had limitations because it was virtual and not face to face."

WHAT THE USERS TOLD US

In phases 1 and 2 of the Library Visit Study, when we analysed the face-to-face library visits in which users reported unsuccessful transactions (declaring themselves either unwilling to return or unsure), it turned out that most of the difficulties could be reduced to a small number of problems. These problems have been reported elsewhere[30] but can be briefly summarized as follows. Before they had even asked their reference question, some users reported barriers in the physical environment, including lack of signage, lack of ways to identify the reference librarians, physical barriers such as high desks, and unwelcoming body language on the part of staff. A frequently reported problem with the reference transaction itself was the tendency of the librarian to accept the user's initial question at face value and to bypass the reference interview. In the 261 face-to-face library visits, the staff member conducted a reference interview only half the time. Secondly the librarian often failed to let the user know what s/he was doing, and so users made observations like, "I had no idea where she was going or why, and it made me feel quite uncomfortable to just follow her, without knowing why." Two additional problems noted were the unmonitored referral, which occurred in 37% of cases and the failure to follow up, which occurred in 64% of cases. In the unmonitored referral, the staff member refers the user to a source, either inside or outside the library, but does not take any steps to check whether or not the source actually contains a helpful answer. Typically the user asks for information and is given a piece of paper listing some call numbers. When the user went to the shelf looking for the books, it often happened that the books were missing or, if found, did not contain the necessary information. A way to give the user a second chance of finding helpful sources is for the librarian to ask a follow-up question, "If you don't find what you are looking for in these books, come back and we can try something else." The literature on reference interviews has long noted that asking a follow-up question is the "single most important" behavior in the reference transaction.[31] However, in the 261 face-to-face reference transactions, staff members chose to ask a follow-up question only about one third of the time.

In phase 3 of the Library Visit study, we are interested in knowing whether the factors that make a difference to the users' satisfaction with their experience with virtual reference are the same or different from the ones we identified as important in face-to-face reference. We examined the Library Visit accounts, focusing on the differences between the successful transactions (where the user was willing to return) and the unsuccessful transactions. The following are features of the virtual reference service that users identified as being helpful as well as features they found unhelpful.

FEATURES OF THE VIRTUAL REFERENCE SERVICE THAT HELPED

- The chat interface is easy to navigate to and from the home page. [Chat]
- I appreciated the [personal] greeting. It acknowledged me as opposed to only concentrating on the question I asked. [E-mail]
- The friendliness of the response was nice to read. The librarian addressed the e-mail with my name and wrote in the first person. [E-mail]
- As soon as I submitted my question, I received a notice thanking me for my question and informing me that a librarian would be with me soon. This reassured me. [Chat]

- [The librarian] gathered sufficient information about my need in order to answer the question. [Chat]
- What I liked most about the e-mail is that there was time to reflect. I could think about my question and write it out clearly and the librarian had time to read it over and think critically about it. [E-mail]
- If the librarian is friendly and patient, many patrons will feel that they have had a successful reference transaction even if they do not get the answer they are looking for.
- The response time was fantastic [3 hours]. [E-mail]
- I realized that digital reference is similar to in person reference in that much of my satisfaction was determined by my assessment of how well I had been treated, as much as by my reaction to the answer I received. [Chat]

FEATURES OF THE VIRTUAL REFERENCE SERVICE THAT WERE UNHELPFUL: CHAT

Barriers in the Environment

- The service was not advertised on the library homepage.
- The technology didn't work.
- There was no guidance on the Webpage about who could use the service, what kinds of questions it was intended to answer, or how soon I could expect a response.

Lack of Acknowledgment and Inclusion

- There were lag times when I was not sure if I had been disconnected.
- At times I was not sure if the librarian was still there.
- This comment [from the librarian] was followed by almost ten minutes of virtual silence. This confused me because it made me wonder if my session was over.
- I waited and waited for a response. In reality it was only four or five minutes but it felt like longer. I was thinking, "Did the librarian forget about me? Something as short as 'Still looking' would have reassured me."

- [The librarian] just started pushing pages at me. He did not explain what he was doing.

Unmonitored Referral

- [After being told to browse the stacks under a particular call number range], I thought to myself about my location. I was chatting on the Internet, why is the librarian asking me to come to the library?
- [After being told that it might work to search Google again, using particular terms], I felt that [the librarian] was going to turn me loose on my own and stop helping me.

Bypassing the Reference Interview

- Many of the files I was forwarded were not at all useful. Had the librarian paused to ask me a little bit more about my question and what I was looking for, this could have been avoided.
- He seemed obsessed with the phrase [in the original question] and did not try other words. I felt rather helpless at this point.

Faulty Assumptions and Communication Accidents

- The librarian's response [advice to look at a book in the library's collection] indicated to me that s/he thought I was within traveling distance to the library.
- As I was looking at the page, I had a real sense that I should let the librarian go. I felt so flustered with the page in front of me that although I was only half way down the page and wasn't sure if it had what I wanted, I said, "This is great. Thank you very much." Just to let the librarian go.

No Follow Up

- I started to reply with thanks. Before I finished typing, however, a message came on the screen reading "Got to go. Someone else is waiting." I was stunned by the abruptness of this termination. I felt rude for not even thanking the person, then annoyed that the librarian hadn't even waited for a reply or made even a token attempt at a follow-up statement.

FEATURES OF THE VIRTUAL REFERENCE SERVICE THAT WERE UNHELPFUL: E-MAIL

Barriers in the Environment

- On the main library page, I could find no mention of virtual reference at all.
- Libraries need to make the digital reference a more welcoming experience.
- Once I clicked "Ask a Librarian," all that appeared was a list of librarians and their corresponding subject specialty. This makes it a little daunting to users who have to determine under which subject their question might be categorized. There were no forms to complete.
- The library site freezes on dial-up loading, has information cluttered everywhere, and has far too many menus.
- I clicked on the Submit Query button but instead of seeing a copy of the reference question I had composed, I was presented with eight lines of error message that all began with the word "WARNING" in bold type. I filled the form a second time and received the same error results . . . The most frustrating part of the experience was not knowing if my form had been received by anyone at [the university].

Lack of Acknowledgment and Inclusion

- It was frustrating not to receive any indication that my question was accepted and someone was working on my question.

Unmonitored Referral

- The response did not actually contain a direct answer to my question. Instead, the response gave me URLs to recommended sites. In the event, however, these sites proved useless to me in search of the information I was seeking.
- Since I was asking something factual, I was surprised to see that my question was not answered but instead I was given a couple of links to sites.

Bypassing the Reference Interview

- The e-mail form used is not conducive to replacing the reference interview. The form isn't detailed enough. The only information that is gained is whether the patron is above or below grade six, their city, and their question.

Faulty Assumptions and Communication Accidents

- The librarian assumed I was in an area that had a local academic library.

Other

- The digital reference service [of the academic library] does not provide reference in the true sense of the term. There is no effort to answer elaborate academic questions that would require time or extensive research.
- After this experience, I think quality is a far better attribute than speed, especially if it means getting a better response.

The Disappearing Reference Interview

The most striking difference between face-to-face reference and virtual reference, as reported in Table 3, is in the area of the reference interview. At physical reference desks, library staff members conducted a reference interview only about half the time. At the virtual reference desk, the reference interview almost disappears, occurring in only 17 accounts of the 85 completed transactions. In the face-to-face transaction, we counted it as a reference interview if the staff member asked at least one question intended to find out more about the user's information need. We used a generous definition, counting any clarifying ques-

TABLE 3. Frequency of Occurrence of the Reference Interview

	Phases 1 & 2 261 face-to-face visits	Phase 3 85 virtual visits
Reference Interview occurred	51% (n = 132/261)	20% (n = 17/85)

tion that was asked at any time during the entire transaction by any staff member, including on a second attempt when the user started over with a second librarian. We also counted responses that were not formally questions but had the performative function of a question, such as repeating the keywords of the user's statement and pausing strategically to encourage further elaboration.[27]

To be counted as a reference interview in e-mail or chat accounts, the transaction had to include either some sort of question to clarify the information need, either on a form or as part of an e-mail or chat exchange with the user (see Table 4). Just as in the face-to-face interview, we did not count as a clarifying question, "Do you know how to use the catalogue?" so in the e-mail and chat context we did not count, "Do you know how to search the Internet?"

Of the eleven interviews recorded for chat transactions, ten took place during chat sessions in university libraries, and only one occurred in a public library. Conversely, of the six interviews conducted with patrons who used e-mail, all occurred in public libraries. In only three of these did the librarian attempt to elicit more information than was initially provided. The remaining three were counted as including a reference interview only because users were required to fill in a good form that served to substitute for an interview. Those responding to e-mail reference in university libraries apparently believed that their users expressed their information needs precisely and completely in their initial e-mail queries.

Were so few interviews conducted because users of virtual reference services are able to formulate an initial question that completely and clearly communicates their real information need? If so, they must differ substantially from face-to-face users who, we know, often initially ask for something general when they really want something quite specific or they ask for something specific when their real information need

TABLE 4. Comparing Frequency of Chat and E-Mail Reference Interviews by Type of Library

	Public Libraries	University Libraries	Total Transactions that Included an Interview
Chat	1 of 9	10 of 16	11 of 25 (44%)
E-mail	6 of 31	0 of 29	6 of 60 (10%)
Total	7 of 40	10 of 45	17 of 85 (20%)

is more general.[33] They may say, "Can you give me information on transportation?" when actually they want pictures of steam engines. We found the same pattern of vaguely formulated initial questions in chat reference sessions. For example, one user of chat reference asked for information on Crohn's disease. The transaction went like this:

User: Hi, I'm looking for information on Crohn's disease and I'm not sure where to start.

Librarian: Crohn's disease? From a patient's perspective, or in the medical literature?

U: From a patient's perspective.

L: www.cfa.org is the US Crohn's organization. You could start there for basic info and coping info. www.ccfc.ca is the same type of thing for Canada.
[item sent: the academic library's Gateway]
Now in terms of journal articles and scholarly information that will help you, I recommend the PUBmed database–it's like MEDLINE except that MEDLINE is the one for doctors and medical students.
[item sent: electronic resources]
So if we look at the health sciences journal sources page . . .
[item sent: EBSCO host]
Is there a specific question you had about the disease or are you just browsing?

U: I just found out a friend has the disease and I would like to learn a little about it.

L: Then I recommend the national organizations–they can provide you with the initial information and point you to further resources too.
[item sent: Crohn's and Colitis Foundation of Canada]
There you go. Does that answer your question for now?

This transaction, which included both a reference interview and a follow-up question, was rated as a highly successful transaction by the user who said s/he would be willing to return to this digital reference site with another question. However, even in this case, the user felt that the reference process would have been more effective if the librarian had done more to clarify the question at the outset: "I think that she could have asked what I needed the information for earlier in the transaction. That would have eliminated the need to search the medical databases . . . the librarian should not assume the users' need. It will only waste the time of the librarian and the patron if you give them inappropriate information."

Another user of chat reference who asked about an ancient Chinese battle tactic called "wall of fire" was not interviewed but instead was sent a barrage of files. The user's comment was: "Many of the files I was forwarded were not at all useful. Had the librarian paused to ask me a little bit more about my question and what I was looking for, this could have been avoided . . . In the end, the one thing that this experience emphasized most for me was the need to ensure that a proper reference interview is conducted over an online medium since, without the physical presence of both participants, communication problems can develop very quickly." Surprised not to be interviewed, several users explained the sparseness of communication in terms of the cumbersome process of having to type everything. One person noted, "I believe that . . . having to type in real time while working a potentially busy Reference/Info desk, militates against an involved interview process. It's as if, as reference librarian, the tendency is to say, 'Let's get to it; there's no time for small talk . . .'"

For whatever the reason, it is apparent that in the virtual environment the reference interview or its equivalent is almost an endangered species. It could be argued that in the case of e-mail reference, questions on the form did the work that would be done in the face-to-face transaction by the reference interview. But is this the case? Unfortunately not often. In some cases, the interface consisted of an icon on the library's home page labeled "Ask-a-Librarian" and a regular e-mail mail-to form. One user who experienced this rudimentary interface, commented, "When I clicked on the link, as it was not clear what sort of 'asking' was involved, I was surprised to have a Netscape e-mail window pop up. There was no guidance on the Webpage about who could use the service, what kinds of questions it was intended to answer, or how soon I could expect a response."

Typically the only structure on the form was an instruction along the lines of, "Submit your question" or "Your question(s) or comment(s)," sometimes with the additional comment, "To help us answer your question, please be as specific as possible." But as one user put it, "A well-designed e-mail form is more than simply a box to put text in and a button to send the text . . . Such a form is far more likely than a simple 'What's your name and what's your question?' form to create a reference interview that is welcoming to the user and helpful to the librarian." Another user commented that the public library e-mail reference form that s/he encountered in the virtual library visit was "extremely simple and did not prompt the user into giving detailed information." This user concluded that "the e-form does not allow for a reference interview to take place." The particular form being criticized said, "Enter your question into the box below. Provide as much detail as possible." The request for detail is certainly better than just a bare "Enter your question here" but is still problematic. Many users simply don't know *what kinds* of detail librarians need or find useful. As Joseph Janes points out in *Introduction to Reference Work in the Digital Age*, simple forms that limit themselves to a "Your question" box "solicit very little information and perhaps even dictate sketchy inquiries from users." He argues persuasively, "If we truly want to take advantage of our collective experience in reference practice, perhaps it would be best to invest forms with what we know about questions that really help in determining what a person wants to know."[34]

And what do we know from a sustained body of research on the face-to-face reference transaction? We know that, in comparison with answering the initial question at face value, that the librarian saves time in the long run by asking open questions or sense-making questions such as, "What aspect of X would you like to find out about?" or "What sort of information about X would help you most?" or "How do you plan to use this information."[35] The best forms among those encountered by the student-users in our study were like the one used by the Internet Public Library that has been refined in the crucible of answering over 50,000 questions through an e-mail reference service. This form imitates the turn-taking of the face-to-face reference interview by providing a number of questions that give users the opportunity to refine their question in a structured way. The Internet Public Library form incorporates, among other things, a series of three open questions deliberately chosen to elicit the type of information the librarian needs to know: "Please tell us your question," "How will you use this information?" and "Sources consulted." Janes explains, "I like to think of it as scaffolding the inquiry; giving the user a level of support in framing and expressing their need."[36]

The vast majority of e-mail reference forms currently available do not succeed in providing this scaffolding for users. The rationale for impoverished forms seems to be that users expect things to be quick in the electronic environment–that they should be able to type in a few keywords and get an answer at the click of a button. The problem is that, if this approach was going to work, the answer would already have been found in Google, since typically users of virtual reference service have already tried and failed to answer the question on their own. We are certainly not advocating long, complex forms containing numerous closed questions. We *do* argue that the reference interview is an indispensable part of the reference transaction that needs to be part of every reference transaction, whether face-to-face or virtual. In e-mail service, the reference interview needs to be incorporated into the form as a series of questions (as is done so effectively on the Internet Public Library form).

THE LOW BANDWIDTH PROBLEM

In the face-to-face Library Visit, users sometimes acknowledged that they got a helpful answer but still said they would not be willing to return because the staff member seemed uninterested in their question or impatient or appeared to be trying to get rid of them. Similarly in the virtual environment, the quality of the communicative exchange sometimes trumped the quality of the information exchange when it came to the users' evaluation of their experience. Just as users in the face-to-face transaction say that the body language of the staff member is very important to their feelings about the transaction, so in the virtual reference transaction many users commented on what they perceived to be the tone of the written exchange. One person said, "I was surprised that the tone of the e-mail made such a difference to me." Another wrote, "I feel the . . . librarian should avoid short answers because they can be construed as sharp and cold answers to the patron."

Here is one example of many we could have chosen that illustrates how users interpret small clues in the written exchange to form impressions, quite possibly erroneous ones, about the intentions, coolness, and lack of friendliness of the staff member. One e-mail reference user asked, "I'm wondering if you can tell me the names of some award-winning First Nations writers from British Columbia?" Within half an hour, the user received an e-mail from a staff member saying she was unable to find this information on any of the awards Websites and had forwarded the question to a subject expert. The user said, "I was impressed that the response was so quick, and found her reply polite, if not exactly friendly, and helpful . . . I appreciated being kept informed of the status of my question and being referred to an expert." On the morning of the first working day after the question was sent, the expert responded with the sentence: "Eden Robinson's *Monkey beach* is the most notable B.C. native to win an award." On the questionnaire, the user responded to the question, "To what extent would you say that the digital librarian was friendly or pleasant?" by giving the librarian a 2 on a 7-point scale where 1 is "not at all friendly" and 7 is "very friendly." In the written account, the user explained, "I appreciated this bit of information, but found the brevity of the e-mail made it feel cold in spite of the fact that she greeted me by name and signed it with her first name. Her grammar was wrong, and there was a typo (beach instead of Beach in the title), which spoke to me of carelessness and impatience. I would have liked it had she shared her sources. I got the feeling that this was a fact that she knew off the top of her head and she had not done any research . . . Quite honestly, I went from being very impressed with the service at my first reply to feeling like I was wasting someone's time and questioning whether I would use this service again at the second reply."

These kinds of communication accidents happen because written messages are low bandwidth, stripping away the nonverbal cues of nodding and smiling and encouraging tone of voice. Users can interpret apparently innocuous statements as negative or critical. For example, a library staff member responded to a request for information with the statement, "There should be some information on ancient Chinese war tactics." Probably the librarian intended the comment as encouraging, but the user commented, "I got the impression that the librarian was slightly exasperated with me, since the phrase 'there *should* be some' seemed to suggest the material was there, I just hadn't bothered looking for it. This put me slightly on the defensive." A number of users thought that the library staff sounded annoyed or irritated in circumstances when, had the same statement been spoken, they probably would not have come to a negative interpretation. One user commented, "The face-to-face interview makes sense. It was hard for them to know exactly what I wanted and it was hard for me to tell them. In fact I wanted them to try and read my mind a little bit."

The importance of the "relational dimension" of the virtual reference transaction has been confirmed in a study by Marie Radford, presented at the Virtual Reference Desk Conference 2003. Radford analyzed 44 award winning chat transcripts submitted to the LSSI Model Virtual Reference Transaction Prize honoring Samuel S. Green.[37] She argues that in the virtual reference environment staff should take special steps to compensate for the lack of non-verbal cues.

IN CONCLUSION, SOME TIPS

Do's and Don'ts for All Virtual Reference Services

- Make sure the technology works, and check it frequently.
- Do provide an automatic response assuring users that their question has been received.
- Be sure that the library's home page indicates that the service is available. The service site should be no more than two clicks away from the home page. Let users know what kinds of questions that can be answered, with examples.
- Don't assume that the user is local and can easily come to the library for additional help or to look at a particular reference tool or print product. Expect questions from people who are far away (even if you indicate that the service is limited to those who are in some way affiliated with your institution).
- Do transfer good reference behaviors from the physical reference desk environment to the virtual environment.
- Don't assume that a reference interview is not needed.
- Pay attention to the relational dimensions of the transaction with users.
- Check URLs that are forwarded . . . do the sites answer the user's question?
- Do ask follow-up questions.

Do's and Don'ts Specific to E-Mail Reference

- Do provide a form that the user can fill in (an example of a good form is the one used by the Internet Public Library at www.ipl.org).
- Do indicate time by which an answer can be expected.
- Do address the user by name and sign your message with your name.
- Do remember that words can sometimes sound cold and unfriendly when you don't mean them to be. Take special steps to make your message friendly.
- Do send an answer to the question in your first reply, but ask if this is what the patron is looking for (e.g., "Does this answer your question?"). Encourage the user to contact you again if the information you provide is not helpful.

Do's and Don'ts Specific to Chat Reference

- Do indicate the hours when the service is staffed.
- Do take time to clarify the question. Don't feel that speed is more important than quality.
- Do let the user know what you are doing with a quick note such as, "still working on your question."
- When pushing pages, explain what the user is to do with them.
- If the transaction is going on for a long time, reassure the patron that this is okay.

NOTES

1. Patricia Dewdney and Catherine Sheldrick Ross, (1994), "Flying a Light Aircraft: Reference Service Evaluation from a User's Viewpoint," *RQ* 34 (2): 217-30; Catherine Sheldrick Ross and Patricia Dewdney, (1994), "Best Practices: An Analysis of the Best (and Worst) in Fifty-two Public Library Reference Transactions," *Public Libraries* 33 (5): 261-66; Catherine Sheldrick Ross and Patricia Dewdney, (1998), "Negative Closure: Strategies and Counter-Strategies in the Reference Transaction," *Reference & User Services Quarterly* 38, 2: 151-63; Catherine Sheldrick Ross and Kirsti Nilsen, (2000), "Has the Internet Changed Anything in Reference? The Library Visit Study Phase 2," *Reference and User Services Quarterly* 40 (2): 147-155; Nilsen, Kirsti (2004). The Library Visit Study: User Experiences at the Virtual Reference Desk. *Information Research* 9 (2). Paper 171. Retrieved 9 January 2005 from http://InformationR.net/ir/9-2/paper171.html; Kirsti Nilsen (2006). "Comparing Users' Perspectives of In-Person and Virtual Reference," *New Library World* 107 (3/4) forthcoming.

2. Catherine Sheldrick Ross, Kirsti Nilsen and Patricia Dewdney, (2002), *Conducting the Reference Interview: A How-To-Do-It Manual for Librarians* (New York: Neal Schuman; London: Facet).

3. American Library Association, (2004). "Guidelines for Implementing and Maintaining Virtual Reference Services." 2004. Prepared by the Digital Reference Guidelines Ad Hoc Committee of the Machine-Assisted Reference Section, Reference and User Services Association. Chicago: ALA. Retrieved 22 December 2005 from http://www.ala.org/ala/rusa/rusaprotools/referenceguide/virtrefguidelines.htm.

4. Bernie Sloan, (2004), "Digital Reference Service Bibliography," Last updated 20 September 2004. Retrieved 224 December 2005 from http://people.lis.uiuc.edu/~b-sloan/digiref.html.

5. See for example the "Registry of Real Time Digital Reference Services" which illustrates numbers of services in different types of libraries as of March 2003. Retrieved 22 December, 2005 from http://www.public.iastate.edu/~CYBERSTACKS/LiveRef.htm. More recently several state and province-wide collaborative virtual reference systems have been established that include public libraries.

6. Bernie Sloan, (2001), "Ready for Reference: Academic Libraries Offer Live Web-Based Reference: Evaluating System Use," Retrieved 22 December 2005 from http://www.lis.uiuc.edu/~b-sloan/r4r.final.htm.

7. Jo Kibbee, David Ward and Wei Ma, (2002), "Virtual Service Real Data: Results of a Pilot Study," *Reference Services Review* 30 (1): 25-36.

8. Marilyn Domas White, Eileen G. Abels, and Neal Kaske (2003), "Evaluation of Chat Reference Service Quality: Pilot Study," *D-Lib Magazine* 9 (2), 14 p. Retrieved 22 December 2005 from http://www.dlib.org/dlib/february03/white/02white.html.

9. Joanne Smyth, (2003), "Virtual Reference Transcript Analysis: A Few Models," *Searcher* 11 (3): 26-30.

10. Sloan, (2001).

11. Donnelyn Curtis and Araby Green, (2004), "A University-Wide Library-Based Chat Service," *Reference Services Review* 32 (3): 220-233.

12. Marie Ruppel and Jody Condit Fagan, (2002), "Instant Messaging Reference: Users' Evaluation of Library Chat," *Reference Services Review* 30 (3): 183-197.

13. Marianne Foley, (2002), "Instant Messaging Reference in an Academic Library: A Case Study," *College and Research Libraries* 63 (1), 36-45.

14. Matt Marsteller and Paul Neuhaus, (2001), "The Chat Reference Experience at Carnegie Mellon University," Presentation at the American Library Association Annual Conference, 2001. Retrieved 22 December 2005 from http://www.contrib.andrew.cmu.edu/~matthewm/ALA_2001_chat.html.

15. Kibbee, Ward and Ma, (2002), p. 34.

16. Corey Johnson (2004), "Online Chat Reference: Survey Results from Affiliates of Two Universities," *Reference and User Services Quarterly* 43 (3): 237-247.

17. Ruppel and Fagan, (2002), p. 190.

18. For example, see Foley, (2002), p. 144.

19. Kibbee, Ward and Ma, (2002), p. 34.

20. Marsteller and Neuhaus, (2001).

21. Saskatchewan Libraries. (2003). "Saskatchewan Libraries: Ask Us! Pilot Project Evaluation." Retrieved 24 January 2004 from http://www.lib.sk.ca/staff/virtref/askusreport.html.

22. Peter Hernon and Charles R. McClure, (1986), "Unobtrusive Reference Testing: the 55 Percent Rule," *Library Journal* 111 (April 15): 37-41; Kenneth D. Crews, (1988), "The Accuracy of Reference Service: Variables for Research and Implementation," *Library and Information Science Research* 10, no. 3 (July): 331-355.

23. Neal Kaske and Julie Arnold, (2002), "An Unobtrusive Evaluation of Online Real Time Library Reference Services," Library Research Round Table, American Library Association, Annual Conference, Atlanta, Georgia, June 15, 2002. Retrieved 24 January 2004 from http://www.lib.umd.edu/groups/digref/LRRT.html.

24. White, Marilyn Domas, Eileen G. Abels, and Jennifer Agresta, (2004), "Relationship between Interaction Characteristics and Answer Quality in Chat Reference Service," 6th Annual Virtual Reference Desk Conference, Cincinnati, Ohio, [PowerPoint presentation], Retrieved 22 December 2005 from http://www.vrd2004.org/proceedings/presentation.cfm?PID=376.

25. White, Abels, and Agresta, slide 21.

26. Bencivengo, Glen, (2004), "A Lawyer's View of Privacy, Surveillance, and the USA Patriot Act," Chapter 12 in David Lankes et al., (eds.), *The Virtual Reference Experience: Integrating Theory and Practice*, 235-257 (New York: Neal Schuman), 251.

27. Joan C. Durrance, (1989), "Reference Success: Does the 55% Rule Tell the Whole Story?" *Library Journal* 114 (April 15): 31-36.

28. Marie L. Radford, (1999), *The Reference Encounter: Interpersonal Communication in the Academic Library* (Chicago: Association of College and Research Libraries).

29. Dewdney and Ross, (1994); Ross and Dewdney, (1994), (1998); Ross and Nilsen, (2000).

30. Dewdney and Ross, (1994); Ross and Dewdney, (1994), (1998); Ross and Nilsen, (2000); Ross, Nilsen and Dewdney (2002); Nilsen (2004); Nilsen (2006).

31. Ralph Gers, and Lillie J. Seward, (1985). "Improving Reference Performance: Results of a Statewide Study," *Library Journal* 110 (8), 32-35.

32. See Ross and Nilsen, (2000).

33. Ross, Nilsen and Dewdney, 2002.

34. Joseph Janes, (2003), *Introduction to Reference Work in the Digital Age* (New York: Neal-Schuman), p. 56.

35. Ross, Nilsen, and Dewdney, (2002).

36. Janes, (2003), p. 60.

37. Marie L. Radford, (2003), "In Synch? Evaluating Chat Reference Transcripts," Virtual Reference Desk Conference 2003, San Antonio, Texas. Retrieved 24 January 2004 from http://www.vrd2003.org/proceedings/presentations.cfm?PID=231.

doi:10.1300/J120v46n95_05

Balancing Statewide and Local Digital Reference Service

Ruth Vondracek

SUMMARY. As digital and chat reference services become established as another way to do business, many libraries juggle the delivery of consortial and local virtual reference services. Balancing services without overtaxing staff and resources presents a number of challenges. How, for example, do libraries staff more than one chat reference service in addition to traditional services? Or more critically, how are subject specialists used to their greatest advantage in a multi-type library service? This article explores the benefits and issues of offering service at the statewide and local level based on OSU's experience and describes how OSU responded to these issues. doi:10.1300/J120v46n95_06 *[Article copies available for a fee from The Haworth Document Delivery Service: 1-800-HAWORTH. E-mail address: <docdelivery@haworthpress.com> Website: <http://www.HaworthPress.com> © 2006 by The Haworth Press, Inc. All rights reserved.]*

KEYWORDS. Digital reference, chat reference, virtual reference, digital reference consortia, statewide reference services, multi-type library services, Oregon State University Libraries, L-net, Answerland

Ruth Vondracek is Head of Reference and Instruction, Oregon State University, 121 Valley Library, Corvallis, OR 97331, and Chair of the L-net Advisory Board, Oregon's statewide digital reference service (E-mail: ruth.vondracek@oregonstate.edu).

[Haworth co-indexing entry note]: "Balancing Statewide and Local Digital Reference Service." Vondracek, Ruth. Co-published simultaneously in *The Reference Librarian* (The Haworth Information Press, an imprint of The Haworth Press, Inc.) No. 95/96, 2006, pp. 81-98; and: *Assessing Reference and User Services in a Digital Age* (ed: Eric Novotny) The Haworth Information Press, an imprint of The Haworth Press, Inc., 2006, pp. 81-98. Single or multiple copies of this article are available for a fee from The Haworth Document Delivery Service [1-800-HAWORTH, 9:00 a.m. - 5:00 p.m. (EST). E-mail address: docdelivery@haworthpress.com].

INTRODUCTION

Three years ago, when QuestionPoint was still the Collaborative Digital Reference Service (CDRS), Oregon was undiscovered country for virtual reference service. Oregon State University Libraries, like most Oregon libraries other than Multnomah County Public Library, did not offer virtual reference service. At OSU we were just beginning to anticipate what it might be like to deliver reference services virtually. Our reference questions showed no signs of the decline that other libraries were reporting. We knew, however, that we were not tapping into those questions we might be able to answer for students studying in their dorms or for those students accessing library resources remotely. Wouldn't virtual reference provide us the means to reach all of our students when and where they needed help?

In response to these needs a grass roots task force consisting of OSU librarians and staff began investigating options for purchasing chat and co-browsing software. As the new Head of Reference, I joined the task force and urged them to engage in a pre-planning effort to examine more thoroughly how it would be integrated into existing services in our library and with other potential regional systems. In addition, we knew that purchasing software would require a well-developed justification, given that it would require funding at a time when budgets were shrinking.

At that time of this planning effort we operated a regional center for the Oregon Reference Oregon Library Information Network for Knowledge (LINK), a library-to-library reference referral service begun in 1994, but that service was beginning to wind down as the number of LINK questions slowly dwindled due to lack of demand, slow response times, and better access to the Internet in many libraries. We were aware that the Oregon State Library was looking for a better way to deliver reference services to the state.

Since 2002, digital and chat reference services have become established as another way to do business and Oregon is no longer a virtual reference wasteland. In fact, there are a plethora of opportunities available for participating in one consortia or another. Determining how and if to participate in this multitude of opportunities is a challenge for us as we consider what best serves our users.

Like OSU, many libraries juggle simultaneous delivery of multiple virtual reference services. Balancing these services without overtaxing staff and resources can be a challenge. How, for example, does the reference staff accommodate two or more different chat reference schedules along with traditional desk, e-mail and phone reference services? Or more critically, how are subject specialists used to their greatest advantage in a multi-type library service? This article explores the benefits and issues of offering service at the statewide and local level based on OSU's experience and describes how OSU has responded to the issues.

Oregon State University Libraries have participated in Oregon's statewide digital reference service, L-net, since its inception in 2002, as a pilot project named Answerland. It is the successor to the Oregon Library Information Network for Knowledge (LINK). L-net was developed primarily to support Oregon's small- to medium-sized rural libraries, many of them with limited staff and even more limited reference services. According to Oregon State Library figures, 9% of Oregonians have no library service. Service providers from academic, public, publicly-funded special libraries, and school libraries operate the current statewide service. Oregon's four largest research libraries, OSU, University of Oregon, Portland State University, and Multnomah County Public Library all participate.

At this time OSU Libraries belongs to three other groups considering establishing digital or chat reference services, the Greater Western Library Alliance (GWLA), an alliance of 30 research libraries located in the Midwest and Western United States and the Orbis-Cascades Alliance comprised of Oregon and Washington academic libraries, and three Oregon University System libraries engaged in L-net. A cluster of GWLA libraries that use QuestionPoint are currently planning to open a chat service. A second GWLA group of libraries that use Tutor.com software is discussing the possibility of developing another service cluster. The hope is that inter-operability standards will in time enable the two groups to work together. OSU is deciding whether to participate in this service. The Orbis-Cascades Alliance has discussed the possibility of establishing a digital reference service in the future, but has taken no formal steps at this time. In Oregon, the three major academic libraries engaged in delivering L-net services, OSU, University of Oregon, and Portland State may set up an academic queue on L-net in early 2005. The advantages of being involved with an academic library virtual reference service include the similarities in reference delivery philosophy and the access to complementary subject collection strengths and librarian expertise. Determining how and if to participate in this multitude of opportunities in addition to a statewide service and a local service is a challenge for us. As we examine these options we must consider how we would mesh services and which configuration of services would benefit our users.

BACKGROUND

OSU is no stranger to statewide reference service or to digital reference. As a land grant university, OSU's responsibilities extend beyond OSU to the rest of Oregon. For this reason, participating in a statewide service is a natural fit for us. In 1994, OSU became one of the regional centers (Oregon Northwest LINK) for the Oregon Library Information Network for Knowledge (LINK) service, a statewide library-to-library reference referral system. Oregon State University's involvement with digital reference began in 1997, when the e-mail reference service was launched. It is now an integrated part of our service.

OREGON LINK

A brief history of OSU's participation in the LINK service is pertinent to this discussion because many of the issues that were associated with operating LINK have carried over to L-net. This suggests that the major issues in providing reference services statewide in a multi-type library system are not related to the technology, but to the delivery of the service itself. As discussed in a short history of LINK by the Library Development Services unit of the Oregon State Library, LINK's mission was to provide effective reference service for all Oregon citizens by routing reference referrals through five regional reference centers and by providing reference training to local librarians.[1] This parallels the vision of the current L-net statewide digital reference service to build a cooperative statewide multi-type library reference service available to all Oregon residents.

LINK operated through library-to-library reference referrals. Grant funding could be used to cover staffing, publication costs, collection, and training costs. Northwest LINK operated independently from OSU's other reference services. Grant funding was used to hire a part-time staff person to manage the Northwest LINK program and to be the primary reference contact. The OSU subject librarians filled in for the NW LINK manager as needed. Grant funds also paid for the cost of printing and mailing the quarterly newsletter, blocks of FirstSearch searches for use by the regional libraries, and travel costs associated with reference training for the regional librarians. We had difficulties with keeping the part-time position filled and there were significant gaps in time when the position was open. Because of this, OSU staff and librarians ended up managing the service and responding to requests when the position was unstaffed. While the LINK program was highly successful initially, the number of requests handled by the service gradually lessened.

One of the major concerns of the librarians was answering general reference questions that were not suited to OSU's subject specialists or the research collections. Particularly before the advent of widespread use of the Internet, the subject specialists found it frustrating to answer questions without the collections to support them. This same concern exists with the current digital reference service and is discussed in more detail later in the Issues section.

STATEWIDE E-REFERENCE PROGRAM

In 2001 the Oregon Library Association released Vision 2010 Call to Action. One challenge to the library community was to "Create a collaborative on-line reference service that is available 24 hours a day, 7 days a week."[2] This call for action, the reduction in requests handled by LINK, and the growing popularity of digital reference services prompted Oregon State Librarian, Jim Scheppke, to appoint the Statewide E-Reference Task Force in April 2002. He charged the Task Force to develop a proposal for statewide digital reference service.[3] Membership on the Task Force included representatives from public, academic, school libraries, as well as representatives from the Orbis and PORTALS consortia and the Oregon Reference Library Information Network for Knowledge (LINK) centers. Anne Gruel of Jackson County Library and I were elected as co-chairs for the Task Force.

The Task Force proposal recommended that Oregon establish a statewide e-reference program using software with chat and co-browsing features.[4] Any library in Oregon would be considered eligible to apply to be providers; a welcome change for many Oregon libraries that had been limited in providing service by the LINK program. In addition, the Task Force recommended that a pilot project be undertaken in 2003 using the Virtual Reference Toolkit from LSSI and that a Program Coordinator position be created to oversee and promote the project. The Oregon State Library Board approved the proposal and later selected Multnomah County Public Library (MCPL) as the fiscal agent. Once LSTA funding was released, MCPL appointed a temporary project manager, Eva Miller, to begin setting up the software and training providers. Under her direction, Answerland, the pilot project, became a reality in April 2002. Eva stayed with the project until MCPL hired Caleb Tucker-Raymond as the service coordinator in June 2003.

Once Answerland was up and running the Task Force disbanded and an Advisory Board was formed. Membership followed the same configuration as the Task Force with representatives from academic, public, and school libraries.

BENEFITS OF PARTICIPATING IN L-NET

While many libraries first started a local e-reference system and then became involved in a multi-library service, Oregon State University decided to gain familiarity with the statewide service before developing our own. This allowed us to learn the software, take advantage of training, and work out the kinks in managing a service of this type. Most importantly, it meant the librarians did not have to learn how to use a different system. At least four of the staff had a year's experience on the statewide system before the local system was launched. The system also required fewer resources, such as staff time. This was a boon as we were in the midst of filling several open positions while the pilot was underway.

ACCESS TO THE SOFTWARE

Participating in the statewide service provides many benefits to Oregon State University Libraries and to the other participants. The primary benefit has been realized with the licensing agreements for Tutor.com's Virtual Reference Toolkit and Altarama's RefTracker. The Statewide e-Reference Task Force recommended that the project cover the full cost of licensing with Tutor.com rather than compensating providers for time spent answering questions or helping set up the system. Multnomah County Public Library arranged the licensing so that providers could eventually set up local queues. This ability to use Tutor.com's Virtual Reference Toolkit and Altamara's RefTracker proved decidedly advantageous to OSU when we set up our local queue, L-net OSU.

ESTABLISHING A REFERENCE NETWORK

Participating in L-net benefits OSU by providing us additional reference assistance for a minimal time investment. Providers and participants use the service to supplement their frequently understaffed reference service, particularly in those libraries that may only have one to two employees, who are responsible for the full gamut of library operations. For OSU, L-net offers us coverage in off hours or during regularly scheduled meetings.

One of the original charges to Statewide E-Reference Task Force was to provide 7-24 service. Because all of Oregon is in the same time zone, offering this type of coverage in the past has been problematic. Even covering evenings and weekends has been a challenge. The service has used Tutor.com in the past to cover Sunday hours, although this was discontinued because of cost and low usage. In October 2004, L-net will be engaged in a pilot with Tutor.com to provide round the clock service with external providers. If the trial is a success L-net may be able to fulfill on that charge.

In the Oregon LINK service only the regional centers were supposed to answer referral questions. L-net broadened that scope to allow any library to provide service that met the application standards, which require a commitment for providing a minimal amount of hours. This decision has been appreciated by many of the medium sized libraries. It has also increased contact among library reference staff across the state. More work needs to be done to take advantage of this resource, such as the development of a knowledge base for referrals and developing means for the provider librarians to meet in person or online.

REDUCED COSTS

In addition to not having to pay for the software, OSU did not need to invest in server time or storage space, since Tutor.com hosts the service. The cost to OSU amounts to staff time the Library Technology and Reference departments invested in setting up the queue, customizing settings, developing a local user satisfaction survey, and designing the linking Web page. Establishing local procedures and scheduling also consumed time. While this has taken many hours of staff time, it is still significantly less than what it would have cost to set up an entirely new system, and it accelerated our set-up time.

TRAINING

During the Answerland pilot, several OSU librarians were able to take advantage of the existing training for the statewide system, and then assist in training the remainder of the library reference staff. Valery King, a social sciences librarian at OSU and coordinator for the OSU virtual reference task force, serves as OSU's contact to L-net and became a member of the original Answerland set-up and training team. This team attended vendor training and took responsibility for conducting regional training sessions and for guiding other local providers through the initial software set up. Valery, along with other members of the current OSU Virtual Reference Task Force coordinated on-going training sessions for OSU and other libraries in the Corvallis area.

QUALITY AND SERVICE GUIDELINES

Another timesaver for OSU was leveraging L-net's service and quality standards. Rather than reinvent the wheel, L-net OSU follows the service and quality guidelines that L-net[5] developed and adapted from the MARS Ad Hoc Committee on Virtual Reference Draft Guidelines for Implementing and Maintaining Virtual Reference Services,[6] RUSA's Guidelines for Behavioral Performance of Reference and Information Service Providers,[7] IFLA Digital Reference Guidelines,[8] and Library of Congress QuestionPoint User Guidelines.[9]

EVALUATION OF SERVICE QUALITY AND USER SATISFACTION

From a manager's point of view I find it critical to have tools available to evaluate the quality of service, to adequately gather usage statistics, and to gauge user satisfaction. As with other aspects of the service, we were able to leverage the work from the statewide service for use in our local service.

Quality of Service: To assess the quality of the service as defined in the standards and guidelines, L-net Service Coordinator, Caleb Tucker-Raymond along with others established transcript evaluation instructions.[10] These were based on QandANJ.org's *Reference Session Evaluation Checklist*.[11] Between February and April 2004 Caleb and volunteers from the statewide service provider libraries reviewed L-net transcripts gathered in a two week period in February.[12] Some OSU librarians assisted in the evaluation and have since begun to use this training in evaluating L-net OSU transcripts. The results of the evaluation indicate that users were satisfied with their reference sessions 58 per cent of the time. The transcripts indicate that while the librarians were perceived to be friendly and professional (84%) only 65 per cent of the transactions included a reference interview and only 50 per cent asked open-ended questions. The results from these evaluations helped the L-net Service Coordinator and the Advisory Board to determine how best to improve the service. Training for the service has focused primarily on familiarizing service providers on how to use the software when answering or referring questions. The results indicated a need to focus on reference service basics, such as how to conduct reference interviews in an online environment and how to ask open-ended questions. In order to meet this need L-net will be offering training sessions on these topics in the near future.

The OSU Virtual Reference Task Force assumed responsibility for reviewing the L-net OSU transcripts in the summer and fall terms. Beginning in winter term a series of brown bag lunches are planned for all of the virtual reference staffers. We are defining these sessions as problem-solving and development opportunities for the virtual reference librarians. The sessions will provide an open setting to discuss how to improve responses and how to conduct effective reference interviews online. They will not be used for individual performance evaluations; however, I may choose to use specific transcripts in one-on-one sessions with librarians as a development tool.

Usage Statistics: The statewide service captures only minimal statistics including the number of chat and e-mail questions, the level of the information, length of transaction, and the zip code of the user. As they initiate a query users are required to give their name (this is then stripped later), zip code, and level of information required. Information level includes a choice of General Interest, College/Research, Elementary/Middle School (K-8), High School (9-12), or Professional. Optional questions include the person's home library and their e-mail address. The L-net Service Coordinator then correlates the zip code data to the appropriate counties. Local library statistics can only be gathered if the library has a separate queue.

As a manager, I did not feel that this would provide us with the type of information we needed. This information was critical for us to be able to tailor the service to meet the needs of students and faculty, and to gauge the volume of service provided to the different categories of users. With the help of Tutor.com we were able to set up the service so that we can identify whether the user is an undergraduate or graduate student, faculty, alumni, belongs to an affiliated unit, or is unaffiliated with OSU. This information combined with information from the exit surveys has already proven useful in helping us assess where to promote the service and how well we are meeting user needs.

User Satisfaction: When setting up L-net OSU we determined that for the first phase of the local pilot we had specific questions that we needed to ask users in order to develop an effective service. For that reason, we decided to use a different, shorter user satisfaction exit survey than that used by the statewide service uses. The problem this presents is that we have to gather and tally the responses manually. For the second phase of the pilot, beginning in January 2005, we are discussing whether or not we will begin using the same survey as the statewide service so that the results can be captured more easily.

Currently the statewide survey asks seven questions:

1. Were you satisfied with the answer you received?
2. Was this the first time you used this service?
3. In what ways have you gotten help from a librarian before today?
4. Are you more or less likely to use this service, now that it is available 24 hours a day, 7 days a week?
5. Would you use this service again in the future?
6. Do you have any additional comments/suggestions to help us improve this service?
7. Would you like to participate in a more in-depth survey regarding our service?

OSU's exit survey asks only four questions:

1. Where did you hear of this service?
2. How helpful was the answer you received?
3. Would you use this service again?
4. What are the hours you would find this service most useful?

The responses to the survey have provided us with important information for improving our service. While the overall number of queries answered is low, the response rate on the OSU surveys has been high, 26 surveys from 83 users (31%). The responses indicate that that the majority of respondents found the Web link (18 of 26), rather than either trying the service because of a recommendation, or for some other reason. This information is useful as it indicates that our publicity (posters, bookmarks with the url, press releases, referrals to the service in classes) has had limited impact. Based on these results we will revamp our promotional efforts during the winter term by timing promotional activities closer to exam times, holding demonstrations in residence halls and in the library, distributing our posters more widely, promoting the service directly to on-campus and distance education teaching faculty, increasing the presence of the link on our Web page, and asking other departments to place links on their pages where appropriate.

Other results indicated that only one of the 26 individuals has used the service before. Not surprising given the newness of the service. Seventy-three percent of the respondents found the service very helpful or helpful (18 very helpful, 8 helpful, and 0 reporting that it was not helpful). These results are higher than I anticipated based on the statewide survey, and I hope to confirm that the users are able to get more focused help from the OSU librarians. Twenty-three individuals indicated that they would use the service again; three would not. For the respondents our choice of service hours appears to be correct, with 11 indicating that noon to 4 p.m. works, and 8 suggesting 2-6 p.m. However, it should be noted that we do not have data for those individuals who were referred automatically to L-net statewide. Also it is a self-selected group of individuals who may typically conduct their research during the time of day that the service happens to be available.

We will continue to collect and evaluate the responses. Our next steps are to compare the results of our evaluations and exit surveys with the statewide service. These evaluation efforts will provide us tools to improve both the local and statewide service delivery through better training and promotion.

ISSUES

Operating a multi-type library service may create difficulties because of the wide range of questions asked, but it is also enriching for libraries and patrons to have the shared expertise available. A highly functioning system could make the best of each library's strengths, be that individual subject expertise or specialized and unique collections.

Issues reviewed in this section represent those that have had the most impact on OSU. These include: how to best use library's subject expertise and issues of trust, whether to use an instructional or direct answer approach to reference, how to use the software to its best advantage, scheduling, maintaining a local identity and promotion. For a more extensive examination of the issues faced by the L-net program see Donna Cohen's "L-net Evaluation and Planning Report."[13]

USE OF SUBJECT EXPERTISE AND ISSUES OF TRUST

As with Oregon LINK, a major concern for OSU and the other academic libraries has been how to best use the expertise of the subject librarians and how to take advantage of the specialized collections. The collections at OSU, both print and digital, are geared to the undergraduate and graduate level researcher rather than the general public. The majority of service providers in the statewide service are public librarians. So for the librarians the question has been, is it more of a service to answer general questions when they have unique subject strengths to offer, or would it be better to build a referral system that could still provide library to patron service?

These questions are not unique to OSU or to academic libraries. Both academic and public librarians in the state have raised similar issues. A recent evaluation of the L-net service comments solicited during focus groups indicates that trust in others answering local questions is a major issue.[14] I would consider these more an issue of lack of confidence than trust. Issues of trust fall into two categories. First, librarians feel a strong commitment to their patrons and want to be assured that if one of their patrons uses the statewide service that the question will indeed be answered, that "it doesn't get lost," that it be answered in a timely fashion, and that it will be answered accurately. OSU Libraries offers a strong instructional program, delivering created courses and individual sessions for a broad range of disciplines. The librarians work hard to build recognition with faculty and students within their assigned academic departments as the person to contact with library research questions. Students are told to contact their subject specialist with questions they may have about research on specific assignments. Librarians keep their colleagues informed of assignments for specific classes and leave instructions with other reference desk staff on how to assist students in particular courses. In addition, many of the librarians hold office hours for students to consult with them on their research. Naturally, the librarians are reluctant to have their students referred to a general statewide system where the student's question may be picked up by a librarian with no knowledge of the assignments or the courses offered at OSU, and who probably do not know to whom they should refer the question or where to locate the information. To expect the providers in the statewide system to track all of the details about assignments for all courses is unrealistic.

The second issue that is of major concern is the lack of knowledge about where to refer questions and to whom. L-net has just begun to develop a knowledge base of libraries' collection strengths and individuals' subject expertise. As a result, librarians must rely on their own experience to figure out who might be able to answer questions appropriately. This is not the most efficient system, particularly if the library of choice is not one of the libraries participating in the service. Questions referred outside the system are even more difficult to track.

Solutions discussed by the statewide service include staffing the service with two individuals, one from a public library and one from an academic library. Another solution would be to develop two queues, one public and one academic, or alternatively developing a subject referral system. University of Oregon, Portland State, and Oregon State University libraries are currently discussing setting up an academic queue. Either of the first two solutions would still require referrals, since the likelihood that the appropriate subject expert would be on at the time a question comes in is slight. Offering different hours for certain subjects such as science has also been suggested. The chance that the schedule would match the times that patrons needed a particular type of answer is unlikely. They would also need to decide where their question fits in the subject schema. This subject-driven service is the equivalent of separate reference desks that were popular in the 1970s and 1980s that have been consolidated since into one general reference point.

An obvious solution is the development of a knowledge base of individual's subject expertise and of library's collection strengths. One of the concerns about developing a knowledge base is the impact on specific individuals' or library's workloads. In a state such as Oregon where forestry is a major industry, being listed as the forestry expert is a daunting prospect. Also, the criteria for being listed as an expert has not been defined. Collection strengths do not always reflect the level of expertise of the reference staff. The question of balance again comes into play. How does the Forestry Librarian, who already has one of the heaviest referral loads from the OSU community, allocate her time between outside referrals and internal referrals?

Plans for the service do include creating a knowledge base, and a list of collection strengths and subject expertise are being compiled. In practice, the question of referrals has not been a major one yet because the volume of questions in both services has been low. Once the L-net promotion kicks off in earnest, we anticipate that the number of questions will increase. We also expect that the number of questions funneled to L-net OSU will rise rapidly in the coming academic year. Both of these scenarios will exacerbate the referral problem and will make developing a knowledge base more urgent.

INSTRUCTION OR PROVIDING ANSWERS

Another issue that L-net participants raise is the perceived differences in the way public and academic librarians approach questions. Some academic librarians feel that the instructional methods that they favor will erode if public librarians simply give patrons the answers they seek. Some public librarians also express anxiety at having to take an instructional approach with every patron. This is a false dichotomy between service delivery academic libraries and public libraries. The approach taken in answering questions in most cases is question specific. Both academic and public libraries instruct when needed and give information directly when it is warranted. The issue really is, whether subject expertise or a specialized collection is needed to answer a question and if the type of question warrants an instructional approach or simply giving the answer. The local library is best prepared to deliver specific local information. Examples of this might be policies or procedures for a specific library, such as "What do I do to get interlibrary loan services?" "How do I conduct research for my class assignment?" and "How do I find genealogical information on my relatives who lived in this county?" Having a strong referral service in place with an accompanying knowledge base of collection strengths and individual subject expertise is critical for success.

USING THE SOFTWARE TO ITS BEST ADVANTAGE

How to use the system to its best advantage is also a challenge. Software functions include referral, question tracking, transcripts, statistics gathering, scheduling meeting rooms, and being able to set up appointments with users. We envision chat reference and co-browsing or file sharing becoming an integrated aspect of our work with students and faculty to support teaching and research. For example, we will be able to set up appointments with students or faculty to meet online, consult one-on-one, set up sessions with an entire class, and link the service to online classes delivered through Blackboard Learning System software. This will also enhance our ability to work with distance learners and researchers. Our librarians could also set up online office hours for specific classes.

In Fall term, four of the OSU librarians intend to set up online office hours for students engaged in their credit courses, such as English 200, and for students from courses where the librarians have conducted a library research methodology session. Using the software in this way is a challenge for us and for our vendor, because it means using the system differently than it has been used in the past.

SCHEDULING–HOW MUCH IS ENOUGH?

Determining how to staff both a statewide and a local service in addition to supporting traditional desk, off-desk referrals, phone, and e-mail services presents challenges for OSU in effective allocation of librarians' time. Because we have opted to provide only the minimal amount of service for L-net, we have focused more on how to staff our local service.

The volume of reference service at the OSU reference desk is heavy, with the number of desk questions averaging about 10,500 each fiscal quarter. Over the past few years OSU has tried to reduce the number of hours subject librarians serve at the desk in order for them to concentrate their efforts on instruction, collection development, and off-desk reference consultations in support of their assigned academic departments. To do so, we staff the reference desk with students trained to answer technical questions and para-professional staff, as well as librarians.

Providing service for L-net has a minimal impact on the librarians. During the Answerland pilot, we staffed the service for as little as 12 hours a month. We staff L-net only two hours a week, the minimum requirement for L-net providers. We opted instead to allocate hours to L-net in other ways, by supplying staff for regional training and being engaged in governance through my involvement with the Advisory Board, which required many hours of our time, but provided more benefit to the service. In addition, OSU librarians have contributed to task forces appointed by the Advisory Board to pursue such issues as establishing the quality and service standards, and exploring options for statewide database licensing.

As a consequence of the low volume of questions on L-net and the minimal hours, the reference staff received little practice using the software, which affected their confidence levels in responding to inquiries. To mitigate this only four individuals were trained as L-net providers. All of the reference staff including the on-call or substitute staff is being trained to deliver service for L-net OSU. This will give each of the librarians two hours of virtual reference service a week and provide the practice that they need to build confidence in responding to reference questions on chat.

For our first foray into offering L-net OSU, we haven chosen to offer only six hours of service per day Monday through Friday, and to develop a separate schedule for digital reference. Doing so means we need to cover an additional 30 hours a week, which impacts the librarians ability to focus on their subject specialties. We are pursuing integrating L-net OSU with our regular desk service once the staff feels more comfortable using the system, in order to eliminate the need for scheduling extra hours, and more importantly to expand our hours of service. Integrating L-net OSU with desk service presents other issues that need to be resolved, such as how to juggle walk-up patrons, phone, and virtual reference at an already busy desk and yet provide high quality service.

MAINTAINING LOCAL IDENTITY AND PROMOTION

Libraries participating in the statewide service have been concerned about maintaining their identity with their users. L-net's solution to this is to have each library link the service off of their individual Web pages and to promote the service directly to their community, even modifying the logo to individualize it or referring to it by a different name. How libraries have chosen to present L-net varies widely. For example, Eugene Public Library kept the logo design but changed the wording; University of Oregon chose not to display the logo.

OSU chose to maintain the linkage to the statewide system by naming our local service L-net OSU. While we retained the original logo for the statewide service, we branded our logo so it reads L-net OSU. On our Ask our Librarian Web page, we list both services, marketing L-net as the place to go when L-net OSU is closed.

Even though the statewide project produced excellent marketing and promotional materials, a lack of promotion has plagued the statewide service since its beginning. During the Answerland pilot, some libraries objected to the name as appealing to children and not an older population.[15] Because of this, they were reluctant to market it to their communities. Another concern was L-net or Answerland's ability to handle volume. Most libraries have simply placed the link on their Web page and waited for users to stumble across it; others announced the service in local newspapers and in their libraries. OSU chose the low-key approach; however, with the advent of OSU L-net we will be promoting it heavily during the beginning of each academic term. As mentioned in the "Evaluation and User Satisfaction Section" based on user exit surveys we are re-evaluating our approach to our promotional activities for the local service.

This overall low-key approach has resulted, as mentioned before, in a low volume of questions. Plans call for either hiring a marketing person for L-net or using consultants in order to develop a more dynamic, ongoing statewide promotional program.

CONCLUSION

While participating in both a statewide system and a local service can be problematic, the experience has helped OSU exploit the opportunity to reach our users when and where they need help the most. Ironically we believe that the greatest opportunity the virtual reference software avails us is the ability to enhance our instructional activities, such as setting up online office hours for specific user groups. For both the statewide and our local service the potential to access outside subject expertise has yet to be realized. OSU faces difficult decisions in the months ahead as we determine what our level of involvement will be with other consortia also interested in our participation in their digital reference services.

NOTES

1. Library Development Services, Oregon State Library, "Oregon Reference LINK: A Short History," n.d., <www.osl.state.or.us/home/libdev/RefLinkHist.html> (August 15, 2004).
2. Vision 2010 Committee, Oregon Library Association, "A Call to Action for the Oregon Library Association," OLA Quarterly 7, no. 3 (Fall 2001), <http://www.olaweb.org/v2010/index.shtml> (August 15, 2004).
3. Statewide E-Reference Task Force, Oregon State Library, "Task Force Charge." Updated September 25, 2002, <http://www.osl.state.or.us/home/libdev/eref/charge.html> (August 29, 2004).
4. Statewide E-Reference Task Force, Oregon State Library, "Establishing E-Reference Services for Oregon: Proposal and Recommendations," October 1, 2002, <http://www.osl.state.or.us/home/libdev/eref/eref.htm> (August 15, 2004).
5. L-net, "Guidelines for Oregon Statewide Digital Reference Service," 2003, <http://oregonlibraries.net/staff/docs/service_guidelines.shtml> (August 1, 2004).
6. RUSA, Mar MARS Ad Hoc Committee on Virtual Reference Guidelines, "Draft Guidelines for Implementing and Maintaining Virtual Reference Services," May 2003, <http://www.ala.org/ala/rusa/rusaprotools/referenceguide/virtrefguideline.htm> (August 15, 2006).

7. RUSA, "Guidelines for Behavioral Performance of Reference and Information Service Providers," Revised June 2004, <http://www.ala.org/ala/rusa/rusaprotools/referenceguide/guidelinesbehavioral.htm> (August 23, 2004).

8. IFLA Reference Work Section, "IFLA Digital Reference Guidelines," revised June 12, 2004, <http://www.ifla.org/VII/s36/pubs/drg03.htm> (August 23, 2004).

9. Library of Congress, QuestionPoint User Group, "QuestionPoint User Guidelines," Revised August 13, 2003, <http://www.loc.gov/rr/digiref/QP_best_practices.pdf> August 23, 2004.

10. Tucker-Raymond, Caleb. "Transcript Evaluation Instructions," n.d. http://www.oregonlibraries.net/staff/docs/evaluation_instructions.shtml (August 15, 2004). L-net Staff Resources Documents.

11. QandANJ.org's. "Reference Session Checklist Transaction", n.d., <http://www.qandanj.org/description/eval_check.pdf> (October 25, 2004).

12. Tucker-Raymond, Caleb. "Results of the February 2004 two-week sampling" n.d. http://www.oregonlibraries.net/staff/docs/feb_04_eval_results.xls (August 15, 2004), Transcript Evaluation Instructions, L-net Staff Resources Documents.

13. Cohen, Donna L., "L-net Evaluation and Planning Report," D.L. Cohen Information Services, Portland, Oregon, August 17, 2004, Report to Oregon State Library and Oregon State LSTA Board <http://oregonlibraries.net/staff/docs/evaluation_report.shtml> (August 23, 2004).

14. Cohen, "L-net Evaluation," 26, 42.

15. Tucker-Raymond, Caleb. "Answerland: Summary and Statistics: April-December 2003," Report to the Oregon State Library and Oregon State LSTA Board, February 24, 2004. http://www.oregonlibraries.net/staff/docs/answerland_pilot_report.doc (August 15, 2004).

doi:10.1300/J120v46n95_06

STANDARDS AND METHODS
FOR EVALUATING VIRTUAL REFERENCE

Looking at the Bigger Picture:
An Integrated Approach to Evaluation
of Chat Reference Services

M. Kathleen Kern

SUMMARY. Virtual reference offers some unique new opportunities for evaluation due to the richness of the transcripts and other automatically collected data. To put evaluation of virtual reference into context, however, libraries should view and evaluate virtual reference as part of the whole of a library's reference service. Holistic evaluation pursues an integrated approach to evaluating the total of a library's reference service. doi:10.1300/J120v46n95_07 *[Article copies available for a fee from The Haworth Document Delivery Service: 1-800-HAWORTH. E-mail address: <docdelivery@haworthpress.com> Website: <http://www.HaworthPress.com> © 2006 by The Haworth Press, Inc. All rights reserved.]*

M. Kathleen Kern is Assistant Professor and Reference Librarian, 300 Main Library, MC-522, University of Illinois at Urbana-Champaign, 1408 West Gregory, Urbana, IL 61801 (E-mail: katkern@uiuc.edu).

[Haworth co-indexing entry note]: "Looking at the Bigger Picture: An Integrated Approach to Evaluation of Chat Reference Services." Kern, M. Kathleen. Co-published simultaneously in *The Reference Librarian* (The Haworth Information Press, an imprint of The Haworth Press, Inc.) No. 95/96, 2006, pp. 99-112; and: *Assessing Reference and User Services in a Digital Age* (ed: Eric Novotny) The Haworth Information Press, an imprint of The Haworth Press, Inc., 2006, pp. 99-112. Single or multiple copies of this article are available for a fee from The Haworth Document Delivery Service [1-800-HAWORTH, 9:00 a.m. - 5:00 p.m. (EST). E-mail address: docdelivery@haworthpress.com].

KEYWORDS. Evaluation, reference services, virtual reference, e-mail reference, chat reference, integration

INTRODUCTION

Virtual reference services provide the library community with a new opportunity to evaluate our services. In fact, chat reference has sparked something of a renaissance in evaluation of reference services. There are many aspects of the virtual reference transaction that can be examined; some of these types of evaluation are unique to the virtual reference environment.

Most of the evaluations of virtual reference have focused exclusively on chat and e-mail transactions, examining only those virtual transactions. As virtual reference becomes less of a novelty and more of a mainstream service, it is important that libraries start to evaluate their virtual services in the context of their reference services as a whole. Holistic evaluation will give us a better picture of our reference services.

TIMELESSNESS OF EVALUATION

The basics of reference evaluation are timeless and classic. We seek to answer the questions: *who are our users and how do they use our service*; *when, how, and with whom should we staff our service*; *are our answers accurate*; and *how satisfied are our patrons with the assistance we provide*? The fundamental questions, the reasons for evaluation, remain the same. Approach to these questions, however, has varied. Librarians have used different research methodologies and have examined different aspects of the questions.

Innovations and new technologies emerge and change the patterns of what and how we evaluate reference service. The Brandeis model of tiered staffing led to evaluations of where and with whom we staff at tiered service points, as well as the efficacy of this model. Telephone reference led to evaluation of the telephone as a communication tool for reference and a separate reference service point. Seminal papers such as Dorothy Cole's 1946 study examining the types of questions asked in public, academic, and special libraries and Joan Durrance's 1989 study of the importance of user satisfaction as a measure of reference service success led to further studies that attempt to look at the same question from a different angle.[i] The results of the "55% study"[1] led to more studies of accuracy and also prompted the more qualitative evaluations of patron satisfaction and willingness to return.

The emergence of virtual reference as a popular service has had a noticeable impact on evaluation of reference. (It is not really a new technology, having been around in some form for over 20 years, but it has only recently gained widespread implementation as a library service.) A search of Library Literature[ii] finds six articles on reference service evaluation for the years 2002-2003. Five of these articles were published in 2003, and only one of these is about in-person reference. None of the articles include evaluations across "traditional" and virtual reference services. Looking at Library and Information Science Abstracts, there were seventeen research articles indexed on reference service evaluation for 2002-2003.[iii] Eleven of these were about virtual reference services. The other six only examined in-person services, with three of these articles being from Norway (there were two articles from the UK about virtual reference). Only one article[2] contained evaluation of both virtual reference and in-person reference services.

Since virtual reference is new, it has turned our heads and we have focused our evaluation efforts in this direction. What is it about evaluation of virtual reference that is distinctive and what is unchanged from the evaluation of other reference services? I will explore the answers to both of these questions, as well as the importance of a holistic approach to reference evaluation that integrates evaluation of virtual reference with other reference services.

DEFINITIONS

For an article on virtual reference services, it is necessary to define a few terms since terminology may be unfamiliar. Terminology in this area is not standardized, so you may see the same words used elsewhere with variation in meaning.

Chat Reference–Real-time communication between two users via computer. Chat reference allows users to communicate instantaneously with librarians, or as it is commonly described, the communication is synchronous.[3]

E-mail Reference–Communication via electronic mail. Patrons can send messages at any time to be answered by operators at another time. Since patrons are not interacting with the librarian in real-time, this mode of communication is asynchronous.

Virtual Reference–An umbrella term that encompasses chat and e-mail reference as well as emerging reference communication technologies such as voice-over-IP and online videoconferencing. Virtual Reference focuses on the interaction between patron and librarian (operator) whereas *Digital Reference* is a broader term that includes online resources as well as virtual communications.

Transcript–The text of a virtual reference interaction. This may take the form of a chat transcript stored in a database of chat interactions, or the e-mail correspondence between patron and librarian. Most commonly in the virtual reference environment, the supporting software automatically collects the transcripts.

Operator–A generic term for the person on the answering end of a virtual reference interaction. The operator may be a librarian, a paraprofessional, a graduate school student, a contracted employee from a virtual reference software company or some other person designated to answer the virtual reference questions at a library or Ask-A service.

UNIQUE ASPECTS OF EVALUATING VIRTUAL REFERENCE

Aside from the newness of these services, there are some distinctive characteristics of the virtual reference environment that make evaluation of virtual reference different from evaluation of other reference services. The most unique, and tantalizing, aspect of evaluation of virtual reference services is the availability of a transcript of the entire reference interaction. It is perhaps this aspect, as much as the newness of virtual reference, which has engendered interest in the evaluation of virtual reference. Most commercial chat software collects and archives the transcripts for either all transactions or selected chat transactions determined by the operator. These transcripts are rich with data and opportunity. The reference interview can be examined in detail as well as the accuracy and appropriateness of the librarians' answers. Tone, typing skill, and jargon are right there in print. There is a ridiculous amount of information that could be mined. It is important to look at the transcripts as the last step of the research design rather than the first; you should know what questions you want to answer before you jump into the transactions as a data source. Starting from the transactions could lead to specious evaluation. For instance, examining typing errors in chat transcripts is possible, but it has questionable value.

The consortial nature of many chat reference services can add a layer of complexity to evaluation of chat reference which is not present in the evaluation of other reference services. If you are a member of a chat consortium, you need to consider if you want to evaluate only your operators answering questions for your institution's patrons, or your operators answering the questions of other institution's patrons (or both). Or maybe you want to evaluate operators at other libraries answering questions from your patrons. There are issues of access to the consortial data, but also issues of operator privacy and inter-institutional collegiality. The drive to evaluate as a way to measure and maintain service quality can create a tension with the desire for harmony within the consortium.

WHAT IS EASIER TO MEASURE?

There is also much data that is collected automatically by the virtual reference software. The exact data will differ by vendor and the preferences of the library. Some common things that are collected: time and date of transaction, operator name, length of time spent in a chat session, user information such as affiliation or status, IP range, and Web browser. From this data a variety of reports can be run. It takes next to no effort to collect and can quickly yield much information. Some of it may be worth the time it takes to evaluate and some of it may be superfluous. Detailed reports of traffics by time of day, day of week, or week of the year can be generated to help with staffing patterns. If your patrons are asked for status or affiliation (undergraduate, public, faculty), a report can be produced to answer the timeless question of "who are our patrons." If IP range is collected, you can determine where your patrons are when they ask questions (inside the library, elsewhere on campus, off-campus). These can be useful facts for training and staffing. Again, specifics vary by vendor, but this kind of patron information is often stored separately from the transcript of the reference transaction to further ensure patron privacy.

One of the ways that libraries and software vendors have made collection of patron data easy is to use a form to collect data up-front (Diagram 1).[iv] How difficult it is to run reports from the data in your system depends on the software, where the data is stored, and what pre-scripted reports are available or the extent to which you can write your own reports to query the database of transcripts and transaction data. Some data may be collected (such as IP), but not pre-scripted into a report or stored in such a way as to make queries of this data straightforward. Extraction of what you want to know can be painful, even when the data exists.

DIAGRAM 1. Sample Patron Question/Data for a Chat Reference Service

Name/Handle required

┌─────────────────────────────
│

Email (optional)

┌─────────────────────────────
│

Status required

┌─────────────────────────────┐
│ UIUC Student   ▼ │
└─────────────────────────────┘

Question

┌───────────────────────────┐
│   ▲ │
│   │
│   │
│   │
│   │
│   ▼ │
└───────────────────────────┘

┌─────────────────────┬─────────┐
│ Login to Live Chat │ Reset   │
└─────────────────────┴─────────┘

Select a Librarian (*Optional*)

┌─────────────────────────┐
│ -- Any Librarian --   ▼ │
└─────────────────────────┘

Reprinted with permission from University of Illinois at Urbana-Champaign and Docutek.

ETHICAL ISSUES

Operator privacy is only one of several ethical issues involved with evaluation of chat reference. Patron privacy is of constant concern, particularly with the automatic retention of transcripts. Are patron identifiers (name, e-mail, etc.) stripped from the transcript? Is this done automatically, or does it need to be done by a librarian? If data is collected about the patron (operating system, affiliation, major, etc.) is it stored separately from the question? How long will transcripts be retained and who has access to view the transcripts? Does your transcript retention policy and privacy safeguards match your library's broader policies on patron privacy? And do you have a publicly stated privacy policy so that patrons know that the data is being collected and the transcripts retained?

Many of the same issues do occur when you collect data for an evaluation of in-person or telephone reference. Evaluation of colleagues can often be sensitive, even within a single library or department. Patron privacy is always a consideration whenever data is collected, be it through a survey, unobtrusive evaluation, or collection of in-person question. Chat (and e-mail) transcripts just heighten this concern, since more data is collected, in more automated ways, and sometimes with less control over who might view the data.

APPROACHING THE BIG QUESTIONS

However, traffic counts and patron affiliation do not make a total plan for evaluation. These measures do not answer the bigger questions of how do patrons use our service, how accurate are our answers, and how satisfied are our patrons with the assistance we provide.

Surveys, which are a popular data collection method, are easily "pushed" to the user in the virtual reference environment. Exit surveys can be sent to the user as a link or a pop-up window when they exit the chat interaction. E-mail users are similarly easy to reach with a survey URL embedded in the e-mail response. These surveys are targeted, reaching actual users of the service immediately after they have used the service. Surveys have enjoyed wide use as a tool to assess patron satisfaction with services.[4]

More difficult to evaluate are the issues of accuracy of responses, question types being asked, and issues involved with communication. These areas of evaluation require an analysis of the total transcript. Virtual reference relieves the tedium of manually collecting transcripts through audio recording or note-taking, but still leaves the work of reviewing the content of the transcripts. Subject assignment, accuracy, and communication style are areas considerably more subjective than traffic counts and require more thought and planning to the research design and evaluation rubric. Some virtual reference software systems allow for assignment of subject headings, keywords, number of questions answered, and other criteria to a transcript. This can be a help in streamlining analysis of content, but the criteria for applying these categories must be developed and if more than one person enters this meta-data, consistency must be enforced. However, if we are to answer the bigger questions about our services, we must undertake this type of content analysis.

These questions of accuracy, traffic levels, types of questions, etc., remain the same regardless of mode of communication. Data collection methods may differ for evaluations of virtual reference and in-person or telephone interactions, but the analysis is parallel. For example, if a question has been correctly answered (setting aside how fraught with difficultly this determination can be) is not dependant on mode of communication. Similarly, looking at communication style has common aspects across communication mediums: approachability, appropriate language, greeting, invitation to return, etc. Approachability is displayed differently in a text-based medium such as chat than in a face-to-face interaction, but the underlying philosophy is the same.

GETTING THE BIGGER PICTURE

Evaluation of chat reference is all the rage. The newness of the service makes it intrinsically interesting, but we also wish to test and prove the concept via evaluation. Additionally, automatic data collection, the ease of pushing surveys, and pre-set reports makes evaluation of chat reference perhaps more appealing than the evaluation of in-person reference transactions. Extensive focus on virtual reference outside of the context of more "traditional" reference services is like looking at the brushstroke and not the entire canvas. Comparison with other aspects of reference service (in-person, telephone) provides depth to the evaluation. It is good to know that your chat service answered 6,000 reference questions last year. But what percent of your overall volume was this: .5 percent, five percent, fifty percent? Pardon the extension of the painting metaphor, but this gives perspective to the data.

Even better than comparison with other reference services, is a holistic approach to evaluation of all of a library's reference services. Several studies[v] have looked at user satisfaction with virtual reference. These studies show that patrons appreciate the service. While this is useful to know, I am more interested in what patrons think about all of our services. Are the perceptions of value the same for all reference services? Do patrons have different expectations of virtual reference? If they are not, then this leads to another place to focus our evaluations and our improvements. If patrons are equally pleased, then we have also learned something valuable: that we have taken a well-liked service successfully into a new medium.

Very few studies have realized the importance of holistic evaluation and have approached their evaluations of virtual reference in relation to their other reference services. Mostly, when evaluations include other reference services it is purely in relation to the numbers of questions asked at the reference desk and through the virtual service. While this is a useful management measure, to be sure, it is somewhat lacking in depth. One notable exception is the aforementioned article by Ruppel and Condit-Fagan. The recently revised Guidelines for Behavioral Performance of Reference and Information Service Providers[5] are a good example of taking the holistic view of reference services. While they are not themselves an evaluation instrument, they form the theoretical basis for many studies of librarian reference behavior and reference success.

A truly holistic evaluation of a library's reference service does not stop with a single study or even an on-going collection of a single set of data across all service points and mediums. As discussed, there are many questions that evaluation can answer. Each of these is important to our libraries at one time or another. During tight budgets, we may need data to optimize our staffing or to prove the worth of a service. At other times, we might be able to focus evaluations to seek directions for improvement of a particular aspect of a service such as communication or accuracy. Changes to a service, such as a new service point (chat!) might turn evaluation toward the impact of these changes on staff or patrons. Training might be the driving factor behind an evaluation, as we seek to understand the complexity of questions asked or the common subject areas of inquiry. We can ask ourselves an enormous number of questions about our reference services.

TOWARD HOLISTIC EVALUATION

Start with examining what you evaluate right now. Why do you use these measures? What questions do they answer about your reference service? Are these still the questions that you want to ask? Is the data still useful or is it time to ask something different? Longitudinal data is great. You may have a well-established and finely honed data collection method. It is still important to examine the evaluation method; don't stay with something just out of tradition.

If you answered "No" to any of the above, or were unable to answer the questions, it might be time to change your approach to evaluation entirely. Radical change may not be necessary if you could answer the questions, but had some "maybe" and "sort of" responses. You can keep doing what you've been doing, but make some additions to update your evaluation and answer your current questions.

How does your current evaluation measure for in-person and virtual reference compare? Are you answering the same evaluation questions? If not, why not? Some evaluations don't translate out of the virtual environment, but many do. Is your evaluation of virtual reference just more in-tune with what you want to know about all of your reference services, or is it so focused on the unique aspects of being virtual that it does not relate to the rest of reference at all?

Most important is to look at a way to bring together the evaluations of all reference services. What do you need to know about all of your services? What do you need to know specifically about virtual services? Is there anything specific for in-person services?

As you determine the questions that you want to answer, you may have more than can be reasonably examined with a single evaluation instrument. What data is important (if any) to collect on an on-going basis? What evaluations could be done as a one-time or infrequently recurring basis? Holistic evaluation is a plan to examine all important aspects of your reference service in an integrated and deliberate way. It might include on-going collection of statistics about reference traffic (for trend analysis) and less frequent examinations of patron satisfaction and accuracy. If your list of evaluation questions is long, your holistic plan should be prioritized. It should also be sequenced if one evaluation is dependant on the results of another.

Determining what is worth measuring involves looking at the ratio of how much you want to know something to the amount of time involved in the evaluation. Some methods of data collection and evaluation are quite time-consuming but are the key to answering important questions. If accuracy is your most important evaluation question, it is up to you to decide if it is significant enough to invest the time in planning the evaluation and in collecting and analyzing data.

The holistic plan is only the beginning. This article is not about the specifics of research design and evaluation methods are someone else's article. Charts 1-3 do provide an example approach to a holistic evaluation plan. Since this is an example, I have thought big: do not be intimidated. The first chart shows working from a broad question about reference service to the determination of a more specific question and the determination of tool for measurement. Chart 2 compares a thought process for working through two of the possible measurements for the question "Are patrons happy with our service?" This is merely an example, and is not meant to suggest that one measurement tool is superior. The emphasis is, in this case, on choosing a measure to be used across all modes of communication and is most likely reflecting an evaluator preference for communication-based research. Chart 3 shows how all three of the questions in Chart 1 can be approached through a multi-layered, holistic approach to reference service evaluation.

CHART 1. Model Decision Tree for Choosing an Evaluation Question and Methodology. White Boxes Are Final Decisions.

CHART 2. Sample Decision Process for Comparing Data Collection Methods.

Exit Surveys		Examination of "thank you" responses	
Easy for chat/e-mail–push web survey at end of transaction	Traditionally poor level of survey return	Easy for chat/e-mail as data is present in transcripts	Time-consuming to analyze transcripts
Multiple-choice responses quickly tabulated	Intrusive to hand out surveys at desk	Actual patron response—not guided by presence of survey	Time-consuming to analyze transcripts–may require transcription
		May gather other data from recorded transcripts (patron displeasure?)	More difficult to collect data for in-person/ telephone (tape record?)
Quantifiable	Not sure how to distribute to telephone patrons		Will this pass university's IRB?
Prior experience with survey method	Survey format may "guide" answers		Not a statistical measure—qualitative (might be a positive aspect?)
			Staff knowledge of data-gathering may affect results
Conclusion: Not at this time/for this question		Conclusion: <ul><li>Will pursue this evaluation method.</li><li>Potential for rich-data collection. Communication based aspect is appealing.</li><li>Need to work out data-gathering aspects; talk to Institutional Review Board; determine how to avoid influencing results.</li><li>Since transcript analysis is labor-intensive, this will be a short duration data-gathering. Likely one-time only.</li></ul>	

BARRIERS TO HOLISTIC EVALUATION

Even if I've convinced you of the need for holistic evaluation, you might still have reservations. Data which is easily collected for virtual reference service might be more difficult to collect for in-person services. This leads, then, back to the equation of what is worth evaluating. You may decide that a question is important, but cannot be answered at

CHART 3. Sample Outline for a Holistic (and Ambitious) Evaluation Plan.

What do we want to know about our services?

1. Are we providing correct answers?
2. Are patrons happy with our services?
3. Are we staffing in the most effective manner?

How often to measure:

Question 1: Snapshot. One time measure (One day? A week? Random sampling?). Might repeat in subsequent years for comparison.

Question 2: Once every year or two.

Question 3. Continuous data collection for at least one year (may continue or repeat) to determine staffing needs over the course of an academic year.

Measurement instrument:

Question 1: Analysis of actual chat and email transcripts. No comparison with in-person/telephone at this time.

Question 2: Survey to virtual reference users with questions about all modes of communication. Follow-up with 2 focus groups with questions about all reference services. Planning study for "thank yous" across all services with data collection next year.

Question 3: (1) On-going, daily collection of traffic statistics for all modes of communication. (2) One week collection of questions asked through all modes of communication to analyze subject and expertise required. Librarians will log in-person and telephone questions and report on difficulty of question.

the current time; if so, move it further in the future of your plans: it might increase in importance and change the balance of the equation, or you might develop an easier way to approach the evaluation.

Not all data, of course, translates across all services. This is okay. Some aspects are unique and this does not mean that these aspects should not be evaluated. Just examine their place within your overall holistic plan. Be sure you have a reason you need to know how many patrons are running Opera on a BeOS operating system.

Indubitably, developing a holistic plan will take some time. Comparable data collection across virtual and in-person services will also take time to develop. Do I need to tell you that anything worth doing is worth doing well?

Perhaps the biggest obstacle faced by a holistic evaluation plan is the cooperation of others. Some methods of data collection and some evaluation questions will require the cooperation of your colleagues and perhaps even of those libraries. Buy-in will start with acceptance of the importance of the evaluation question. If they see the question as important, they will be more willing to participate. Since evaluation can be wide-reaching in the impact of its data collection and its outcomes, involving colleagues during the development of the holistic evaluation plan is advisable.

BRINGING IT ALL TOGETHER–NOW

Designing a holistic evaluation plan starts with thinking about your reference services as *a single reference service* with many modes of communication. With this perspective in mind ask *why evaluate?* What is it that you want to know about the reference service? From the answers to this question will evolve the research design of what to evaluate and how to collect these measures. The practical considerations of what is easy or difficult to measure will factor into your research design, but should not drive your planning. It is most important, from a management viewpoint, to answer the questions that will help to improve the library's reference service.

Reference services are complex and a single library's service might be open to several areas of evaluation. Multiple questions may become apparent as you develop a holistic plan for evaluation. Aspects of your service long unexamined might present themselves as opportunities for evaluation. A single method of data collection is unlikely to be able to effectively measure for too diverse a set of evaluation goals. Plan for multiple evaluations. Each different *why evaluate* may lead to a different *what* and *how*. Prioritize what will be evaluated. Prioritization may be based on a critical concern, or what is easiest and quickest to measure first while future evaluations are planned. A series of evaluations may be structured so that the later evaluations can build on the results of earlier evaluations.

The future of reference evaluation looks a lot like the history of reference evaluation; it just includes a few new pieces.

NOTES

i. For an extensive annotated bibliography of reference evaluation, see *The Reference Assessment Manual*. While almost ten years old, it is a wonderful introduction to this extensive and historically deep body of literature.

ii. Search performed October 22, 2004 using the string Reference Services [as a subject] AND Evaluation. I then examined the subjects, abstracts, and articles to determine which included discussion of chat or e-mail reference. Some results were false hits (such as one evaluating Web sites) and are not included. Note that because of indexing lag time, 2004 was not examined.

iii. The search in LISA was for reference work AND evaluation. This change in terms was because of the indexing terms used in LISA. Again, a few false hits (in this case, articles that were not reports of research) were taken out of the search result.

iv. Virtual reference patron login form courtesy of University of Illinois at Urbana-Champaign Ask-A-Librarian service (http://www.library.uiuc.edu/askus) and Docutek Information Systems.

v. For example, articles by Kibee (2001), Janes and Mon (2003) and Stoffel (2004).

REFERENCES

1. Terence Crowley, The effectiveness of information service in medium size public libraries. *Information service in public libraries: Two Studies.* Metuchen, NJ: Scarecrow Press, 1971.

2. Margie Ruppel and Jodi Condit-Fagan, "Instant messaging reference: users' evaluation of library chat," *Reference Services Review.* 30 no. 3 (2002): 183-197.

3. Library and Archives of Canada. *Virtual Reference Canada Glossary*, http://www.collectionscanada.ca/vrc-rvc/s34-151-e.htm. Accessed October 24, 2004.

4. Marjorie Murfin, Assessing library services: the reference component. In *The Reference Assessment Manual.* Ann Arbor, MI: Pieran Press, 1995.

5. Reference and User Services Association. Guidelines for Behavioral Performance of Reference and Information Service Providers. Revised June, 2004. http://www.ala.org/ala/rusa/rusaprotools/referenceguide/guidelinesbehavioral.htm.

BIBLIOGRAPHY

Dorothy Cole, "Some characteristics of reference work," *College and Research Libraries* 7(1946): 45-51.

Terence Crowley, "The effectiveness of information service in medium size public libraries," *Information service in public libraries: Two Studies.* Edited by Terence Crowely (Metuchen, NJ: Scarecrow Press, 1971).

Joan Durrance, "Reference success: Does the 55% rule tell the whole story?" *Library Journal* 114 (1989): 31-36.

Josephine Z. Kibbee, David Ward, and Wei Ma, "Virtual service, real data: Results of a pilot study [real-time online reference at the University of Illinois]," *Reference Services Review* 30 no. 1 (2002): 25-36.

Lori Mon and Joe Janes, "The Thank You Study: User Satisfaction with Digital Reference Service," 2003 OCLC/ALISE research grant report published electronically by OCLC Research. Available online at: http://www.oclc.org/research/grants/reports/janes/jj2004.pdf.

Margie Ruppel and Jodi Condit-Fagan, "Instant messaging reference: Users' evaluation of library chat," *Reference Services Review* 30 no. 3 (2002): 183-197.

Bruce Stoffel et al., "E-mail and chat reference: Assessing patron satisfaction," *Reference Services Review* 32 no. 2 (2004): 120-40.

doi:10.1300/J120v46n95_07

Budget Planning and Performance Measures for Virtual Reference Services

Andrew Breidenbaugh

SUMMARY. The Tampa-Hillsborough County Public Library, as a county government agency, is required to follow a specific budget planning process in order to obtain funding for library programs and services. One tool of this planning process–the "decision unit"–requires advanced planning and continued evaluation of potential and existing library services. Prior to receiving funds for any new service, performance measures must be established in order to measure the success of the service in relation to the public money invested. This article will look at the evaluation process built into the funding of the library's participation in a statewide virtual reference service and the implications for continuation and/or expansion of this service based on continued assessment. doi:10.1300/J120v46n95_08 *[Article copies available for a fee from The Haworth Document Delivery Service: 1-800-HAWORTH. E-mail address: <docdelivery@haworthpress.com> Website: <http://www.HaworthPress.com> © 2006 by The Haworth Press, Inc. All rights reserved.]*

KEYWORDS. Evaluation, assessment, digital reference, virtual reference, reference services

Andrew Breidenbaugh is Coordinator of Reference & Information Services, Tampa-Hillsborough County Public Libraries, 900 North Ashley Drive, Tampa, FL 33602 (E-mail: breidenbaugha@hillsboroughcounty.org).

[Haworth co-indexing entry note]: "Budget Planning and Performance Measures for Virtual Reference Services." Breidenbaugh, Andrew. Co-published simultaneously in *The Reference Librarian* (The Haworth Information Press, an imprint of The Haworth Press, Inc.) No. 95/96, 2006, pp. 113-124; and: *Assessing Reference and User Services in a Digital Age* (ed: Eric Novotny) The Haworth Information Press, an imprint of The Haworth Press, Inc., 2006, pp. 113-124. Single or multiple copies of this article are available for a fee from The Haworth Document Delivery Service [1-800-HAWORTH, 9:00 a.m. - 5:00 p.m. (EST). E-mail address: docdelivery@haworthpress.com].

Public libraries nation-wide endeavor to offer a wide range of creative services to meet the current and future needs of their customers. Prior to investing the time and resources into these services, we should also invest the time in doing the background research and planning necessary to ensure success and customer satisfaction. We often fall short in this respect–libraries often provide new services to our customers without first setting standards for performance measurement and continued success. Libraries generally expend greater effort in securing the funding for their services than in their planning. This article will take a look at one aspect of the process of budget planning for a countywide, public library system in which the mandated steps for evaluating performance and measuring success are part of the process to receive funding. We will examine budget and service development, specifically the creation of a "decision unit" within the library's overall budget for the participation in a statewide, collaborative virtual reference (chat and e-mail) service. The decision unit sets the level of required inputs and sets the measures for success for this new service, showing its effectiveness and potential for expansion or removal based on funding and stated outcomes.

BACKGROUND

The Tampa-Hillsborough County Public Library System provides countywide library services to the 1.1 million residents of Hillsborough County, on Florida's west coast. The main library in the city of Tampa is the focal point for the system of 23 geographically dispersed library branches of varying size. In addition to traditional library branches and a bookmobile, the library has partnered with 34 city and county recreation and senior centers that host smaller, computer based "E-Libraries." The library's approximately 30 million dollar annual budget ($29 per capita) provides for a robust collection of well-used programs and services throughout the county. Nearly 65% of county residents are library card holders.

Since January, 2000 the library system has offered reference services to residents outside of traditional library branches through a centralized *Electronic Reference and Information* department that handles telephone, e-mail, and (now) virtual reference services. This centralized approach has allowed for services to remote users–reference, library information, electronic resource instruction–to be tailored to meet their specific needs. These same services have been extended to our E-Library locations which have no library staff. E-mail reference has been offered since late 1999 and has experienced a doubling of traffic each year since. The library answers approximately 230 e-mail questions each month.

The Tampa-Hillsborough County Public Library system provides access to a growing collection of about 80 subscription databases through the library's Web site–www.hcplc.org. The databases collection is not only available in the library, but most resources are available remotely with a library card number. The library has worked vigorously to market its online resources and has conducted library card sign-up campaigns to promote their use from home, school, or office. The subscription databases have proven very popular. They have been accessed nearly 175,000 times with about 3.1 million full-text documents retrieved–including 2,000 monthly e-book checkouts. Hillsborough County library customers have shown that they are very willing and able to use the library's virtual collection and services.

It was in this context that we began our investigation into expanding our virtual services to include chat-based virtual reference. We spent nearly two years watching, researching, following the growing body of literature on virtual/digital reference, attending conferences, and looking at various virtual reference packages. We looked at several models of providing chat-based reference services. In May of 2004, we joined the Florida state-wide virtual reference service, *Ask a Librarian*–www. askalibrarian.org.

The Florida's *Ask a Librarian* program is a collaborative service made up of public, academic, and special libraries throughout the state. About 80 different libraries participate in *Ask a Librarian* including all of Florida's community college libraries, public libraries from small municipal locations to county-wide systems, and the Florida Virtual High School. The service is open weekdays 10 a.m.-10 p.m. and weekends 10 a.m.-5 p.m. Each participating library provides coverage for the collaborative desk and has the capability to directly serve local customers for extended hours. *Ask a Librarian* uses the Dokutek VRL*plus* service which provides chat-based reference integrated with e-mail services and a knowledge base, currently used for library specific information. The service currently handles about 1,500 sessions each month.

Ask a Librarian began serving customers in July, 2003. Florida's statewide live virtual reference service started as an LSTA grant funded project of the Center for College Library Automation and the Tampa Bay Library Consortium. It has now become component of the Florida Electronic Library–www.flelibrary.org. Participation in this collaborative reference service currently requires only staff time, Internet access, and local computer equipment. The fact that providing virtual reference services through *Ask a Librarian* requires no dedicated budgetary expenditure makes the discussion of budget planning and evaluation an academic one. It is, however, a discussion that we have indulged in order to prepare for possible expansion of this service, changes in the current funding of the service, or the possibility of moving to a different model of providing virtual reference service altogether.

PLANNING FOR A NEW LIBRARY SERVICE

As a part of county government, the library's spending is based on a two year budget cycle. The amount of funding received for the operation of library services from the special taxing district is dependent on the number of successfully funded programs. Each program or service is outlined and justified by a decision unit (see Appendix 1). The decision unit describes the funding amounts needed, staff required, equipment and any materials necessary to provide a service. In addition, it must also spell out how the service relates to the strategic plans of the county and library. Decision units must be written for every new or continuing service, building one upon the other to lay out the level of service to be offered, how the organization's goals are to be met, and to outline performance measures for each service. Each decision unit is rated at a "minimum," "continuation," or "desired" level based on its importance to the overall budget. Minimum services are funded at a basic level not reflecting growth or demands. A reference example would be a decision unit for the core print collection and the number of staff required to handle in-person reference transaction. All subsequent reference units would build on this. Continuation and desired level units take into account demands for services, continuing enhanced services, and new services. Continuation units could be built for telephone and e-mail reference, database funding, public informational programs, etc. A desired level service might include additional staff, software, and new equipment required to begin providing virtual/chat reference services to customers. The creation of these decision units for each budget cycle provides for a continual re-evaluation of library services and service levels. The decision unit also requires that performance measures and evaluation steps be built into the planning of all library service and programs.[1] This aspect of the decision unit will be discussed in greater detail in the next sections.

It is with this process in mind that we began to plan for virtual reference services. We did not actually write a decision unit and seek funding for participation in Florida's *Ask a Librarian*. The collaborative model that we chose to join as our entry into virtual reference services did not require new or additional staff and resources. We have been, however, doing the research necessary and building the trend data to set performance measures for evaluation of virtual reference should we decide to expand our program (for example to work with existing outreach services such as our bookmobile or e-libraries), change software, or provide this service not in a collaborative effort. A separate decision unit would then be required.

CHOOSING PERFORMANCE MEASURES

One of the more important aspects of the decision unit, other than to garner funds for library services, is to show the impact of those funds on performance–the value of the money being spent. The goal of the decision unit is not necessarily to show growth, but increased efficiency and effectiveness in the use of public money. Each decision unit is required to demonstrate, through statistical and qualitative analysis, all inputs, outputs, and outcome performance measures. Inputs–costs of staff, equipment, facility, software–are not difficult to provide with some background research. These are the expected costs of providing the service. Outputs–workload, demand, efficiency, effectiveness–are built using the statistical data collected by actually providing the service. Outcomes–decreased costs, increased satisfaction, fewer errors, shorter response times–are the desired goals of the service. These can be evaluated by comparing inputs and outputs, customer surveys, and librarian interviews. Outcome performance measures can often be evaluated along with quality standards to help assess the results of the service. Output and outcome evaluation measures are more of a challenge and require two key components: choosing which measures to evaluate, and being able to collect the data and statistics effectively.

In choosing relevant performance measures, we have looked not only at the growing body of literature on evaluating virtual reference, but also at materials for evaluation of general library and traditional reference services. *Evaluating Reference Services: A Practical Guide* by Jo Bell Whitlach is a good general book to help you decide how and what to measure. Chapters on selecting the best evaluation method and working with data have been useful. A more recent and general work is *Mea-*

suring for Results: The Dimensions of Public Library Effectiveness by Joseph R. Matthews. The purpose of this book is to help assess the value of the public library to the community. It provides a good overview of input, process, and output performance measures. Especially helpful is *Appendix A* which contains a list of input, output, process, and satisfaction measures and how they are defined and calculated.[2]

In the last few years there has been an increasing amount of literature dealing specifically with evaluation, performance measures, and satisfaction for virtual reference services. Much of this literature is coming from names attached to the Information Institute of Syracuse (sponsors of the Virtual Reference Desk Project) and the Information Use Management Policy Institute at Florida State University (developers of the E-Metrics Instructional System). The focus of this literature is shifting from the basic questions of "What do you count?" and "How do you count?"–the technical statistics–toward solving issues involved with outcomes assessment and quality standards.[3]

Developing performance measures often comes down to what data can be captured. Most virtual reference services can generate a broad list of statistics, assist in pushing surveys to users, and allow for the archiving of session transcripts. Docutek VRL*plus* is able to generate statistics that can be used to form and evaluate performance measures based on reference sessions and questions. Most of the reports can be limited from the full collaborative to the institution or specific librarian. The date range for the reports can be defined by the user.

By session we currently track:

- Number of sessions per day
- Number of sessions by hour of the day
- Session duration
- Time spent by customer in the queue
- Customer's browser and operating system
- Customer affiliation (based on entry point)

By question we currently track (for both e-mail and chat):

- Number of questions received per day
- Number of questions answered per day
- Number of questions by status (various)
- Questions transferred from chat to e-mail
- Response times

We are able to customize the customer entry page to also capture data from users that we can define–age, education, affiliation, ZIP code, etc. Currently we only ask for ZIP code.

The important thing to remember is not *what* can be tracked, but *that* you track at all. Building trend data is the key for creating the performance measures that will ensure that a decision unit receives funding. We were recently able to get additional staff funded for our centralized telephone reference service, not based on the addition of virtual reference to their list of activities, but by building trend data and relating it to established performance measures. We could show that over the past three years customer wait times for assistance, and the volume of transactions for each staff member had risen to levels exceeding our target performance. Collected data, or estimated data prior to having built up any significant trends, can be used to establish a baseline for setting tangible and realistic standards. Most of the statistical material we can collect will help set efficiency and workload related goals, such as:

- % increase in the number of customers (session) annually
- % increase on the users per capita (awareness of the service)
- % decrease in the wait time for customers to receive assistance
- % increase in the number of questions answered (completed) at time of original transaction

Most statistical, workload measures can be used to gage efficiency. Efficiency is a ratio that expresses the relationship of inputs (time, cost, staffing) to workload. Keeping track of inputs and outputs will let you determine productivity measures such as: cost per question, question per staff, cost of questions per capita, etc. Collecting and evaluating this type of information about your service, over a period of time, can show the value of a service in easily understandable terms and help set future improvement goals.

These measures can help define the success of the service, but will not give a complete picture of the effectiveness and definitely not customer satisfaction or quality. There are two other methods of evaluation that can be used to create this more complete picture–user surveys and transcript analysis. Docutek VRL*plus* has the ability to push user surveys to customers after a session, or e-mail them at a later time. The surveys are user defined, enabling to collection of relevant feedback. By asking customers for their input, better effectiveness measures can be created. Customers could be asked about their impression of the reference transaction:

- Was the librarian helpful, courteous?
- Did they get the information they needed?
- Was the response timely?
- Was this method of delivery easy to use?
- Have they used the service before?
- Would they use the service again?

Transcript analysis is another technique to assess effectiveness and quality.[4] This may be something that you already have done with existing e-mail reference programs. Most virtual reference systems, e-mail and/or chat, allow for the archiving (even if temporarily) of reference transactions. These "artifacts" can be examined for completeness, accuracy, sources used, subject, etc. Docutek VRL*plus* allows for our review of transcripts as a group or sorted by librarian. We can not only assess quality of response, but look for reference interview skills, resource knowledge, and skill with virtual reference. The ability to examine professional skills also lets us add staff training goals to our possible evaluation points. After we established our e-mail reference program in 1999, we archived our e-mail responses (without customer information) and review two six month periods, a year apart. We were able to see trends in subjects of questions and ways to help customers that had not previously been apparent in a face-to-face reference setting.

By looking at these factors combined with user feedback from surveys, our list of potential effectiveness and quality performance measures expands to include measure such as:

- % increase in the use of subscription databases in virtual reference transaction
- % customers expressing satisfaction with service
- % repeat customers for the service
- % increase in the number of genealogy related questions (targeted awareness)
- % of questions answered correctly
- % found the service easy/intuitive to use

When we build a decision unit, it is not necessary to provide quite this many evaluation points. The three main areas of output measures need to be addressed–workload, efficiency, effectiveness. The written decision unit has a narrative component to include quality measures and additional impact statements and justifications. As stated before, we have not created a decision unit for virtual reference since our current resource allocation is limited. When the need to submit one becomes a reality, it might potentially include the following minimal performance measures:

1. 5% increase in sessions annually
2. 30% repeat customers annually
3. 85% customer satisfaction with the service
4. Provide subscription database instruction/awareness in 50% of sessions

Even though we may not use all of the trend data to evaluate our virtual reference service for the purposes of funding justification, having the statistical data and customer feedback would be worthwhile. The data can be used later for additional assessment and training, and to make continual improvements.

The reasons for choosing measures may vary greatly. It will depend on how you define "success" and set quality goals for your service. Success in virtual reference can be defined as increased use, short response times, customer satisfaction, correct answers, etc.–your performance measures should reflect what you intend to get out of the service. The potential measures given above evaluate both outputs (increase in use) and outcomes (repeat use and customer satisfaction). These measures are required by the decision unit. The choice to examine the volume of instruction for subscription databases would let the library use its virtual reference service to work toward the added goal of raising the awareness and use of (often) expensive databases. Like the use of the librarian as expert help in the virtual environment, the use of authoritative library resources in the virtual environment is an information literacy goal we are working toward.

CONTINUAL EVALUATION

The importance of gathering statistics and building trend data for a virtual reference service cannot be underestimated. Even if there is no clear use for certain statistics, assessments, or user feedback now, their use may become important for later evaluation and will definitely be useful in setting service standards and performance measures. There can be problems with the collection of data. Technical problems can obscure the origins of your statistics by date, time, institution, or librarian. The nature of collaborative services can also add challenges to data collection. Often the local data needed for budget justification is difficult to gather within a statewide service. Survey clarity can also cloud customer responses. Surveys pushed through the virtual reference service are only answered by the willing (i.e., those who chose to get help virtually), skewing the results. Keep the data anyway, making note of the issues.

Regardless of the ultimate goals in evaluating virtual reference services–required or not–the need to continually review the effectiveness of the service exists. The mandated evaluation of our services for the budgeting process in Hillsborough County has forced us to maintain the mechanism for regular re-evaluation of the library's services. Through continual evaluation and the review of trend data, we hope to avoid the need to ever create a separate decision unit for our virtual reference service. By showing increased use, customer acceptance, quality and/or "success" based on established performance standards, virtual reference may one day be part of our "minimum" level of services, secure in funding, that we can build other decision units upon.

NOTES

1. For a more thorough discussion of the budgeting process for Hillsborough County, Florida and to review the actual budget and decision units, see Eric R. Johnson. *Taxpayer's Guide to the Hillsborough County Budget* (Tampa, FL: Hillsborough County Management and Budget Department, 2003) and visit the budget online at http://www.hillsboroughcounty.org/.

2. Joseph R. Matthews. *Measuring for Results: The Dimensions of Public Library Effectiveness.* (Westport, CN: Libraries Unlimited, 2004), 193-213.

3. See for example John Carlo Bertot and Charles R. McClure. "Outcomes Assessment in the Networked Environment: Research Questions, Issues, Considerations, and Moving Forward." *Library Trends* 51, no. 4 (Spring 2003): 590-613; and R. David Lankes, Melissa Gross, Charles R. McClure. "Cost, Statistics, Measures, and Standards for Digital Reference Services: a Preliminary View." *Library Trends* 51, no. 3 (Winter, 2003): 401-413. See bibliography for additional examples.

4. See Joanne Smyth. "Virtual Reference Transcript Analysis: a Few Models." *Searcher* 11, no. 3 (March, 2003): 26-31.

SUGGESTED READING

Bertot, John Carlo and Charles R. McClure. "Outcomes Assessment in the Networked Environment: Research Questions, Issues, Considerations, and Moving Forward." *Library Trends* 51, no. 4 (Spring 2003): 590-613.
Gross, Melissa, Charles R. McClure and R. David Lankes. "Assessing Quality in Digital Reference Services: An Overview of Key Literature on Digital Reference." In

Lankes, R. D., McClure, C. R., Gross, M., & Pomerantz, J. (eds.). *Implementing Digital Reference Services: Setting Standards and Making It Real*. New York: Neal-Schumann Publishers, 2003.

Information Institute of Syracuse. 2004. Internet Online. <http://iis.syr.edu/> [August, 2004].

Information Use Management and Policy Institute. 2004. Internet Online. <http://www.ii.fsu.edu/> [August, 2004]. See specifically the E-Metrics Instructional System at <http://www.ii.fsu.edu/emis/>.

Janes, Joseph. *Introduction to Reference Work in the Digital Age*. New York: Neal-Schumann Publishers, 2003.

Johnson, Eric R. *Taxpayer's Guide to the Hillsborough County Budget*. Tampa, FL: Hillsborough County Management and Budget Department, 2003. Internet Online. <http://www.hillsboroughcounty.org/mbd/recommended/fy05/publications/taxpayers.pdf> [August, 2004].

Kasowitz, A., B.A. Bennett, and R.David Lankes. "Quality Standards for Digital Reference Consortia." *Reference & User Services Quarterly* 39, no. 4 (2000): 355-63.

Lankes, R. David, John W. Collins III, and Abby S. Kasowitz (eds.). *Digital Reference Service in the New Millennium: Planning, Management, and Evaluation*. New York: Neal-Schumann Publishers, 2000.

Lankes, R. David, Melissa Gross and Charles R. McClure. "Cost, Statistics, Measures, and Standards for Digital Reference Services: a Preliminary View." *Library Trends* 51, no. 3 (Winter, 2003): 401-413.

Matthews, Joseph R. *Measuring for Results: The Dimensions of Public Library Effectiveness*. Westport, CN: Libraries Unlimited, 2004.

Maxwell, Nancy Kalikow. "Establishing and Maintaining Live Online Reference Service." *Library Technology Reports* 38, no. 4 (July-August, 2002): 1-76.

McClure, Charles R., R. David Lankes, Melissa Gross, and B. Choltco-Devlin. *Statistics, Measures, and Quality Standards for Assessing Digital Reference Library Services: Guidelines and Procedures*. Syracuse, NY: Information Institute of Syracuse, School of Information Studies, 2002.

Smyth, Joanne. "Virtual Reference Transcript Analysis: a Few Models." *Searcher* 11, no. 3 (March, 2003): 26-31.

Virtual Reference Desk. 2004. Internet Online. <http://www.vrd.org/> [August, 2004].

White, M. "Digital Reference Services: Framework for Analysis and Evaluation." *Library and Information Science Research* 23, no. 3 (2001): 211-231.

Whitlatch, Jo Bell. "Evaluating Reference Services in the Electronic Age." *Library Trends* 50, no.2 (Fall, 2001): 207-217.

Whitlatch, Jo Bell. *Evaluating Reference Services: A Practical Guide*. Chicago: American Library Association, 2000.

doi:10.1300/J120v46n95_08

APPENDIX 1

FY 06 and FY 07 Decision Unit Description & Cost

Office:	Human Services
Department:	Library Services

Fund:	
Subfund:	
Index Code:	

SERVICE LEVEL

Continuation

CATEGORY:

(M1, M2, E, D)

PRIORITY	
Funding Source Priority #:	
Department Priority #	

C.I.P.#:	

BUDGETARY DECISION UNIT:	Virtual Reference Services
SERVICE:	Reference & Information

RESOURCES:

Total Positions (Listed by Job Class)
(Use separate sheet if necessary.)

	Total Costs						
	FY 06	FY 07		Class #	Description	FY 06	FY 07
				3821	Librarian	2	2
Personal Services							
Operating Expenses							
Capital Outlay							
TOTAL	$	$			TOTAL		

IMPACT ON FY 06:

IMPACT ON FY 07 (if different from FY 06):

REVENUE IMPACT:

Revenue Description	FY 06	FY 07	Narrative:
Fines, Fees & Misc.			

(Continue on separate page, if necessary.)

VET:
The Virtual Evaluation Toolkit

Buff Hirko

SUMMARY. Between October 2003 and July 2004, the Statewide Virtual Reference Project (a Washington State Library initiative funded by LSTA) developed the Virtual Evaluation Toolkit, or VET. The purpose of VET was to help libraries improve virtual reference services, with resulting increased awareness, usage, and customer satisfaction. VET includes three levels of evaluation tools with information on their implementation and examples of the use of results, along with a generic final report based on three test site evaluations (an academic, public, and special library). The complete manual is available on the Web in order to provide practical and meaningful tools and recommendations that encourage libraries to use them and also to report on their use. doi:10.1300/J120v46n95_09 *[Article copies available for a fee from The Haworth Document Delivery Service: 1-800-HAWORTH. E-mail address: <docdelivery@haworthpress.com> Website: <http://www.HaworthPress.com> © 2006 by The Haworth Press, Inc. All rights reserved.]*

KEYWORDS. VET: Virtual Evaluation Toolkit, virtual reference, service evaluation, evalution criteria, checklists, Washington State Virtual Reference Project

Buff Hirko is Statewide Virtual Reference Project Coordinator, Washington State Library, P.O. Box 42460, Olympia, WA 98504-2460 (E-mail: bhirko@secstate.wa.gov).

[Haworth co-indexing entry note]: "VET: The Virtual Evaluation Toolkit." Hirko, Buff. Co-published simultaneously in *The Reference Librarian* (The Haworth Information Press, an imprint of The Haworth Press, Inc.) No. 95/96, 2006, pp. 125-148; and: *Assessing Reference and User Services in a Digital Age* (ed: Eric Novotny) The Haworth Information Press, an imprint of The Haworth Press, Inc., 2006, pp. 128-148. Single or multiple copies of this article are available for a fee from The Haworth Document Delivery Service [1-800-HAWORTH, 9:00 a.m. - 5:00 p.m. (EST). E-mail address: docdelivery@haworthpress.com].

Evaluation–everyone talks about it, but relatively few libraries do it. Evaluate what, when, and how? And who will do it? This article outlines activities and materials developed in Washington state to support a variety of library virtual reference services. It starts with a description of the circumstances under which the work began and the players involved in developing evaluation tools. The discussion follows the evolution of the process and modification of the materials, with the logical progression to testing VET in different types of libraries and the preliminary results of those tests. Three tools and checklists that exemplify the information provided in the manual are included at the end.

When the Steering Committee[1] of Washington's Statewide Virtual Reference Project (VRS) met in October 2003, Joe Janes suggested that we tackle the problem as a logical next step. The success of the project's previous work with training and marketing provided incentive, and the Needs Assessment Subcommittee[2] began work the following month. Many of the challenges were identical to those presented by the training program. VRS works with multi-type libraries in geographically far-flung places–urban, suburban, and rural–with wide-ranging community sizes and diverse staff education/experience levels. All needed our product. We set a tight timeline, since we wanted to make materials available as soon as possible to the VRS project libraries, whose grants would end in September 2004.

Several important suggestions were made at the October meeting, most based on the idea of building on existing activities rather than inventing new ones.

- Virtual reference must be assessed in the context of overall reference service.
- The "Anytime, Anywhere Answers" curriculum used in VRS training included online exercises that could provide the basis for evaluation tools.
- The skills of VRS trainers could be utilized to evaluate chat reference services both remotely and on site. (A "SWAT" team approach was envisioned.)
- VRS grant libraries had participated in additional activities that could be translated for our purposes–notably the peer transcript review process implemented by Matt Saxton (University of Washington Information School) at Seattle Public Library.

Assessment interests focused in two directions–internal (management information, professional development) and external (customer needs and satisfaction). At the same time, we recognized the need to place evaluation in the context of service standards currently in use. The intent was to provide information that libraries would find relevant, clear, and useful. Subcommittee members volunteered to assemble lists of sample customer service survey questions and send copies of related documents to the project coordinator. Above all, we wanted to design tools that would be easy to use and understand, ones that actually would result in *improved service*. There was no interest in evaluation for the sake of evaluation; we intended to write practical guidelines. It was a solid start.

Despite some wheel-spinning and changing views of checklist design, we made progress in the next two meetings. Shared documents included draft evaluation checklists based on VRS training activities, the 24/7 Reference Cooperative Policies and Procedures Manual, Seattle Public Library's Reference Service Protocols (under revision at that time), and survey questions and topics compiled from many services. A number of other resources were consulted by individual subcommittee members that informed our discussions. We agreed to call the result of our process the Virtual Evaluation Toolkit (VET), and also identified two important goals. First, the final document would be posted to the VRS Project Web page. Second, a program proposal to describe the process and test site evaluations would be submitted for the 2004 Virtual Reference Desk Conference. (Note: This presentation will be made at VRD in Cincinnati.) To underscore that assessment is a useful process, everyone was tasked with bringing examples of ways in which libraries had used similar findings to improve services and/or make them more responsive to customer needs. These would be incorporated into VET.

There was an acute awareness of the calendar, and meetings increased. Prior to the March meeting, the project coordinator compiled and distributed a more complete draft document. This promoted detailed discussion and decision-making, including:

- Contracting with two VRS trainers to conduct test evaluations at three library sites–academic, public, and special,
- Organizing the VET manual into three levels, based on the resources (staff, time, funds, etc.) required to implement the tools, and
- Targeting May-June as the test evaluation period.

The three library evaluations were intended to test the tools in actual use so that shortcomings could be corrected prior to posting to the Web.

The site reports would be included in the manual to illustrate VET implementation.

The evaluation tools were modified at every meeting. In some cases changes were reversed; other areas were eliminated as too labor-intensive to be practical. We didn't want to take the kitchen sink approach of including every possibility, but rather wanted to recommend specific approaches that would elicit focused results. At the same time, we expected libraries to select from the tools those which seemed most appropriate to local needs. The March draft included:

Introduction and Pre-Evaluation Preparation

Level I: Web Site Evaluation Checklist
            Virtual Reference Transaction Checklist
            Virtual Reference Policy Checklist
            Customer Use and Satisfaction Survey

Level II: Web Site Usage
            Provider Self-Evaluation

Level III: Peer Transcript Review
            Transcript Analysis
            Focus Groups
            Usability Testing
            Cost

Test Site Libraries: Report Template and Results

Each tool is preceded by an introductory section that includes purpose, methods for implementation, and examples of the use of results. Level I was designed as a basic set of tools that would allow a good overview of virtual reference service. Web site evaluation covered branding, accessibility, scope of service, and confidentiality/data gathered. The virtual reference transaction, in which evaluators log onto a service and act in the role of user (using a set of questions taken from real chat reference sessions), considered setting the tone, getting the question straight, keeping the user informed, providing information, and follow-up. The policy checklist identifies essential written policies which ensure consistent, equitable, and legal terms of service that are readily available to remote patrons. Because legal and institutional requirements vary widely, the checklist is not meant to assess policy content. The section on surveys provides several recommended packages of questions intended to elicit specific information (e.g., administrative, clarity, speed, demographics, target groups, satisfaction) and also a long list of prepared questions, arranged topically. These primary Level I tools were identified for use in the test site evaluations.

April arrived all too soon. We invited two VRS trainers to attend. They were contracted as the test site evaluation team, selected for their expertise and varied backgrounds.[3] This was a crucial decision that made us look very smart in the end. They would use checklists for the "Virtual Reference Transaction" (based on the VRS training "Secret Patron" exercise), "Web Site Evaluation" (based on "Virtual Field Trips"), and "Virtual Reference Policies" (also based on an online training activity),[4] as well as an on-site visit with managing and staff librarians at each library. The evaluators and subcommittee members carefully reviewed each tool, the final report, and the assessment process in detail.

The project coordinator contacted the libraries that had volunteered to participate, outlining evaluation activities, a timeline for events, and a short list of information needed in order to begin the test. The latter included hours of service and operator schedule for virtual reference, preferred dates and times for an on-site visit, library Web site URL, name and telephone number of library contact person, electronic copies of any library policies not posted to the Web site, user survey reports for the most recent three months (if available), and a short list of staff expectations for the evaluation.

Fortunately, we had enthusiastic participation by grant project libraries. In each test site library, some staff members had participated in the VRS training classes, so the activities and evaluators were familiar. With the end of the academic year looming, the trainers were asked to begin in mid-May and complete their activities by mid-June. That request was met, but the time squeeze resulted in some confusion and less than optimum task organization. The evaluators had full-time jobs, and VET activities had to be scheduled during non-work time and also coordinated with library staffs at three different institutions.

Each of the evaluators completed multiple chat reference transactions with each of the test site libraries. This activity proved difficult. In order to assume identity-neutral patron roles (i.e., not use names and addresses that were obviously library-connected), the evaluators needed several e-mail personas. In the case of the public library, authentication requirements almost doomed the test. Luckily, the library's reference coordinator came to the rescue with a list of temporary card numbers with fictional identities that were used for test purposes. Similar problems arose when student numbers were requested during academic library sessions. Even more troublesome was the problem of initiating a great number of chat sessions during the evaluators' off work hours. Chat sessions, examinations of Web sites and policies, and site visits–added to the requirement to write a coordinated report of the results and recommendations for each library–proved to be a workload far greater than originally envisioned.

On July 8, the evaluators met again with the subcommittee to present their preliminary reports. Despite the time crunch and overwork, they were enthusiastic about the process and all that they had learned from it. They stressed the appropriateness and usefulness of the checklists. They also noted that the on-site visits offered the opportunity to share the high quality of service they had received from staff members at each of the test libraries. The subcommittee was equally impressed with the final reports, which were both pragmatic and insightful. The value of objective evaluators (that is, librarians not associated with the test sites) was underscored. In addition, the evaluators offered pointed, valuable advice on refining the tools, the process, and the report to make them easier to implement. Among the recommendations were lengthening the time available to complete an evaluation, completing the assessment of a single library before starting another, answering authentication requirements before beginning any virtual activities, and modifying the report template to reduce repetition.

The final draft of the VET Manual was sent to a number of virtual reference experts around the U.S. and Canada for comment and suggestions. A preliminary version also was posted to the Anytime Anywhere Answers training curriculum Web site in August and the URL [http://vrstrain.spl.org/textdocs/VETmanual.pdf] was shared on the DIG_REF discussion list, requesting comments. When the responses are reviewed and appropriate recommendations are incorporated, the manual will be posted to the Web in fall 2004. Three months after the completion of the original test site evaluations, a questionnaire will be sent to each of the participating libraries to determine their reaction to and use of the reports. A summary of results will be added to the Web posting.

In the following pages, excerpts from the VET manual illustrate both tools and organization, as well as an executive summary for a sample report. The final manual (70+ pages) includes a bibliography,[5] index, and three sets of question scenarios (public, academic, legal) used for test site chat transactions.

PRE-EVALUATION PREPARATION

Assemble a Team

The evaluation process requires one or more staff members who will:

- Develop the evaluation plan/select tools to be used
- Collect and compile data (new or existing)
- Implement evaluation tools
- Analyze the results
- Communicate progress
- Write and distribute a final report
- Recommend improvements based on the report

There are a number of skill sets needed to complete these tasks. Planning requires both an understanding of evaluation methods and an overview of service components, such as: quality control for customer service, the effectiveness and efficiency of procedures, economic concerns, marketing, appropriate use of resources. Data collection needs attention to detail and timeliness. Analytical skills are critical to the process of correlating and breakdown of results. Those who communicate progress and write reports must be articulate both orally and in writing, be sensitive to deadlines, and understand distribution methods. All of the work requires the support of administration and the trust of subordinates (see Staff Buy-In on next page). Communication efforts throughout should follow the old public relations rule: "Tell them what you're going to do, tell them what you're doing, tell them what you did."

If any of these areas of expertise are not available among library staff members, then consideration should be given to using outside evaluators or consultants. Such persons may be paid or recruited from colleagues in partner/consortium libraries in exchange for similar or other duties.

Identify Expectations

Prior to beginning the evaluation, library staff members should list their expectations for the process and results. Examples:

"The evaluators should be as objective as possible."

"The process should not interrupt normal library operations."

"The process should not create extra work for those not involved in the evaluation."

"The final report must be complete, well-organized, and clear."

"The final report should offer recommendations for using the results."

When the evaluation is complete, the results should be compared to the preliminary list of expectations. A close match is reason for applause; consequences that diverge from those that were anticipated can help improve or tweak future efforts.

Staff Buy-In

Involve staff and stakeholders, such as Board members, in planning for the evaluation. Be sure that everyone who might be affected by it contributes to the goals of the project and also understands their role in the evaluation process. Consider offering a general information meeting for all staff.

Determine in advance any anticipated barriers that might be encountered during the evaluation process. Examples:

- staff availability
- language barriers
- timing of evaluation activities

These are all potential obstacles that can be handled proactively to make the process run smoothly.

Establish a method for obtaining feedback from them–e-mail, suggestion box, meetings, etc. Whenever possible, assign responsibility for responding to feedback to someone involved in the evaluation process. Compile a list of feedback gathered and notify staff when their ideas have been incorporated. Keep staff apprised of progress at regular intervals, including notification of important benchmarks. For example, an e-mail to all staff might read:

> We completed Evaluation Phase I on schedule on Friday, May 28 with a higher than anticipated return rate for surveys. In the next step, the Evaluation Committee will compile the results. We anticipate that the final report will be issued by June 15. If you have questions, please contact Lotta Smarts at 123-4567 or e-mail lsmarts@usalib.org.

When the evaluation is completed, the final report should be shared with all staff and their comments solicited. These can be incorporated into considerations for improving virtual reference service, and noteworthy observations communicated to the staff.

TOOLS

Level I

This level provides a set of basic tools, with an emphasis on evaluating customer service. It was used in our 2004 test site evaluations. Note that whenever possible, evaluators should be recruited from outside the department or library being assessed, in order to ensure reasonably objective results.

Virtual Reference Transaction Checklist (See Table 1)

Purpose: To provide a snapshot of virtual reference service from the customer perspective.

Method: Using an identity-neutral e-mail account (e.g., Carfan@ hotmail.com–something that does not readily identify a library/staff member), each evaluator logs on to the library's virtual reference service on four to six (4-6) separate occasions, scheduled at different times on various days to ensure that the same library provider is not contacted repeatedly. In the case of a library that requires authentication (e.g., library card number), it will be necessary to establish a mock card number or use a card number belonging to a non-library staff member. In either case, the evaluator should log on with a different, neutral name that does not indicate gender or profession.

For each visit, a different question is selected from the list of scenarios provided. The checklist is used to determine whether specific service concerns are answered. Unusual, extreme (good or bad), and/or especially useful experiences, as well as overall insights, can be added in the comments section. Complete *all* sections of the checklist.

Recommendations: Use real questions that have been asked by customers in the past. If possible, obtain questions from another library of the same type. It is useful to develop a scenario or context for each question that provides the evaluator a logical way to proceed through the transaction. Note practices and issues (good and bad) that are repeated in or common to different transactions that can be used to focus on ser-

TABLE 1

VIRTUAL REFERENCE TRANSACTION CHECKLIST

Evaluator: _____

Library: _____

Date/Time: _____

Question used: _____

PLEASE CHECK ALL THAT APPLY

SETTING THE TONE:

Identification: a personal name was used for the service provider	
Greeting: the service provider greeted me personally and used my name.	
Readiness: it was clear that he/she was interested in my query and ready to provide assistance.	
Use of scripts: he/she thoughtfully integrated any scripted messages into the transaction.	

GETTING THE QUESTION STRAIGHT

The service provider clarified my question using:

☐ An open probe ☑ A closed probe ☐ Both open and closed probes ☐ Did not clarify my question

KEEPING ME INFORMED:

Options offered: he/she asked me whether I wanted to see how to find the answer.	
Clarity: the service provider's responses were clear, easy to read, and free of library jargon or personal opinion.	
Time management: the service provider kept me informed about his/her progress in finding an answer, providing a time estimate when needed.	
Responsiveness: he/she let me know what he was doing, e.g., still looking, pushing a Web page, escorting, etc.	

PROVIDING INFORMATION:

Quality: he/she identified authoritative information appropriate for my need and interest.	
Pacing: the service provider gave me time to determine whether the information found actually answered my question to my satisfaction. Didn't rush me by pushing too much information.	
Citation: cited the source of the information.	
Completeness: asked if I wanted to be shown more sources.	
Referral: recognized if my question needed to be referred elsewhere.	

FOLLOW-UP:

Relevance: asked if the information found answered my question to my satisfaction.	
Further needs: asked if I had any other questions.	
Marketing: encouraged me to use the service again.	
Appreciation: thanked me.	
Survey/evaluation: I was asked to evaluate my experience with the service. This evaluation was/was not an effective tool to express my opinion of the service.	

COMMENTS:

vice improvement. Consider the bottom line–as a customer, would you use this service again? If "yes," why? If "no," why?

Sample Question Scenarios

1. You are: An employee working on a training manual for your boss. You are proofreading it and can't decide whether to use who or whom in a sentence. You need to have the corrected version done ASAP.

> Question: When do you use who, when do you use whom?
> Follow up: What's correct? The Tester should behave like the person who needs to implement the next phase of the product life-cycle.

2. You are: A 65-year-old woman who has persistent pain in her foot and hasn't gotten a lot of help from her doctor.

> Question: What is the real name for heel spurs?
> Follow up: How can I find medical advice? I want some advice for getting rid of the pain in my heel. I have been wearing orthotics but they don't help.

Examples (Use of Results): Following their experiences as "Secret Patrons" in the VRS Training classes, several learners reported their discomfort with the unwelcoming and robotic feel of chat sessions when the service provider was identified only as "Librarian" or other generic term (e.g., "BPLibrarian18"). Opening a discussion of this concern on return to the library resulted in several libraries switching to the use of real first names or pseudonyms in order to make the customer experience friendlier and more personal.

When the lack of question clarification is a frequent characteristic of chat sessions, libraries often provide or enroll staff in appropriate training to improve their use of appropriate scripts and/or reference interview techniques.

To counter over-reliance on Google as a starting point for searches, staff can be trained in the use of licensed databases.

Web Site Evaluation Checklist (See Table 2)

Purpose: To ensure that the Web site works well, meaning that John and Mary Patron, who are average folks in terms of ability and experi-

TABLE 2

WEB SITE EVALUATION CHECKLIST		
Evaluator: _____		
Library Web Site visited: _____		
Date/Time: _____		
BRANDING (includes the name, logo, tagline and descriptions of the service. A brand makes a promise, then consistently delivers):	Yes	No
Name of service (appealing, memorable, descriptive)		
Tagline (jargon-free, relevant)		
Logo (attractive, visible, appropriate)		
Links to service (easy to locate, on main page)		
Other links to service (from additional Web pages, such as catalog, online databases, and/or circulation page)		
Consistency (page layout, use of graphics, and message are uniform throughout Web site)		
Comments on service branding:		
ACCESSIBILITY:	Yes	No
Navigability (minimal scrolling and clicks to point of question entry)		
Service availability (clear statements on availability -- to anyone, library card or ID required for access, other)		
Restrictions (clearly stated, visible)		
Service hours (limited, coincide with library open hours, 24/7, holidays)		
Technology requirements (clearly described--browser, plug-in, etc.)		
Disability alternatives (Bobby approved or ADA compliant)		
Comments on Accessibility:		
SCOPE OF SERVICE:	Yes	No
Service description (clear, complete, jargon-free)		
Questions (limitations, if any, for type or length of questions)		
Information literacy (service offers to demonstrate how to find answers or navigate the Web)		
Links (starting points for Web searching, Web source citation)		
Staffing (description of service providers, qualifications, subject expertise)		
Disclaimers (statements about medical or legal advice, copyright restrictions, citing online sources)		
Databases (statements regarding quality, use, limitations)		
Comments on Scope:		

CONFIDENTIALITY and DATA GATHERED	Yes	No
Explanation of requested personal information (minimal--name, email address; or detailed-i.e., level of information sought, homework assignment, phone number, etc.)		
Anonymity (anonymous logon possible, alternatives to providing name/email address)		
Privacy policy (clearly stated, complete, easy to find)		
Data statement (how data is used, how long it is retained)		
Explanation of requested personal information (minimal–name, email address; or detailed–i.e., level of information sought, homework assignment, phone number, etc.)		
Comments on Confidentiality:		

ence, can use it for its intended purpose without getting hopelessly frustrated.

Method: Log on to the library's Web site, then carefully examine all pages for usability. The checklist focuses on a number of facets of Web site design that affect customers' remote interaction with the library–collections, services, and staff. For each of the categories, offer comments that underscore positive characteristics of the site and/or clarify problems. When the checklist is complete, provide an overall review of the Web site, highlighting pages or aspects that are excellent, unusual, or that need improvement.

Note that this activity is related to the Reference Policy Checklist which follows. While exploring the Web site, look for references and/or links to any formal library policies related to the service and bookmark any pages where they are found.

Recommendations: One of the most important considerations for VR is consistency. On a Web site, this means that the same term is used for the service wherever mentioned, that page layout is fairly uniform, that navigation tools (e.g., tabs, breadcrumbs, button bars, etc.) are consistent, and that content is well-edited. In the following paragraphs, questions are posed that may help put the evaluation in context.

Branding: A brand includes all of the associations a user makes with a service or product, from name and logo to descriptions. Successful brands evoke a lasting emotional response that underscores the value of the service. A strong brand makes a promise, then delivers. As you explore the Web site, ask these questions: What is the name of the service? What image or logo is used to "brand" the service? How is the service described? Is library jargon used? Do you think the name, image, and description are appealing and attention-getting? Is the link easy to find on the main library Web page? Are there links to the virtual reference service from all areas of the library's Web site? From the catalog? From the online databases? From the circulation information page?

Accessibility: Remember that people won't use a Web site if they can't find their way around it. Good site design offers high visibility and clear, simple, consistent navigation. Questions to ask: Is the service open to anyone? Is a library card or student ID number required for access? What other restrictions exist? Where are these restrictions stated? When is the real-time reference service open? What are the user's options when the service is closed? Is the service available on holidays? Are disability requirements taken into account?

Scope of Service: Is there a clear statement about the kinds of questions that are appropriate for this real-time reference service? Does it offer more than simple, factual answers? If targeted to college students, is it clear how much research help will be provided? Does the service promote information literacy by offering to demonstrate how to find answers or use the Web more effectively? Are links to starting points for Web searching provided? Links to how to cite Web sources? Who are the staff providing answers through this service? What are their qualifications? Subject expertise? Is there any disclaimer about providing medical or legal advice? Are there any statements about copyright restrictions or about citing online sources?

Confidentiality and Data Gathered: What kind of information is gathered in advance about the user or about the question? Reading level or level of information sought? Homework assignment? Phone number? How is this information used? What is the privacy or confidentiality policy? Where can a user find the privacy policy? Is there an option to remain anonymous? If so, is there an explanation of what that option means?

Examples (Use of Results): Branding–For nearly two years, the digital reference service at Seattle Public Library provided a little-noticed link at the top of the Web site home page. The link was in plain, small-font type, "Ask a Question." Assessment over time resulted in re-design in March 2004. SPL added a large, square blue button with a centered question mark and bold text "Ask a Question" at the center right of the page. The e-mail traffic doubled, almost overnight–and for e-mail, that was the only change made. (The chat service underwent a number of simultaneous changes, making it impossible to determine the exact effect of the new link.)

Level II

Provider Self-Evaluation

Purpose: To improve individual performance in providing virtual reference service, including skills in communication, reference interview, customer service, Internet searching, and other relevant aspects.

Method: The purpose of the self-evaluation must be explained to the provider before it is undertaken. The Virtual Reference Transaction Checklist can be offered as a guide, but it should be made clear that no paperwork will be collected at the end of the exercise. This is a private, individual process.

Use or select questions from the lists of Self-Evaluation Questions. If the transcripts for review are selected by the provider, they should meet set criteria. For example:

- Six to ten transcripts should be reviewed
- Transcripts should represent a variety of complex transactions
- Transcripts should be selected over a specified time period, representing different days and times

At the end of the self-evaluation, the provider should be asked to identify one area in which he or she needs improvement, suggesting methods for doing so if appropriate (e.g., training, additional practice, work with mentor).

Examples (Use of Results)

Library staff members find reading their own transcripts revelatory. Phrases that seemed reasonable and appropriate when typed often evoke a different, sometimes unpleasant tone when read. They also recognize awkward wording and over-use of scripted messages. Self-evaluation is a good preliminary step for peer review of chat transcripts.

Virtual Reference Service Provider Self-Evaluation Questions

A List Based on the "Guidelines for the Samuel Swett Green Exemplary Virtual Reference Award"

1. How long did you keep the caller waiting?
2. Were you dealing with more than one caller when involved in this session?

3. Did you use open-ended questions at the outset of the session to clarify the information needed?
4. Did you ask what other resources the caller had already checked?
5. Did you use a close-ended question during the reference interview process to determine that you understood the caller's inquiry?
6. Did you tell the caller what you were doing as the session progressed?
7. Did you use a close-ended question such as "Did this answer your question" before ending the session?
8. Did you answer the question correctly?
9. Did you answer the question completely?
10. Did you need more time to answer the question?
11. Did you have to refer the caller to other resources based on the caller's inquiry?
12. Did you cite specific, authoritative source(s) to support your answer?
13. Is there evidence of the caller's satisfaction with information provided or help given?

A List Based on a Librarian Survey from Wright State University Libraries

How satisfied do you think the caller was with the chat service?

☐ Very satisfied

☐ Somewhat satisfied

☐ Somewhat dissatisfied

☐ Very dissatisfied

A List Based on the Reference Session Evaluation Checklist from QandANJ.org

1. Did you use open-ended probing questions to elicit the caller's specific question?
2. Did you maintain a steady dialog with the caller?
3. Did you keep the caller informed about your activities?

4. Did you communicate what steps the caller was expected to do next?
5. Did you make appropriate use of scripted messages?
6. Did you inform the caller you were sending a Web site in answer to the inquiry before actually sending it?
7. Did you explain to the caller what you sent?
8. Did you provide the caller with instructions on how to use the resource, site, or information sent?
9. Did you explain where the caller could find the answer within the site or information sent?
10. Did you appropriately refer the call?
11. If you needed to contact the caller later via e-mail, phone, or other means, did you do so?
12. Did you ask the caller if you had completely answered his/her question?
13. Did you send a Web page or only a URL?
14. Did you successfully send files, Web sites, proprietary database information, or screen shots?
15. Did you evaluate the information, Web site, or proprietary database information before sending it to the caller?

A List Developed by Nancy Huling for Use at the Suzzallo/Allen Libraries, University of Washington

1. Personalized or friendly greeting?
2. Reference Interview? Is it thorough enough?
3. Allows time for user to ask questions and waits for user to confirm when question is asked?
4. Source for answer is cited?
5. Guidance/instruction provided if appropriate?
6. Use of co-browsing/escort feature used appropriately?
7. Follow-up needed? Any indication of doing so, if necessary?
8. Closing interaction–asks if user has any other questions?
9. Other comments?

Level III

Focus Groups

Purpose: Focus group interviewing provides qualitative data based on personal experience. The face-to-face interaction of participants encourages brainstorming from different perspectives and is an ideal way for libraries to hear directly from the "horses' mouths." They can be used to determine customer assumptions, expectations, and preferences. Understanding these concerns helps us tailor virtual reference service to meet the real needs (rather than our perceptions of them) of the library community (see Table 3).

Method: Begin by asking these questions:

1. What kind of information are we seeking?
2. What customers should be represented in the groups?
3. Where should the groups meet?
4. Who should convene the groups?
5. How much project money should be spent on such an effort?

Focus groups should be limited to six to ten members who share common knowledge, experience, or characteristics. Recruitment will be the most time-consuming part of this undertaking. Select members for each focus group from priority customer audiences (such as businessmen, parents, arts and humanities faculty, distance students, etc.). There are innumerable possibilities for recruiting volunteers:

- A group of teens: Contact a high school teacher, youth organization, or YA librarian for a list of recommended names. Consider convening the group via chat (but be prepared for silliness).
- A group of senior citizens: Contact the genealogy or local history society.
- A group of businessmen/women: Contact Rotary Club, the Business & Professional Women's Association, or Chamber of Commerce.
- A group of current VR customers: Provide a script asking for volunteers at the end of transactions with repeat VR users, such as

   "We are looking for volunteers to participate in a focus group that will discuss our chat service to improve it and find new ways to help our customers. Would you be interested?" If the answer is "yes" (and be prepared for a lot of "no's"), you can request a telephone number or e-mail address for exchanging needed information.

Even if you contact volunteers by telephone, send a personal invitation to each participant–include brief description of the event, the date

TABLE 3

PLANNING AND IMPLEMENTING A LIBRARY FOCUS GROUP PROJECT	
Phase I	Identify and discuss the problem/question to be researched
	Decide that focus groups are the appropriate method to collect data
	Identify those who will be involved in implementing the project and what roles each will play
	Decide on the participant pool and criteria for selections
Phase II	Begin to formulate questions
	Draw up a budget, time-line, and plan of action, including a list of tasts, and equipment and supplies if needed
	Decide if and how participants will be remunerated
	Estimate number of sessions to be held
	Develop screening questions as needed for selecting participants
	Decide on sites, dates, and times of sessions
Phase III	Work with appropriate groups, individuals to identify possible participants
	Screen potential participants and get commitments for more people than the minimum required
	Finalize questions
Phase IV	Call to remind participants 1-2 days before session
	Set up room with table, chairs, refreshments, recording equipment
	Run session(s) and record discussion
	Hold debriefing immediately after session(s)
Phase V	Have notes and tapes transcribed
	Review transcription, notes, and tapes as needed to analyze data
	Discuss findings with team members, check back with participants as needed for verification
	Write up findings and prepare report (oral or written) for library management
	Discuss findings with management
	Make decisions based on project findings and convey decisions to staff
	Thank participants and inform them of results and decisions made

and time, location, contact names and numbers. Postcards work well–they display nicely on a refrigerator. Meeting in a library setting underscores the connection between the online service and the library institution. The session should last ninety minutes to two hours, maximum, with a planned fifteen-minute break.

Prepare five to ten jargon-free questions. These should be asked in a logical order from general to specific, and should be open-ended to encourage maximum participation. Choose a moderator who is sociable, interested in virtual reference, has good communication skills (especially listening), is well-organized, and has a good short-term memory. If group members do not have experience using virtual reference service, ask them to try it out once or twice prior to the session. Alternatively, it can be useful to ask customers questions that elicit their vision of an online, real-time information service, then compare their ideas to the actual service offered.

Refreshments are mandatory and incentives highly recommended. For tight budgets, consider asking local merchants or library vendors to donate items–anything from mousepads to latté coupons will be appreciated. Some libraries pay participants a small stipend for participation.

Recommended equipment:

- Poster board/markers for recording ideas.
- Tape recorder to record entire session. A video camera can be used, but may discourage participation or be distracting.

Informal seating is preferred, although many participants like a writing surface for doodling, placing personal items, etc.

The most difficult part of conducting focus groups is interpreting the findings. If an outside consultant is employed, they should provide an objective analysis. Tips for analysis include:

- look for themes that are common to all groups
- identify areas or issues that stimulated the most discussion
- pay attention to unexpected and/or creative approaches

Examples (Use of Results): The Statewide Virtual Reference project convened four focus groups (re-entry workers, folks aged over 50, Hispanics, and teens) in early 2002. Eight questions were asked, ranging from "What type of questions do you need help with in your day-to-day life?" and "If you have a computer at home, what is it mainly used for?" to "What would be your dream of getting information in the simplest way?" A number of key points were made that helped shape project activities, especially marketing:

- "I didn't know the library could help with that"
- We are a 24 hour-7 day society
- Yellow Pages work–library classifications are too confusing
- Libraries need to advertise and market
- Need library signage that is simple and clear
- We have the mentality of fast food–it has to be quick

A university library convened five focus groups of undergraduate and graduate students, asking these potential users what they wanted in a virtual reference service and how the library could get their attention. The results offered a wealth of information. Especially useful were answers to questions that covered expectations for Web site design and marketing, such as:

- "Provide a design suitable for scanning–don't want to read"
- "Must have user friendly appearance that appeals to even the non-computer literate"
- "Give me the simple stuff"
- "Advertise who VR works for, what they can expect"
- "Word of mouth the best marketing tool of all"
- "Be better at getting the idea out there–many don't know"

SAMPLE REPORT– GENERIC PUBLIC/ACADEMIC/SPECIAL LIBRARY– ANYWHERE, WASHINGTON EXECUTIVE SUMMARY

Virtual Reference Transactions

Transactions were exemplary–personal, helpful tone; effective reference interviewing; excellent information literacy and instructional practices; accurate, appropriate answers. Use of opening scripts could be improved.

Web Site Evaluation

Generic Library has a good start on branding the service, but the use of the logo could be more effective and consistent. References to the name of the service are not standardized. Information provided to patrons is generally thorough and easy to find.

Virtual Reference Policies

Privacy Statement could be more thorough. Rules of Conduct are excellent but should be revised to include online behaviors. Policies should all be checked for date, authority, or method of revision.

Site Visit

The Site Visit was a good opportunity to touch base with administrators and staff. Staff members were able to gain some insights into the process. Meeting the evaluators face-to-face may have helped humanize the process.

Recommendations (Includes many possible examples)

- Greet the patron by name and consider using staff names or aliases.
- Improve sequence of scripts at the beginning of transactions.
- Clarify questions more consistently.
- Before closing, ask if patron has any further questions.
- Revise closing messages so that they are not repetitive.
- Create a closing script that thanks the patron and invites him or her back.
- Experiment with sending the Survey as a separate e-mail after the chat session has ended.
- Variety of "help" links needs to be simplified.
- Decide on a name for the service and use it consistently throughout.
- Eliminate all references to previous service name.
- Standardize references to the service throughout the page ("Ask Us Now").
- Use the logo more visibly and consistently.
- Revise "Rules of Conduct" to include online behaviors.
- Add a disclaimer about legal and medical information.
- Strengthen statement about staff qualifications and expertise.
- Check policies for date, authority, and method of revision.
- Review Privacy Statement for completeness.

NOTES

1. Members, 2003-2004: Linda Fenster, Director of Library Operations, City University; Alice Goudeaux, Central Reference Manager, Timberland Regional Library; Jean Holcomb, Director, King County Law Library; Nancy Huling, Head of Reference and Research Services, University of Washington Libraries; Joseph Janes, Assistant Professor, University of Washington Information School; Lisa Oberg, Library Council of Washington (University of Washington Health Sciences Library); Lorena O'English, Reference Librarian, Washington State University Library; Barbara Pitney, Reference Services Manager, King County Library System; Buff Hirko, Washington State Library.

2. Members, 2003-2004: Steve Hiller, Library Assessment Coordinator, University of Washington Libraries; Keith Knutsen, Supervising Librarian, Pierce County Library System; Craig Kyte, Managing Librarian, Seattle Public Library; Barbara Pitney, Reference Services Coordinator, King County Library System; Buff Hirko, Washington State Library.

3. Anne Bingham, University of Washington and Nancy Foley, Seattle Public Library.

4. Complete information about curriculum materials is available in Hirko, Buff and Mary Bucher Ross, *Virtual Reference Training: The Complete Guide to Anytime, Anywhere Answers.* Chicago: ALA Editions, 2004.

5. Complete VET Bibliography shown on following page.

BIBLIOGRAPHY

Bertot, John Carlo et al., "Capture Usage with E-Metrics," *Library Journal,* May 1, 2004. Available at: http://www.libraryjournal.com/article/CA411564.html.

Cohen, Laura B., "A Two-tiered Model for Analyzing Library Website Usage Statistics, Part 1: Web Server Logs," *Portal: Libraries and the Academy,* April 2003.

Hirko, Buff and Mary Bucher Ross, *Virtual Reference Training: The Complete Guide to Anytime, Anywhere Answers.* Chicago: ALA Editions, 2004.

How Libraries and Librarians Help: Putting Outcome Evaluations in Context, University of Michigan and University of Washington, 2002. Available at: http://www.si. umich.edu/libhelp/.

Glitz, Beryl, *Focus Groups for Libraries and Librarians.* New York: Forbes Custom Publishing, 1998.

Krug, Steve, *Don't Make Me Think: A Common Sense Approach to Web Usability.* Indianapolis, IN: New Riders Publishing, 2000.

Lipow, Anne Grodzins, *The Virtual Reference Librarian's Handbook.* New York: Neal-Schuman Publishers, 2002.

Marsteller, Matthew and Susan Ware, "Models for Measuring & Evaluating Reference Costs: A Comparative Analysis of Traditional and Virtual Reference Services," November 17, 2003. PowerPoint presentation available at http://www.vrd2003. org/proceedings/presentation.cfm?PID=255.

McClure, Charles R. et al., *Statistics, Measures and Quality Standards for Assessing Digital Reference Library Services: Guidelines and Procedures.* Syracuse: Information Institute of Syracuse, 2002.

Meola, Marc and Sam Stormont, "Evaluating Your Live Virtual Reference," (Chapter 10) in *Staring and Operating Live Virtual Reference Services.* New York: Neal-Schuman Publishers, 2002.

Owens, Patricia, "Statewide Virtual Reference Project Focus Group Results," March 2002. Available at: http://www.secstate.wa.gov/library/libraries/projects/virtualRef/ textdocs/VRSFocusGroup.htm.

Rubin, Jeffrey, *Handbook of Usability Testing: How to Plan, Design, and Conduct Effective Tests.* New York: John Wiley and Sons, 1994.

Sterne, Jim, "Measuring Your Success," (Chapter 6) in *Customer Service on the Internet: Building Relationships, Increasing Loyalty, and Staying Competitive.* New York: John Wiley and Sons, 2000.

"Virtual Reference Transactions," Section 7.3.1 of EMetrics Instructional System (beta), Florida State University, 2004. Available at: http://ii.fsu.edu/emis.

Wasik, Joan M., "Digital Reference Evaluation," Virtual Reference Desk Conference, 2003. Available at: http://www.vrd.org/AskA/digref_assess.shtml.

Whitlach, Jo Bell, "Evaluating Reference Services in the Electronic Age," *Library Trends*, Fall 2001.

doi:10.1300/J120v46n95_09

Assessing Digital Reference
and Online Instructional Services
in an Integrated Public/University Library

Lauren Miranda Gilbert
Mengxiong Liu
Toby Matoush
Jo Bell Whitlatch

SUMMARY. In spite of the explosion of interest in virtual reference and instruction, assessment of digital reference remains relatively uncharted territory in the library literature. What standards exist for online reference and instruction and how can they be used to assess the innovative new merged online reference environment at the Dr. Martin Luther King, Jr. Library? Led by co-unit heads from the former San Jose Public Library Main Branch and the San Jose State University Clark Library, the merged reference unit is a unique testing ground for perceived differences between public and academic reference service. Evaluation of both the online and the live merged reference environment is crucial

Lauren Miranda Gilbert (San Jose Public Library), Mengxiong Liu (San Jose State University Library), Toby Matoush (San Jose State University Library), and Jo Bell Whitlatch (San Jose State University Library) are all Librarians, Dr. Martin Luther King, Jr. Library, San Jose, CA 95192-0028.

The authors wish to thank their many colleagues, particularly Sandra Belanger, Charity Hope, Bridget Kowalczyk, Ronna Nemer, Tina Peterson, and Lisa Rosenblum.

[Haworth co-indexing entry note]: "Assessing Digital Reference and Online Instructional Services in an Integrated Public/University Library." Gilbert, Lauren Miranda et al. Co-published simultaneously in *The Reference Librarian* (The Haworth Information Press, an imprint of The Haworth Press, Inc.) No. 95/96, 2006, pp. 149-172; and: *Assessing Reference and User Services in a Digital Age* (ed: Eric Novotny) The Haworth Information Press, an imprint of The Haworth Press, Inc., 2006, pp. 149-172. Single or multiple copies of this article are available for a fee from The Haworth Document Delivery Service [1-800-HAWORTH, 9:00 a.m. - 5:00 p.m. (EST). E-mail address: docdelivery@haworthpress.com].

and will be necessary to determine what is working and what is not. This paper will discuss plans for current and future assessment of digital reference including e-mail, live online reference, and online instruction. doi:10.1300/J120v46n95_10 *[Article copies available for a fee from The Haworth Document Delivery Service: 1-800-HAWORTH. E-mail address: <docdelivery@haworthpress.com> Website: <http://www.HaworthPress.com> © 2006 by The Haworth Press, Inc. All rights reserved.]*

KEYWORDS. Digital reference, assessment, online instruction, merged reference, joint libraries, e-mail reference, live online reference, QandACafe, 24/7 reference, TILT (Texas Information Literacy Tutorial)

INTRODUCTION

In 1996, the mayor of the City of San Jose and the President of San Jose State University met for breakfast to discuss how they might strengthen relationships between the City and the University, which is located in downtown San Jose, California. The next day the newspapers and media announced that the mayor and president had agreed upon a combined City/University library as the beginning of building a stronger relationship between "town and gown." Seven years later, the Dr. Martin Luther King, Jr. Library opened its doors to the public and university community on August 1, 2003.

Although the University and City Library administrations remain separate and the building is actually co-managed by the two library directors, several services in the King Library building are integrated including Access services (circulation, information desk, call center, and periodicals), Information Technology, Reference Services, and Technical Services. Part of the planning for the integrated Reference Services unit established a service for remote users that is separate from Reference Desk services. This service is called "The Reference Connection" and is responsible for telephone, e-mail, and live online reference services. Public and academic reference librarians are staffing the Reference Connection together to provide the entire range of reference assistance to remote users.

Leadership and organization of each service within the Reference unit is provided by small teams of academic and public librarians (generally 3 people). As with other teams the team for the Reference Connection is responsible for recommending policies, guidelines, and procedures for delivering reference services to remote users to the Co-Unit Heads (Heads of Reference from the public and academic library). However, because the evaluation of this unique library partnership between the City and the University is essential to determine the success of this innovative arrangement, within Reference Services, there is a separate Assessment Team. The Assessment Team is responsible for developing the plans and overseeing the evaluation of reference and instructional services offered both to users within the King Library and to remote users.

The merging of two large libraries that serve different populations is an unprecedented arrangement, and as this article is being written we are still in the early months of our "marriage." Because of this, we are all still feeling our way and experimenting with what works and what doesn't. However, early assessment studies point to strengths we may build upon in the coming years. Before merging, an assessment of both organizational cultures was created and implemented by consultant Sheila Creth, who found that differences between San Jose State University librarians and San Jose Public librarians were more perceived than actual.[1] To be sure, there are dissimilarities between the two cultures, but our overall goals are remarkably similar, including a strong commitment to service, a solid base of long-term staff, respect for one another as professionals, and a generally informal work environment. Additionally, consultant Tom Childers has found that participants in two surveys conducted before we merged felt they were given a similar amount of instruction with their research from both institutions, thus dispelling the common perception that public librarians tend to simply provide answers whereas academic librarians focus on instructing.[2]

Nevertheless, assessment of merged reference services is an interesting challenge, both because we are still evaluating what needs to be assessed (what *aren't* we counting that should be counted?), and also because we remain two separate institutions with differing institutional requirements for keeping statistics and assessing services.

This article will describe the plans that the Assessment Team has established to evaluate digital reference services, including e-mail, live online reference, and instructional services offered to remote users.

ASSESSMENT OF REFERENCE E-MAIL SERVICE

Literature Review

Developing the standards most useful in assessing remote reference service is challenging. Two very useful documents that can be used to develop standards and measures for assessing reference services are the RUSA Guidelines for Behavioral Performance of Reference and Information Services Professionals (http://www.ala.org/rusa) and SERVQUAL. However, the RUSA guidelines were developed for assessing face-to-face encounters although work is underway to incorporate the assessment of digital reference services as well. SERVQUAL and its application for libraries, LIBQUAL, are also based on face-to-face encounters or customer experiences in physical buildings. SERVQUAL[3] looks at the service process. The measure of satisfaction is based on the relationship between customer expectations and outcomes. Satisfaction is calculated as the difference between perceptions and expectations. The dimensions are not universal across all services and studies have found a high degree of correlation between the five most common dimensions (see Figure 1). Although these dimensions are not stable across all services, they are useful as background for setting service standards. The best-known instrument for assessing face-to-face reference services is WOREP, the Wisconsin-Ohio Reference Evaluation Program (http://worep.library.kent.edu/about.html). WOREP collects data from both staff and patrons on the same set of reference transactions and has been widely used in both academic and public libraries. WOREP administrators have a long term goal to evaluate online reference service.

However, the major dimensions so important in face-to-face encounters must be reviewed and redefined in an environment without any nonverbal clues. Facets of Quality for Digital Reference Services (http://www.vrd.org/facets-10-00.shtml) is a document that has been developed specifically for digital question answering services and may be easiest to utilize in developing standards and measures for assessing digital reference services.

FIGURE 1. Five Common SERVQUAL Dimensions

Reliability	Consistency of service performance and dependability
Responsiveness	Willingness and readiness of staff to deliver service and respond to the customer's requirements
Tangibles	Physical facilities–the environment in which the service actually takes place
Assurance	Trustworthiness, believability, and honesty experienced
Empathy	Understanding and relating to individual customer needs and requirements

One of the great advantages of digital reference services is that records of reference transactions remain and may be archived, after identifying data has been stripped from the transactions to protect the privacy of both user and librarian. These archival records of reference transactions may be sampled to evaluate the quality of digital reference services. David Carter and Joseph Janes analyzed logs of over 3,000 questions from the Internet Public Library[4] to determine subject area, means of submission, self-selected demographic information, how these questions were handled and answered or rejected.

Reference librarians across the Cornell University Library system blind-reviewed Google responses to test questions and compared these responses to answers prepared by Cornell reference librarians.[5] Ask-an-Expert services were tested by asking 240 questions of 20 expert services to evaluate factors such as response rate, response time, and verifiable answers.[6]

Assessment Plan for Reference E-Mail Service

E-mail reference is one component of services offered through the Reference Connection. The Library homepage (http://www.sjlibrary.org) includes an "Ask a Librarian" choice under Quick Links. Ask a Librarian brings the user to a page that allows the user to choose from a variety of reference services: e-mail reference, live online reference, telephone reference, walk-in help, and reference consultations with a subject expert in support of University research. To facilitate the online reference interview, the e-mail reference form asks the user to describe the subject, provide detailed information on the subject, and list any sources already consulted. Users are advised that a librarian will try to respond within 24 hours during the workweek. Public and academic reference librarians answer e-mail questions twice a day between 11-12 and 4-5. Internal procedures for e-mail questions set the standard of providing a response within 24 hours and when necessary, a final answer within 72 hours. Additional guidelines are that librarians should spend no more than 30 minutes per question and balance the provision of facts and instruction in the answer. Reference questions that cannot be answered within that time may be referred to the System Reference Center for additional work. Complex reference questions requiring a significant subject expertise are to be referred to a librarian with subject expertise related to the question.

As part of the planning for reference services in the combined library, the RUSA Guidelines for Behavioral Performance of Reference and Information Services Professionals were adopted as the guidelines for reference services. Therefore, approachability, interest, listening/inquiring, searching, and follow-up behaviors will be a significant focus for assessment of services. An important goal in developing the plan to assess e-mail reference is to use more than one method for collecting information and to collect information from both librarians providing the service and users receiving the service. Utilizing different methods and sources for information collection helps ensure that the results of the assessment will be valid. An important procedure for preserving validity of the results is to compare data collected from different sources and by different methods. For example, collecting descriptions of questions asked and answers provided from both participants in the face-to-face reference encounter serves to compensate for the partial views of both librarian and user. This strategy permits a more complete description of the reference encounter that includes perspectives of both parties.

Developing standards for evaluating reference services by modifying the face-to-face dimensions is quite challenging. Fortunately some excellent work in identifying standards for digital reference services has already been published as Facets of Quality for Digital Reference Services (http://www.vrd.org/facets-10-00.shtml). Figure 2 provides a brief description of each facet. These facets can be utilized to develop measures that collect data on each of the facets of reference service quality.

For e-mail reference two different methods will be utilized in assessing the service. The first method will be an online user survey. Use of surveys will provide information to e-mail reference providers on user perspectives and values.

When sending a response to users, a brief pop-up survey will be randomly administered that asks users to respond to 4-5 brief questions. The Facets of Quality for Digital Reference Service was used as a guide to establish the categories of questions for the brief survey. Users will be asked about service facets related to accessibility, responsiveness (clear response time), quality of communication in terms of interaction and instruction, and effectiveness of publicity. After these general categories were identified, instruments available in *The Reference Assessment Manual*[7] were used as resources for question development. Sample questions are included in Figure 3.

The second method will be peer review analysis of the questions and answers for the same set of questions used for the online user survey. Peer review is "a process where reference librarians review and critique e-mail question-answer sets and/or the transcripts from chat reference sections performance by their peers and provide each other with feed-

FIGURE 2. Facets of Quality for Digital Reference Services

User Transaction–guidelines for the question answering process
Accessibility: easily accessible and navigable
Quick Turnaround: respond to questions as promptly as possible
Clarity of Response Policy: clear communication on question scope, types of answers
    provided, and expected turnaround time
Interactivity: allow opportunities for an effective reference interview
Instructiveness: guide in subject knowledge and information literacy

Service Development & Management–guidelines for creating & maintaining service
Authoritativeness: experts with necessary knowledge and educational background
Availability of Trained Experts: provide training processes to prepare experts
Privacy: complete privacy between users and experts
Evaluation: regularly evaluate processes and services
Accessibility to Related Information: supporting resources and information
Publicity: inform potential users of value of service

From: Facets of Quality for Digital Reference Services http://www.vrd.org/facets-06-03.shtml

back and, where applicable, suggestions for improvement."[8] Use of these reference transaction logs will provide objective data that is less susceptible to respondent bias.

Personal information for both the librarian and users will be removed from the questions and answers prior to using the data for the analysis. This procedure ensures that patron privacy is protected and that the results cannot be used to review the performance of individual librarians. Although user perceptions of service success are essential in evaluating and improving services, users generally cannot judge the factors such as the authority of answers and whether the best sources were used. Review by experts in the field is a more appropriate method than user perceptions in these areas. Therefore, peer review will focus on the authority and reliability of answers provided, number of sources provided, selection of the most useful and relevant sources, the quality of the search strategy and process provided to the user, and the turnaround time between receipt of question and provision of answer. Authority of answer will be measured by having the peer group judge whether the answer was correct, incorrect, referred, or cannot be determined.[9] Questions will also be coded into categories. The first set of categories will be related to the type of answer: (1) factual/ready reference/short answer and (2) instructional, how to get started on a topic and so forth. The second type of categories will be related to the nature of the question: (1) school coursework, (2) research

FIGURE 3. E-Mail Reference Survey for Users

SAMPLE QUESTIONS (ALL 7-POINT SCALES)

Information sources suggested were:
Useful . . . . Useless
Relevant . . . . Irrelevant
Complete . . . . Incomplete

Instructions by the librarian on how to locate information were:
Easy to follow . . . . Hard to follow

Answer provided:
Too much information . . . Just the right amount . . . Too little information

Communicating with the librarian was
Very easy . . . . Very difficult

The e-mail reference service was:
Easy to locate on the Web site . . . . Hard to locate on the Web site
Easy to use . . . . Hard to use

The initial response of the librarian to your question was:
Enthusiastic . . . . . Indifferent
Very interested . . . . . Not at all interested

How did you find out about the e-mail reference service?
- A friend
- By searching the library Website
- Publicity about the service
- Other (please tell us how:_____)

How satisfied were you with the time it took to provide an answer:
Very satisfied . . . . Very dissatisfied

or publication, (3) other job related, (4) information needed for daily living, e.g., health, housing and so forth, and (5) pursuit of personal, leisure, or recreational interests. Reliability of answers will be measured through peer review by assessing the extent to which users with similar questions received similar answers (i.e., consistent answers). A coding protocol sheet will be developed to tell the peer reviewers what to look for and how to code their observations. A checklist that clearly delineates the categories will also be developed. Two reviewers will code each question-answer set in order to verify reliability of the coding.

One of the Facets of Quality for Digital Reference Services is "Reviewed." The discussion under this facet notes that ongoing review and assessment help ensure quality, efficiency, and reliability of transactions as well as overall user satisfaction. In addition, regular monitoring of service quality is vital to improving delivery service methods and processes. Evaluation of service by both users and librarians also ensures that all perspectives are considered when making changes to present services.

ASSESSMENT OF LIVE ONLINE REFERENCE

Live online reference is another component of the merged services offered remotely. Access to it and e-mail reference is available by means of the "Ask A Librarian" link on the library Web site.

Prior to merging, both the academic and public libraries participated separately in QandACafe, the live online reference service provided by northern California's Golden Gate Library Network (GGLN), in conjunction with southern California's Metropolitan Cooperative Library System (MCLS). QandACafe is managed by the now nationwide 24/7 Reference Service (using its software of the same name), and is funded by state and federal grants. Due to the consortial nature of this service, we are able to provide it 24 hours a day, 7 days a week. MCLS librarians are available to assist northern California library patrons at night, on weekends, and during holidays.

In the King Library, all merged reference projects are managed by one lead and one liaison. For QandACafe, the lead (a public librarian) coordinates the overall project. The liaison (a university librarian) oversees monitoring the project's academic queues. Both librarians work with the northern California QandACafe manager. University librarians monitor the academic queues 4 hours a week and the public queues 2 hours a week. Public librarians monitor the public queues 5 hours a week. Substantial training in the use of 24/7 software and techniques for engaging in live online reference interviews is necessary for those additional staff providing the service.

QandACafe librarians follow the policies and procedures created by 24/7 Reference Service. The service was designed to answer brief, factual questions, suggest sources for finding the answers, and guide patrons in the use of library electronic databases and Internet Web sites.

This ability to "co-browse" online resources with patrons sets live online reference instruction apart from both e-mail and telephone reference.

The university liaison plans to provide an online platform of instruction and consultation via QandACafe for distance education students, which will serve to simulate a face-to-face on-site appointment in a traditional reference consultation. Out of this, she is planning an assessment project that examines the information competency aspect of live online reference, which is based on ACRL's information competency standards.

Assessment Plan for Live Online Reference

Because the merged aspect of the service is in its initial launching stage, it is premature to assess its effectiveness. Rather, our assessment plan would first focus on collecting general descriptive statistics and use them to examine staffing levels, volume of service, training needs, and the cost of service. One advantage to assessing live online reference is that the data are more readily available than traditional reference service statistics. The 24/7 software stores all reference transactions and they can be retrieved at any time. For general descriptive statistics, the following data should be collected from public/academic queues. Items noted in parentheses are library processes that are affected or need to be considered.

- Day and time of live online reference sessions (scheduling)
- Number of questions received (determining the volume of service, staffing needs, and promotion of service)
- Number of questions completed (interview effectiveness, resources available, staff training)
- Number of questions not completed (limitations of service, quality of communication skills, technical problem or human error)
- Type of questions received (expertise, consider improving service with FAQs)
- Number of referrals (note to whom referred, acknowledge and assess cooperation)
- Number of sources used per question (budget allocation for databases)
- Number of repeat users (return rate, user satisfaction)

At the traditional reference desk, the reference interview is a very important aspect of the communication between the librarian and users. Through both spoken and body languages, librarians can determine what the user wants. However, in live online reference, the communication between the user and the librarian is mediated through the software, and the actual reference transaction takes place on the Web. According to Meola and Stormont,[10] the lack of visual and oral cues in virtual reference means that the chance for miscommunication is greater. Therefore, finding out the level of user satisfaction is very important. With QandACafe, the users are given a brief survey after each transaction (see Figure 4).

As noted, with QandACafe, each transaction is recorded and transcripts can be retrieved from the archive. The next stage of assessment will focus on peer review analysis of the transcripts. The same method used for e-mail reference peer review will be employed to assess live online reference. As with e-mail reference, peer review will focus on:

- authority and reliability of answers provided
- number of sources provided
- selection of the most useful and relevant sources
- quality of the search strategy and direction provided to the user
- turnaround time between receipt of question and provision of an answer

In addition to the above measures, assessment will also examine the online reference interview between the librarian and the user. Librarians' communication skills will be analyzed and compared with user satisfaction.

ASSESSMENT OF ONLINE TUTORIALS

Another important tool in the milieu of digital reference and instruction is the online instruction tutorial. Although online instruction takes many forms, this discussion will be limited to online tutorials and exclude such online teaching environments as WebCT and others.

Instruction and Information Competence Programs at the Dr. Martin Luther King, Jr. Library

Although both San Jose State University (SJSU) and San Jose Public Library (SJPL) have successful and thriving instruction and information

FIGURE 4. Brief QandACafe Survey

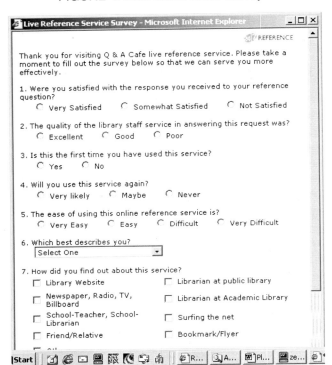

Note: The data collected from this survey can be used to assess user satisfaction, users perception of the quality of service offered, the effectiveness of the service and its accessibility. A systematic approach will be developed to regularly analyze the survey and gather the statistics.

competence programs, there is no merged instruction program currently in place. San Jose State University has implemented a library information competence program as part of both English 1B and Writing 100W classes, which are required writing classes for many majors. San Jose Public Library has Internet instruction classes for seniors and adults, as well as specialized classes in genealogy and other areas. Classes are also offered in a variety of languages that include Chinese and Spanish. The above classes are now taught in the merged environment of the new library. Instructors share four state-of-the-art classrooms that feature remote projectors, Altiris, a teaching software that enables instructors to freeze the screens of students during instruction, and flat-screen terminals for 20-47 students. There are plans to create merged instructional classes in such areas as business but these have not yet been implemented. SJPL has not yet implemented online instruction but SJSU is currently making strides with the use of *InfoPOWER* and online modules.

Online Tutorials: An Introduction

The online tutorial has gone through a variety of manifestations and began as computer assisted instruction in the 1970s, took a giant step forward with the development of the personal computer in the 1980s, and with the advent of the Internet in 1990, assumed its current form of interactive online module written in a variety of programming languages. It is clear that the online interactive tutorial has become a regular staple of information literacy instruction. Yet how is this relatively new form of instruction assessed? Assessment of online tutorials is still in its nascence and a literature search reveals a consensus that this is an area that is greatly in need of development. According to Ianuzzi[11] assessment is essential to program development as well as increasingly necessary in the current world of library budget cuts and accountability. Information competency programs in a time of extensive library cutbacks must be assessed and proven effective in order to justify their existence. Peters[12] sees public services as the necessary third leg of the digital library stool after bibliographic records and collections, which must be in place before evaluation and assessment of digital library services can take place. He hypothesizes that it is the lack of attention to digital library services that has hampered attempts to evaluate them. Evaluation of online or digital instruction certainly fits into this category and a study of such services would start work on building the necessary third leg of the metaphoric library stool. It is an excellent time to evaluate what types of assessment of online tutorials exist, survey how they are working, and propose future improvements.

Literature Review

A preliminary literature search revealed a wealth of scholarship on online library tutorials but very little in the area of assessment of such tutorials. Both Churkovich and Oughtred[13] and Michel[14] state that little research exists assessing effectiveness of online tutorials or evaluation of them. Samson[15] also states that a literature review found little on "the use of a Web-based evaluation tool." The Library Instruction Roundtable section of the Association of College and Research Libraries has a site that lists seven reviewed interactive tutorials (see http://www3. baylor.edu/LIRT/lirtproj.html). A more extensive list of reviewed tutorials can be found online at the *LOEX Clearinghouse for Library Instruction/Instruction Links/Tutorials* Website (see http://www.emich. edu/public/loex/tutorials.htm). However, neither of these sites provide guides for the assessment of online tutorials. The lack of information in the literature makes it difficult to determine how many of these tutorials have been assessed although some of the articles on the tutorials briefly discuss evaluation. Evaluation of tutorials can take the form of pre- and post-tests which evaluate the entire library instruction learning experience. This includes the tutorial, quizzes built into tutorials which evaluate information resources learned based on the module just taken, feedback opportunities for students to contribute qualitative evaluation at the end of the tutorials, and other methodology. The literature on the efficacy of online tutorials seems to mirror much of the classroom information literacy instruction literature and provides many examples of formative assessment evaluating a single library class session or tutorial. However, it offers very little in the way of summative assessment or evaluation of information competency skills developed and incorporated into the learning skills of the students.

Model Tutorials

Before delving into the assessment of online tutorials it is first necessary to look at some of the model library tutorials that have impacted the library world. The creators of the *Texas Information Literacy Tutorial* or *TILT* revolutionized the information literacy world (http://tilt.lib.utsystem.edu) with an online interactive tutorial composed of an introduction and three modules covering specific aspects of information competency. Module one covers selection of appropriate information sources, module two covers efficient searching, and module three the area of evaluation and citation. *TILT* builds on the concept of Bloom's taxonomy[16] that hypothesizes that using problem-based learning will increase both the relevance and long-term retention of information learned. Students incorporate the learned information by applying the concepts learned in the first module through active searching and evaluation of the information in the second and third modules. Assessment of *TILT* consists of quizzes taken at the end of each module as well as student feedback in the form of the question "What is the most important thing you learned from this module?"

TILT administrators keep a database of use statistics and continually improve *TILT* based on statistics.

Online Tutorials at San Jose State University: InfoPOWER

In February 2002 the San Jose State University Library implemented *InfoPOWER* (see http://tutorials.sjlibrary.org/tutorial/index.html), an adaptation of *TILT* created by SJSU librarian Charity Hope and Information Competence Specialist Bridget Kowalczyk. It is now regularly used as part of the English 1B Information Competence Program through the university library and consists of three interactive modules which cover selecting, searching, and evaluating information. Each module incorporates a final quiz and requests student feedback on the most important concept learned in the module. Assessment works much in the same manner as *TILT* with a database of use statistics, collection of student feedback, and continual development of the tutorial based on assessment of *InfoPOWER* quizzes, student feedback, and print evaluation forms given to English 1B students, faculty, and instruction librarians asking "What was the most important thing learned?"

Tutorials As Pre-Assessment

The tutorial usually exists only as a subset of an information literacy program but in some cases serves as the only library instruction students receive. Since they are quick, convenient, and do not necessitate the use of a library classroom or librarians to take, both faculty and students have welcomed them and even in some cases, chosen to do tutorials as an alternative to classroom library instruction. This is especially true when tutorials build on progressive information competency skills. Yet optimally tutorials can serve as both vehicles to teach necessary information competency skills like effective searching and evaluation of information resources and pre-tests to measure student's information competence levels prior to an in-class library session. Online tutorials that serve as pre-tests can free valuable time for library instructors to focus on course-integrated instruction rather than basic concepts of information competence. They also serve as an evaluation of which information competency concepts librarians should cover in the class session: those concepts which students score high on do not have to be covered while those which are difficult for students should be covered. *TILT* and *InfoPOWER* as well as other model tutorials are used as both tutorials teaching necessary library skills and as pre-assessment tools in information literacy programs.

Assessment Methodologies

Assessment of instruction has certain models that can translate to the online environment. These include such methodologies as pre- and post-tests, focus groups, portfolios, and performance appraisals evaluated by Pausch and Popp.[17] Other evaluative tools include evaluation forms or surveys distributed to student or faculty and instruments such as minute papers, muddiest points, one sentence summaries, directed paraphrasing, and applications cards surveyed by Fenske and Roselle,[18] which are less applicable. Currently, one of the most common assessment tools for online tutorials seems to be the evaluation form filled out by students, faculty, and librarians either in the online environment or in a print form. Librarians at San Jose State University use this form for both evaluation of the library component of the Metropolitan University Scholar Experience (MUSE) (see http://www.sjsu.edu/muse/), a freshman community program, and the library component to the English 1B program which integrates information literacy into English 1B, a required English course for all students. The other most commonly used evaluative tool for the online tutorial is the post-test that measures the efficacy of the tutorial immediately afterward. Many tutorials contain post-tests or quizzes that assess formative learning. This is true of *TILT*,[19] *InfoPOWER*, Colorado State University's Information Competence Module,[20] Deakin University's *Smart Searcher*,[21] and the version of *KNOWLEDGE MAZE*[22] used by Araphoe Community College among others. The post-test works well as an indicator of how well the student remembers the skills just learned but it does not usually measure how, or if, the student retains those skills when they finish the class that incorporated the library tutorial. Clearly, the task for librarians is to determine if students retain the skills learned in the tutorial and if not, what is the best way to refresh and reinforce that learning. Assessment that measures the learning outcomes of the students at the end of the class or summative assessment similar to the model discussed by Colborn and Cordell[23] needs to be implemented. Since many library tutorials are given at the freshman level, assessment needs to also measure information literacy levels of students at the junior and senior level. This could be implemented with a more advanced, course-integrated tutorial that incorporates and builds upon the basic information literacy skills of searching, finding, and evaluating information resources taught to freshman in tutorials such as *TILT* and others. San Jose State University is currently working on tutorials that integrate information literacy skills into tutorials on particular subjects such as nursing, biology, and business to be used in required 100W writing courses for many majors, but there is not yet a consistent library program to assess the library skills of students in the upper grade levels. The Health Professions 100W tutorial is complete and can be viewed at http://tutorials.sjlibrary.org/tutorial/index.html.

Pedagogical Guidelines As Assessment

Assessment of tutorials must begin with learning objectives and outcomes since a successful program must be informed by guidelines to be followed. The most informative set of pedagogical guidelines for online library instruction were created by Nancy Dewald[24] and can be used to guide both the development and the assessment of online tutorials. Using pedagogical guidelines which inform and guide traditional classroom instruction, Dewald determined three main areas which can be used to assess online tutorials (also see Figure 5): (1) Learner motivation, (2) Organization of modules, and (3) Levels of interactivity. Learners must be motivated both intrinsically and extrinsically; the tutorial should be organized in such a way that it encourages different paths of learning and facilitates multiple learning styles, and it should be highly interactive since according to Hall[25] "interactivity is what distinguishes an information source from a learning experience." Other pedagogical guidelines that can be used to guide online tutorials include those considered best practices of traditional library instruction. Nancy Dewald in her 1999 article entitled "Transporting Good Library Instruction Practices into the Web Environment: An Analysis of Online Tutorials"[26] develops Web-based pedagogical guidelines based on an analysis of several sets of published instructional guidelines including *Read This First: An Owner's Guide to the New Model Statement of Objectives for Academic Bibliographic Instruction*[27] edited by Carolyn Dusenbury and *Conceptual Frameworks for Bibliographic Instruction: Theory into Practice*[28] edited by Mary Reichel and Mary Ann Ramey. Dewald's guidelines should be used to assess online library instruction (see Figure 6). With the exception of collaborative learning, all of these can and should be adopted as guidelines for assessment of instruction through online tutorials. One other

FIGURE 5. Three Main Areas for Assessing Online Tutorials

Nancy Dewald has created three areas for development of Web-based library instruction:

- Motivation of Learner: the learner is highly motivated since they must complete the module as part of their grade. The module teaches them how to find a specific information resource for a graded class assignment or research paper. It is not merely an introduction to library services and resources.
- Module Organization: Modules are tiered and build on Bloom's concept of problem-based learning.
- Levels of interactivity: The module is highly interactive and students are introduced to concepts that they must then incorporate into exercises and a post-test.

pedogical assessment tool for the development of online tutorials is the set of guidelines developed by the ACRL Instruction Section Teaching Methods Committee (see Figure 7).

Future Assessment Goals

Assessment of online tutorials needs to be driven by clearly defined learning objectives and outcomes. The pedagogical guidelines developed by Nancy Dewald can be used to assess both the development of and continuing effectiveness of the tutorials. Secondly, librarians using the tutorials should have a list of learning outcomes for each module or section of their tutorial based on ACRL information competency standards. For example, the student who completes section one of *TILT*, which teaches how to search for information resources, will be able to accomplish the following activities: (1) select the catalog to look for a book, (2) select the online databases to find an article, (3) learn how to limit to scholarly journal or peer-reviewed journal in order to find a scholarly journal, and (4) select the library resources rather than the Web to quickly find reliable information, etc. Finally, online library tutorials should not mimic the one-shot library session and therefore need to be assessed not only formatively but summatively. How many of those library skills do students retain after their English 1B class or whatever class using a library tutorial is over? Post-tests that are given at the close of the class can serve as tools using summative evaluation and a more advanced, course-integrated tutorial given during student's junior or senior year can be used to either refresh or build upon important information competency skills. Since lifelong learning is the goal of the university, the library should help teach it with information literacy programs and online tutorials that are informed by clear learning objectives and outcomes that are routinely assessed.

FIGURE 6. Guidelines for Assessing Online Library Instruction

Nancy Dewald has created the following guidelines for web instruction based on best practices for classroom instruction:

- The online module includes active learning and post-tests that measure concepts learned.
- The online module uses media such as *Flash* to keep the module exciting and visually informational.
- There are clearly defined objectives for each step of the module.
- There is a focus on conceptual learning rather than on mechanical concepts.
- There is an opportunity for follow-up learning in the format of contact e-mail or phone for the instruction librarian.

Although Dewald also includes collaborative learning in her guidelines this is more difficult to implement in an online environment and has therefore not been included.

FIGURE 7. Tips for Developing Effective Web-Based Library Instruction

The ACRL Instruction Section Teaching Methods Committee has created the following guidelines for developing effective web-based library instruction (See http://www.ala.org/ala/acrlbucket/is/iscommittees/webpages/teachingmethods/tips.htm)

- Clearly defined objectives and outcomes which establish a purpose and realistic expectations.
- Inclusion of a clearly defined structure.
- Provide interactive exercises.
- Attention paid to the concepts behind the mechanics in order to make information skills applicable to other search interfaces.
- Use of contemporary language and topics which are also entertaining and succinct.
- Include librarian contact.

Development and Assessment Plan for Online Tutorials and Instruction

LIBRARY-WIDE LEVEL INFORMATION COMPETENCY ASSESSMENT PLAN

Library Information Competency Plan is tiered and measures cumulative information competency levels rather than memorization of library resources and services:

A. *InfoPOWER* used to assess Freshman level Information Competency levels. (Develop an online summative information competency post-test to administer to a select group of English 1B students near the end of the English 1B class. Administer to students and use statistics to continually revise *InfoPOWER*.)

B. Develop online tutorials to be given to juniors or seniors in major classes. These can be integrated into the 100W library instructional program. Tutorials should be guided by common pedagogical online instructional guidelines (see Figures 1 and 2).

C. Develop summative online information competency assessment that measures learning outcomes at the end of the 100W classes. These can be developed from the model online survey used in the *Standardized Assessment of Information Literacy Skills Program* online survey that is currently being testing in libraries throughout the U.S. San Jose State University is one of the participants (see http://sails.lms.kent.edu/index.php).

D. Work with SJSU University Assessment Team to integrate use of online modules and summative online tests into the university curriculum.

DEPARTMENTAL LEVEL INFORMATION COMPETENCY ASSESSMENT PLAN

1. Set up learning objectives and outcomes by major. Librarian works with liaison faculty in department to develop learning objectives and outcomes which fit the unique major but also conform to the Association of College and Research Libraries Information Competency Standards (see http://www.ala.org/ala/acrl/acrlstandards/informationliteracycompetency.htm).

A. Use the *California State University Information Competency Initiative* Projects as models (see http://library.csun.edu/susan.curzon/infocmp.html for model information competency programs within the CSU system).

ONLINE INSTRUCTION PEDAGOGICAL GUIDELINES

Develop online tutorials for 100W classes based on Dewald's guidelines and those set up by the ACRL Instruction Section Teaching Methods Committee. Integrate Dewald's guidelines into a development plan for all library online tutorials.

CONCLUSION

Effective review of digital reference services requires setting standards for each type of service offered: e-mail reference, live online reference, and instruction through interactive online modules. Assessment results will provide the library staff with essential information for enhancing reference and instructional processes and practices. Understanding how users interact with and assess these services will assist the integrated Reference staff in the King Library in evaluating an important aspect of the innovative partnership, which goes far beyond the physical confines of the King Library building

NOTES

1. Creth, Shelia D. *Organization Culture Assessment: San Jose State University Clark Library and San Jose Public Library.* Unpublished Report. August 2001.

2. Childers, Thomas A. *King Library of San Jose Metrics Project: Service Benchmarks, Round 2. Unpublished Report.* October 30, 2001.

3. A. Parasuraman, V.A. Zeithaml, and L.L. Berry, "SERVQUAL: A multiple-item scale for measuring customer perceptions of service quality." *Journal of Retailing* 64:1 (1988): 12-35.

4. David S. Carter and Joseph Janes, "Unobtrusive data analysis of digital reference questions and service at the Internet Public Library: An exploratory analysis." *Library Trends* 49:2 (Fall 2000): 251-265.

5. Anne R. Kenney, Nancy Y. McGovern, Ida T Martinez, and Lance J. Heidig, "Google meets eBay: What academic librarians can learn from alternative information providers." *D-Lib Magazine* 9:6 (June 2003). Available at: http://www.dlib.org/dlib/june03/kenney/06kenney.html. Accessed on 9/15/03.

6. Joseph Janes, Chrystie Hill and Alex Rolfe, "Ask-an-Expert Services Analysis." *Journal of the American Society for Information Science and Technology* 52:13 (2001): 1106-1121.

7. *The Reference Assessment Manual.* Ann Arbor: Pierian Press, 1995.

8. McClure, Charles R. et al. *Statistics, Measures and Quality Standards for Assessing Digital Reference Library Services: Guidelines and Procedures.* Syracuse, N.Y.: Information Institute of Syracuse, School of Information Studies, Syracuse University; Tallahassee, Fla.: School of Information Studies, Information Use Management and Policy Institute, Florida State University, 2002, p. 59.

9. McClure, Charles R. et al. *Statistics, Measures and Quality Standards for Assessing Digital Reference Library Services: Guidelines and Procedures.* Syracuse, N.Y.: Information Institute of Syracuse, School of Information Studies, Syracuse University; Tallahassee, Fla.: School of Information Studies, Information Use Management and Policy Institute, Florida State University, 2002, p. 60.

10. Meola, Marc and Sam Stormont, *Starting and Operating Live Virtual Reference Services.* New York: Neal-Schuman Publishers, 2002.

11. Ianuzzi, Patricia. "We Are Teaching But Are They Learning? Accountability, Productivity, and Assessment." *The Journal of Academic Librarianship.* Vol. 25 No. 4 (1999): 304-305.

12. Peters, Thomas A. "Current Opportunities For The Effective Meta-Assessment of Online Reference Services." *Library Trends.* Vol. 49 No. 2 (Fall 2000): 334-349.

13. Churkovich, Marion and Christine Oughtred. "Can an Online Tutorial Pass the Test for Library Instruction? An Evaluation and Comparison of Library Skills Instruction Methods for First Year Students at Deakin University." *Australian Academic and Research Libraries.* Vol. 33 No. 1 (March 2002): 25-38.

14. Michel, Stephanie. "What Do They Really Think? Assessing Student and Faculty Perspectives of A Web-Based Tutorial to Library Research." *College and Research Libraries.* Vol. 62 No. 4 (2001): 317-332.

15. Samson, Sue. "What and When Do They Know: Web-based Assessment." *Reference Services Review.* Vol. 28 No. 4 (2000) 335-342.

16. Bloom, B.S. *Taxonomy of Educational Objectives: The Classification of Educational Goals, Handbook I: Cognitive Domain.* Longmans: New York, 1956.

17. Pausch, L.M. and M.P. Popp. "Assessment of Information Literacy: Lessons From The Higher Education Assessment Movement." ACRL 8th National Conference, Nashville, Tennessee, 1997.

18. Fenske, R. and Roselle, A. "Proving the Efficacy of Library Instruction Evaluation." *Research Strategies.* Vol. 16 No. 3 (1999): 175-185.

19. Fowler, Clara S. and Elizabeth A. Dupuis. "What Have We Done? TILT's Impact On Our Instruction Program." *Reference Services Review.* Vol. 28 No. 4 (2000): 343-348.

20. Hayworth, Gene, and Malcolm Brantz. "Developing An Online Library Instruction Program: ACC's Online Library Tutorial." *Colorado Libraries.* Vol. 28 No. 4 (Winter 2002): 39-42.

21. Churkovich, Marion, and Christine Oughtred. "Can an Online Tutorial Pass the Test for Library Instruction? An Evaluation and Comparison of Library Skills Instruction Methods for First Year Students at Deakin University." *Australian Academic and Research Libraries.* Vol. 33 No. 1 (March 2002): 25-38.

22. Hayworth, Gene, and Malcolm Brantz. "Developing An Online Library Instruction Program: ACC's Online Library Tutorial." *Colorado Libraries.* Vol. 28 No. 4 (Winter 2002): 39-42.

23. Colborn, Nancy Wootton and Rosanne M. Cordell. "Moving From Subjective to Objectives: Assessments of Your Instruction Program." *Reference Services Review.* Fall/Winter 1998: 125-137.

24. Dewald, Nancy. "Web-based Library Instruction: What is Good Pedagogy?" *Information Technology and Libraries.* Vol. 18 No. 1 (1999): 26-31.

25. Hall, Brandon. *Web-Based Training Cookbook.* New York: John Wiley and Sons, 1997.

26. Dewald, Nancy. "Transporting Good Library Instruction Practices into the Web Environment: An Analysis of Online Tutorials." *The Journal of Academic Librarianship.* Vol. 25 No. 1 (January 1999): 26-32.

27. Wright, Carol A. "Application of The Model Statement To A Basic Information Access Skills Program at Penn State University." In *Read This First: An Owner's Guide to The New Model Statement of Objectives for Academic Bibliographic Instruction*, edited by Carolyn Dusenbury et al. Chicago: American Library Association, 1991, pgs. 22-33.

28. Reichel, Mary and Mary Ann Ramey, Eds. *Conceptual Frameworks for Bibliographic Instruction: Theory Into Practice*. Littleton, CO: Libraries Unlimited, 1987.

BIBLIOGRAPHY

Bloom, B.S. *Taxonomy of Educational Objectives: The Classification of Educational Goals, Handbook I: Cognitive Domain*. Longmans: New York, 1956.

Churkovich, Marion and Christine Oughtred. "Can an Online Tutorial Pass the Test for Library Instruction? An Evaluation and Comparison of Library Skills Instruction Methods for First Year Students at Deakin University." *Australian Academic and Research Libraries*. Vol. 33 No. 1 (March 2002): 25-38.

Cotton, Nancy Wootton and Rosanne M. Cordell. "Moving From Subjective to Objectives: Assessments of Your Instruction Program." *Reference Services Review*. Fall/Winter 1998: 125-137.

Dewald, Nancy. "Transporting Good Library Instruction Practices into the Web Environment: An Analysis of Online Tutorials." *The Journal of Academic Librarianship*. Vol. 25 No. 1 (January 1999): 26-32.

Dewald, Nancy. "Web-based Library Instruction: What is Good Pedagogy?" *Information Technology and Libraries*. Vol. 18 No. 1 (1999): 26-31.

Facets of Quality for Digital Reference Services (http://www.vrd.org/facets-1000.shtml).

Fenske, R. and Roselle, A. "Proving the Efficacy of Library Instruction Evaluation." *Research Strategies*. Vol. 16 No. 3 (1999): 175-185.

Hall, Brandon. *Web-Based Training Cookbook*. New York: John Wiley and Sons, 1997.

Hayworth, Gene, and Malcolm Brantz. "Developing An Online Library Instruction Program: ACC's Online Library Tutorial." *Colorado Libraries*. Vol. 28 No. 4 (Winter 2002): 39-42.

Ianuzzi, Patricia. "We Are Teaching But Are They Learning? Accountability, Productivity, and Assessment." *The Journal of Academic Librarianship*. Vol. 25 No. 4 (1999): 304-305.

McClure, Charles R. et al. *Statistics, Measures and Quality Standards for Assessing Digital Reference Library Services: Guidelines and Procedures*. Syracuse, N.Y.: Information Institute of Syracuse, School of Information Studies, Syracuse University; Tallahassee, Fla.: School of Information Studies, Information Use Management and Policy Institute, Florida State University, 2002.

Michel, Stephanie. "What Do They Really Think? Assessing Student and Faculty Perspectives of A Web-Based Tutorial to Library Research." *College and Research Libraries*. Vol. 62 No. 4 (2001): 317-332.

Pausch, L.M. and M.P. Popp. "Assessment of Information Literacy: Lessons From The Higher Education Assessment Movement." ACRL 8th National Conference, Nashville, Tennessee, 1997.

Peters, Thomas A. "Current Opportunities For The Effective Meta-Assessment of Online Reference Services." *Library Trends*. Vol. 49 No. 2 (Fall 2000): 334-349.

Reichel, Mary and Mary Ann Ramey, Eds. *Conceptual Frameworks for Bibliographic Instruction: Theory Into Practice*. Littleton, CO: Libraries Unlimited, 1987.

Samson, Sue. "What and When Do They Know: Web-based Assessment." *Reference Services Review*. Vol. 28 No. 4 (2000) 335-342.

Wright, Carol A. "Application of The Model Statement To A Basic Information Access Skills Program at Penn State University." In *Read This First: An Owner's Guide to The New Model Statement of Objectives for Academic Bibliographic Instruction*, edited by Carolyn Dusenbury et al. Chicago: American Library Association, 1991, pgs. 22-33.

doi:10.1300/J120v46n95_10

Costing Reference:
Issues, Approaches, and Directions
for Research

Melissa Gross
Charles R. McClure
R. David Lankes

SUMMARY. The Assessing Quality in Digital Reference project is a first step toward understanding the cost of digital reference services in libraries. This article presents three measures isolated by project participants as being most useful for their immediate needs: total cost of providing digital reference service, the cost of digital reference service as a percent of the total reference budget, and the cost of reference as a percent of the total library or organizational budget. In addi-

Melissa Gross is Assistant Professor, Florida State University, School of Information Studies, and Senior Research Fellow, Information Use Management and Policy Institute, 246 Louis Shores Building, Tallahassee, FL 32306-2100 (E-mail: mgross@lis.fsu.edu). Charles R. McClure is Francis Eppes Professor, Florida State University, School of Information Studies, and Director, Information Use Management and Policy Institute (E-mail: cmcclure@lis.fsu.edu). R. David Lankes is Assistant Professor, Syracuse University, School of Information Studies, and Director, Information Institute of Syracuse (E-mail: rdlankes@ericir.syr.edu).
Address correspondence to Melissa Gross.

[Haworth co-indexing entry note]: "Costing Reference: Issues, Approaches, and Directions for Research." Gross, Melissa, Charles R. McClure, and R. David Lankes. Co-published simultaneously in *The Reference Librarian* (The Haworth Information Press, an imprint of The Haworth Press, Inc.) No. 95/96, 2006, pp. 173-186; and: *Assessing Reference and User Services in a Digital Age* (ed: Eric Novotny) The Haworth Information Press, an imprint of The Haworth Press, Inc., 2006, pp. 173-186. Single or multiple copies of this article are available for a fee from The Haworth Document Delivery Service [1-800-HAWORTH, 9:00 a.m. - 5:00 p.m. (EST). E-mail address: docdelivery@haworthpress.com].

174 ASSESSING REFERENCE AND USER SERVICES IN A DIGITAL AGE

tion, it reviews selected outstanding issues in the ongoing question of how to determine the cost of reference services in libraries and offers direction for further study toward a general cost model for information services. doi:10.1300/J120v46n95_11 *[Article copies available for a fee from The Haworth Document Delivery Service: 1-800-HAWORTH. E-mail address: <docdelivery@haworthpress.com> Website: <http://www.HaworthPress.com> © 2006 by The Haworth Press, Inc. All rights reserved.]*

KEYWORDS. Digital reference, cost studies, information service evaluation, reference services standards

INTRODUCTION

In 1936, Louis R. Wilson predicted that in ten years' time libraries would have methods in place for determining the costs of services and would be able to use them to defend their work (Lopez, 1973). It was a grand thought; however, here at the dawn of the new millennium we still do not have a clear idea of what reference services cost and no standard costing model that libraries can adopt to collect this data in a uniform way. The proliferation of electronic resources and the development of digital reference services have further complicated the problem of how to determine what it costs to deliver reference services. Nonetheless, the perceived benefits of understanding the cost of providing these services remain much the same.

Costing data is needed for:

- Planning
- Cost/benefit analysis
- Determining the effectiveness of service
- Determining the efficiency of service
- Determining the allocation of resources
- Evaluation
- Substantiation of funding
- Determination of fees
- Comparison of services within and across organizations.

The current reference environment is an eclectic mix of delivery modes in which traditional reference is only one service point. E-mail and chat reference services have become increasingly commonplace, as have consortium relationships that allow libraries to expand service hours and to offer the expertise of subject specialists and special collections to a wider user base. In the meantime, librarians continue to experiment with other technologies, such as video conferencing and instant messaging, to determine their usefulness in the never-ending effort to improve access for users.

Because understanding cost is such an important component of service evaluation, it was one of the measures of primary interest in the Assessing Quality in Digital Reference Study undertaken by the Information Use Management and Policy Institute at Florida State University and the Information Institute of Syracuse at Syracuse University supported by OCLC and the Digital Library Federation and a wide range of library organizations (http://quartz.syr.edu/quality/). The overall goal of this project was to better understand and describe the nature of quality digital reference services in order to develop practical and reliable methods, measures, and quality standards to assess these services. This project represents a first step toward the collection of cost data on digital reference services in libraries. There are, however, larger problems in the collection and analysis of cost data than could be resolved within the constraints of this study. This article summarizes selected outstanding issues and current approaches offered for collecting cost data for electronic services and offers direction for further study.

DETERMINING THE COST OF A SERVICE

Cost analysis is the process of determining the expenses associated with the provision of a service or the production of a product. These expenses can also be described as inputs and can include a range of items such as raw materials, physical facilities, and labor. At the simplest level, the cost of a service can be described as the total of all expenses incurred in the process of providing the service (Kingma, 2001).

While this explanation appears simple, the truth is that the processes it describes become highly complex when considered in detail. For instance, the determination of expenses requires being able to differentiate between fixed costs and variable costs. Fixed costs are those libraries have to pay no matter how much business they are doing (such as the cost of the building). Variable costs are expenses that fluctuate depending on how much business the service is generating. For instance, the number of reference transactions received will affect the number of personnel needed to provide this service. During quiet periods at the desk, minimal coverage makes sense. During peak periods, more personnel are required and so this variable cost goes up.

However, the issue of assigning costs becomes even more complicated when the issue of time on task is involved. For instance, it is common for reference librarians to do other work at the desk, when they are not actively engaged in reference service. Should the labor costs associated with staffing the reference desk be charged to reference services when activities such as committee work, general collection development, outreach activities, and the like are being performed there?

Other activities are harder to categorize such as the time reference librarians spend with users troubleshooting hardware and software problems. When this activity is considered in the realm of electronic resources it becomes even more complex. What percentage of the library's information technology infrastructure should be considered as in direct support of digital reference services? How do we identify and track use of electronic resources, such as online databases, that are tied to reference services?

Murfin (1993) called for definition of the nature of reference activities and the outputs associated with them. For instance, reference work involves not only answering questions, but also the development of reference findings aids, such as bibliographies and the notes created and shared by reference librarians based on the day's experience as well as time in training to learn about new technologies used to provide reference services. Then too, how much of the cost of the reference collection should be charged to reference services? It is certainly needed to support this function, but it is also used directly by users who do not seek reference services. For additional discussion of the issues surrounding the determination of cost for information services, see Abels (1997), Kingma (2001), Murfin (1993), and Murfin and Bunge (1989).

. Beside the technical issues mentioned above, there are affective barriers that keep libraries and librarians from engaging in the process of costing reference. There has been an ongoing fear that this service is too expensive and that an investigation into cost would prove detrimental to a library's ability to provide reference services (Gross, McClure, & Lankes, 2002a; Lopez, 1973; McClure 1986; Murfin, 1993).

Approaches to Costing Reference

There is a major gap in the literature on Digital Reference Services in the area of economic models and accounting. Unfortunately, there is also a gap in this area as concerns the cost of providing traditional reference services. This means that currently it is not possible to extrapolate an existing standard procedure or measure to the provision of digital reference services. It also means that if it is desirable to compare the costs of different modes of providing reference, an extensive cost analysis of each method may be required to provide this information. Some examples of approaches that have been used in the literature to date include the input/output model, functional cost analysis, the library costing model, the equivalent valuation approach, and the cost minimization model.

The Input/Output Model. As concerns traditional reference services, Sayre and Thielen (1989) offer a cost analysis process for use in small public libraries. This is a very straightforward method in which the inputs necessary to support library services are isolated, measured, and accounted for and used to compute the per unit cost of a service based on the extent to which a service is utilized, i.e., how many people attend a program, number of items circulated, number of questions received at the reference desk.

Functional Cost Analysis. As noted above, assigning costs to library services is a much more complicated process than the input/output model suggests and for larger libraries this approach is likely too simplistic. Functional cost analysis is a related approach that has been explored in larger libraries that provide a variety of electronic resources as well as mediated searching with users (Abels, Kantor, & Saracevic, 1996).

This is another form of analysis in which the various costs of providing a service are defined and allocated to that service. In a study applying functional cost analysis to nine different reference services, the cost of reference service is reported to range from $1.16 to $35.52; the variation likely being due to how close an individual service came to operating at full capacity (ibid.). A great deal of the detailed work needed to ascertain costs performed in this study will also apply to the processing of costing out of various types of digital reference services.

The Library Costing Model. Hayes (1996) reports on the intricacies of assessing the costs related to the provision of electronic resources in support of reference within the framework of the Library Costing Model (LCM). While the LCM does not provide a detailed breakdown of the costs of digital reference, Hayes provides an interesting discussion of approaches to the problem of costing and provides insight on what might be involved in determining the true cost of providing digital reference services in libraries.

The Equivalent Valuation Approach. This approach, recently refined by Ryan and McClure (2003), is based on identifying an equivalent commercial service to the library service being costed. For example, the value of providing answers to digital reference questions is whatever a similar commercial form is able to convince users to pay. If a particular commercial firm charges $15.00 for answering a "basic" reference question then the value of the library digital reference question activity is estimated to also be $15.00 per correct answer.

The Cost Minimization Model. Hegenbart (1998) writes about cost minimization as part of an interesting analysis of the Internet Public Library (IPL) meant to determine if and how it might become self-supporting. This article provides a detailed discussion of the cost structure and cost components of the IPL and its potential economic viability from a business perspective. Her analysis is pertinent not only to the IPL, but also to the question of how any Web-based, not-for-profit information service can be economically viable.

In addition to the approaches discussed above, Murfin and Bunge (1989, pp. 17-35) offer four methods for assessing the cost of traditional library services in academic libraries. They are:

- *Method One:* Formula for Determining the Full Cost of the Reference Transaction.
- *Method Two:* A Reference Service Cost Effectiveness Index Based on Success, Helpfulness, Accessibility and Time/Cost.
- *Method Three:* Cost (time taken) per Successful Question.
- *Method Four:* A Cost Benefit Formula.

These formulas were tested in academic libraries in a project funded by the Council on Library for research purposes and used in the Wisconsin-Ohio Reference Evaluation Program. There may be value in using this work as a starting point for addressing the current issue of how to evaluate digital reference services from a cost standpoint.

CURRENT ISSUES IN DETERMINING COSTS

As discussed above, there are many issues concerning how to assign costs to reference service that were identified early on, but have yet to be resolved in regard to either traditional or digital reference service.

- What costs should be included in the equation? What portion of materials, overhead, personnel, equipment (Abels, 1997; Kuhlman, 1995; Murfin, 1993)?

- Are there agreed upon definitions for reference and reference activity (Abels, 1997; Lopez, 1973; Murfin, 1993)?
- How do we cost unmediated reference uses of equipment, software, and collections (Murfin, 1993)?
- Do new services require more specialized intervention on the part of staff (Evans, 1995)?
- Are digital reference services more time consuming (and costly) than traditional reference services (Janes, 2002)?
- How can reference service costs that are not easily identified in the traditional library budget such as telecommunication and equipment, software, fees, royalties, etc., be identified (Abels, Kantor, & Saracevic, 1996; Evans, 1995)?
- How can one establish costing criteria in terms of the goals and objectives of the service (Evans, 1995)?
- Necessary data is often not available or not gathered (Evans, 1995).
- Without national standards, inter-institutional comparisons are difficult to make (Evans, 1995; Kantor, 1981). This is especially troublesome in the current environment where various partnerships and consortium arrangements require the sharing of resources.
- To what degree are libraries willing to invest the time and resources to perform such cost studies (Evans, 1995)?
- Staff may be reluctant to participate in cost studies due to concerns about how such data will be manipulated and used and the perception that collecting such data is more trouble than it is worth (Lopez, 1973; McClure, 1986; Murfin, 1993; Gross, McClure, & Lankes, 2002a).
- Library management may be reluctant to engage in cost studies out of fear that the true cost of these services will be difficult to substantiate to funding bodies (Gross, Lankes, McClure, 2002a; Lopez, 1973; Murfin, 1993).

These are but a few of the issues that have yet to be addressed in terms of costing library reference services–but they offer a flavor of the work that has yet to be done in this area.

The Assessing Quality in Digital Reference Approach

The Assessing Quality in Digital Reference Services project used a "best practices" approach in which base line data was collected using a variety of methods during site visits at various types of libraries around the country. Data concerning current approaches to evaluating digital references services were also collected from librarians across the country through the project's "What's Your Story?" Web site. In addition to asking libraries to share current practice, they were also asked to share what they want to know about their services, but have not developed methods of assessment for, and also what do they need to know about their services in order to assess, improve, and promote them. This data on actual practices was also informed by an extensive and ongoing review of the literature on digital reference evaluation (Gross, McClure, & Lankes, 2002b).

The data collected in this process were used to inform the development of a set of measures, statistics, and metrics designed to evaluate various aspects of digital reference. The project advisory committee reviewed draft measures and statistics that the project team then revised. These measures were then field tested by a number of the libraries participating in the project and revised again, based on their feedback. The result of this project is the manual, *Assessing Digital Reference Library Services: Guidelines and Procedures* (McClure, Lankes, Gross, Choltco-Devlin, 2002).

The main finding of this process as pertains to the question of cost, is that the collection of cost data is only minimally performed by libraries and tends to be reported in very general terms. Digital reference is not normally considered separately from traditional reference for accounting or budgeting purposes. Both the cost of traditional reference and the cost of digital reference tend to be unknown. While participants in the project acknowledged the need for cost data mainly to meet demands from their funding agencies, they also voiced some fear that if the cost of providing digital references services were known, the low initial volume of transactions served through the new media might make it impossible for these services to continue. These concerns, coupled with a strong belief in the importance of providing reference service, echo an attitude toward the collection of cost data that has long been a stumbling block to understanding the costs of traditional reference services.

While the above issues need to be taken into account in order to address the question of how to successfully determine the cost of services, there are additional concerns and opportunities that previous work could not have anticipated, when reference services are migrated to the digital realm.

For example, there is a need to establish definitions for the types of reference services being provided in order to categorize services for the purpose of determining costs and making comparisons. In practice, it is not necessarily easy to differentiate between traditional reference services and electronic reference services or between electronic reference services such as e-mail or chat because they are not always provided as separate, distinct services. For example, reference transactions that begin in a traditional face-to-face mode may be completed electronically through the electronic delivery of a PDF file or an e-mail response that follows after the user has left the building. Chat services may move to an e-mail-based format or even result in a face-to-face reference interview in some cases. How are these hybrid transactions to be categorized for costing purposes?

In the Assessing Quality in Digital Reference project a digital reference transaction is defined as one in which all communication between user and staff is conducted electronically or digitally (2002). Hybrid questions are accounted for separately in order to provide a measure of control and consistency in assessing this new and growing service role.

On the opportunity side of the new reference environment, the nature of much of the media used to provide digital reference has the effect of doing away with the ephemeral nature of the traditional reference transaction where the reference librarian often summarizes the question, its negotiation, and the result of the interaction with a hash mark. With digital reference comes the ability to capture the reference question, the reference process, and its resolution in a fixed format for later assessment. Records of reference transactions can now be harvested to feed Frequently Asked Question pages, inform collection development, and for a variety of evaluation uses such as determining the correct answer fill rate, facilitating peer review of reference work, and providing exact statistics on the number of questions received and answered, how long it takes to answer a reference question, and the number of transactions by day of week and time of day, which can make the calculation of cost more accurate and improve management functions such as determining staffing levels.

Determining the Cost of Digital Reference–A First Level Solution

As stated above, the manual produced by the Assessing Quality in Digital Reference project is the beginning of an ongoing process to develop statistics, measures, and quality standards to assess and improve digital reference services. The measures included in the manual are based on literature reviews, input from advisory committee members, and were field tested by a number of libraries participating in the project. Its overall purpose is to improve the quality of digital reference services and assist librarians to design and implement better digital reference services, which meet user information needs.

In the area of cost, three measures were isolated by project participants as being most useful for their immediate needs. These are the total cost of providing digital reference service, the cost of digital reference service as a percent of the total reference budget, and the cost of reference as a percent of the total library or organizational budget.

Cost of digital reference service. This statistic summarizes the total cost of providing digital reference service at the level and to the extent that an individual library is able to calculate this cost. There are many barriers to the collection of this data including problems with how in-house records are kept and the relative difficulty of prorating costs where reference services are completely integrated (the same staff provide traditional and digital reference at the same time) and where cost factors, such as subscriptions and licenses to online resources and databases, are available for use in other departments or by users at home.

The stakeholders in the Assessing Quality of Digital Reference project recognize that there are many issues and considerations that need to be resolved in the costing of reference service, but also strongly feel it necessary to begin collecting this data at whatever level they can. There is increasing recognition that achieving understanding of cost factors, at whatever level they are available, is crucial when developing budgets, planning, and making decisions about the allocation of resources.

Cost of digital reference service as a percent of total reference budget. This measure looks at the total cost of reference, to the extent that it can be described, in relation to the total budget used to support all reference services (traditional, digital, hybrid). This measure is useful, as it provides a picture of the relative cost of digital reference to the total reference budget allowing for appropriate allocations to be maintained for all reference services. Among project participants, this measure was important to the digital reference setting because the cost of digital reference can often be comparatively high due to possible staffing issues, costs of resources, and training needs.

This measure can be difficult to compute relative to a library's ability to determine the real costs of the overall reference budget. For instance, it has been found that in the overall budget, automation and reference budget lines may be separate and the prorating of the cost of fee-based online databases may not allow for differentiations between use by digital reference, use by traditional reference, or use by patrons in the library or in remote locations. Additional problems may result when digital reference service is provided within a consortium arrangement.

Cost of digital reference as a percent of total library or organizational budget. This measure looks at expenditures for digital reference as a percent of the total budget for the total library. This measure is another aid to understanding the relative cost of this service to the organization as a whole. As stated above, informed decision-making relies on understanding the cost of providing services. This measure, like the others, will improve with the library's ability to agree upon the prorating and assignment of the cost of inputs such as staff and electronic resources. However, the process of collecting the data and beginning to work through these issues organizationally is an important step toward developing budgeting and accounting procedures that allow for the development of standard costing models for information services.

WHERE TO NEXT?

Clearly, the measures suggested above are only preliminary steps toward helping libraries collect cost data that will help them describe, improve, and promote reference services. A cost analysis model is still needed that will provide a method that supports cost comparisons by service type, between institutions, and for the appropriate assignment of costs in consortium arrangements. In the Assessing Quality for Digital Reference project it was determined that in addition to the issues outlined above a cost analysis model must provide a process that:

- Allows for the accounting of costs in a standardized way that makes the collection and analysis of data as uncomplicated as possible.
- Is accurate and reliable.
- Allows libraries to make accurate comparisons between different types of reference services.
- Allows for comparison of costs across libraries.
- Allows for appropriate value assignment to work completed in consortium relationships.
- Allows for the inclusion of cost data in the electronic transaction.
- Is meaningful to decision makers.
- Is meaningful to staff.
- Helps libraries to continue to build a culture of evaluation that includes continuing education for staff that demonstrates the value of evaluation.

It must also be remembered, however, that understanding the cost of providing service does not mean that minimizing cost is the ultimate goal of cost analysis. Assessments of cost must include assessments of service quality in order to provide a balanced view of library operations (Murfin, 1993). The Assessing Quality in Digital Reference project provides measures to assess service quality and a process for libraries to use in developing quality standards for digital reference services. This manual also gives guidance in the assessment of impacts and benefits that are needed to provide a context for determinations of cost and cost efficiency. Outcomes as well as outputs need to be measured and considered.

It may be that as interest in the service aspects of digital libraries grows, the economics of providing this service will get more attention. As it is, there is little to inform libraries that want to consider this issue. Further, as collaborative models continue to develop, the question of how to share the costs of providing 24/7 digital reference services, in what will inevitably be a global forum, has already come to light as an issue that will soon need resolution (Kresh, 2001).

Murfin (1993) points out that the development of cost data for reference services must be part of an overall effort to assign costs to all services provided by libraries in order to place the cost of reference services in perspective and to allow for a full understanding of service costs in libraries. But in fact, the degree to which libraries are committed to developing and maintaining such cost data as an overall ongoing evaluation effort is unclear.

In completing the Assessing Quality in Digital Reference Project, one reference librarian commented to a member of the study team that the evaluation–and costing–of digital reference was a procedure in search of practitioners. Until there is greater interest among library administrators–or perhaps greater pressures to justify services–research in costing library reference services is likely to be slow. Nonetheless, such research is essential and as budgets continue to tighten, increased concern about costing reference services may occur.

ACKNOWLEDGEMENTS

Research for this paper was performed as part of the Assessing Quality in Digital Reference Services conducted by the Information Institute of Syracuse at Syracuse University and the Information Use Management and Policy Institute at Florida State University and funded by OCLC, The Digital Library Federation, and a wide range of library organizations. The authors would like to thank all the participants in this study for their support and participation.

REFERENCES

Abels, Eileen G. "Improving Reference Service Cost Studies." *Library & Information Science Research*, 19 (1997): 135-152.

Abels, Eileen G., Kantor, Paul B., and Saracevic, Tefko. "Studying the Cost and Value of Library and Information Services: Applying Functional Cost Analysis." *Journal of the American Society for Information Science* 47 (1996): 217-227.

Evans, John E. "Cost Analysis of Public Services in Academic Libraries." *Journal of Interlibrary Loan, Document Delivery, and Information Supply* 5 (1995): 27-70.

Gross, Melissa, McClure, Charles R., and Lankes, R. David. "Assessing Quality in Digital Reference Services: Preliminary Findings." In *Implementing Digital Reference Services: Setting Standards and Making It Real: Proceedings of the 2001 VRD Conference*, edited by R. D. Lankes, C. R. McClure, M. Gross, and J. Pomerantz. NY: Neal-Schuman Publishers, 2002a.

Gross, Melissa, McClure, Charles R., and Lankes, R. David. "Assessing Quality in Digital Reference Services: An Overview of the Key Literature in Digital Reference." In *Implementing Digital Reference Services: Setting Standards and Making it Real. Proceedings of the 2001 VRD Conference*, edited by R. D. Lankes, C. R. McClure, M. Gross, and J. Pomerantz. New York: Neal Schuman, 2002b.

Hayes, Robert M. "Cost of Electronic Reference Resources and LCM: The Library Costing Model." *Journal of the American Society for Information Science* 47 (1996): 228-234.

Hegenbart, Barbara. "The Economics of the Internet Public Library." *Library Hi Tech* 16 (1998): 69-83.

Janes, Joe. "Digital Reference: Reference Librarians' Experiences and Attitudes." *Journal of the American Society for Information Science and Technology* 53 (2002): 549-566.

Kingma, Bruce R. *The Economics of Information: A Guide to Economic and Cost-Benefit Analysis for Information Professionals*, 2nd edition. Littleton, CO: Libraries Unlimited, 2001.

Kresh, Diane N. "Libraries Meet the World Wide Web: The Collaborative Digital Reference Service." *ARL Newsletter* 219 (December 2001): 1-6.

Kulhman, James R. (1995). "On the Economics Of Reference Service: Toward a Heurustic Model for an Uncertain World." In *Library Users and Reference Services*, edited by J. B. Whitlatch. New York: The Haworth Press.

Lankes, R. David, McClure, Charles R., and Gross, Melissa. (2001). Assessing Quality in Digital Reference Services. Syracuse, NY: Information Institute of Syracuse at Syracuse University and the Information Use Management and Policy Institute at Florida State University. http://quartz.syr.edu/quality/.

Lopez, Manuel D. Academic Reference Service: Measurement, Costs, and Value. *RQ*, 12 (1973): 234-242.

McClure, Charles R., Lankes, R. David, Gross, Melissa, and Choltco-Devlin, Beverly. *Statistics, Measures, and Quality Standards for Assessing Digital Reference Library Services: Guidelines and Procedures*. Syracuse, NY: Information Institute, 2002.

McClure, Charles R. "A View from the Trenches: Costing and Performance Measures for Academic Library Public Services." *College and Research Libraries* 47 (1986): 323-336.

Murfin, M. E. "Cost Analysis of Library Reference Services." *Advances in Library Administration and Organization* 11 (1993): 1-36.

Murfin, Marilyn, and Bunge, Charles. *A Cost Effectiveness Formula for Reference Service in Academic Libraries*. Washington, DC: Council on Library Resources, 1989.

Ryan, Joe, and McClure, Charles R. *Economic Impact of the Hawaii State Public Library System on the Business and Tourism Industries*. Honolulu, HI: Hawaii State Public Library System, 2003.

Sayre, Ed, and Thielen, Lee. "Cost Accounting: A Model for the Small Public Library." *The Bottom Line* 3 (1989): 15-19.

doi:10.1300/J120v46n95_11

Instruction in a Virtual Environment: Assessing the Needs for an Online Tutorial

Wendy Holliday
Sharolyn Ericksen
Britt Fagerheim
Rob Morrison
Flora Shrode

SUMMARY. In 2002, librarians at the Utah State University (USU) Libraries were awarded a grant to develop online tutorials. The major design challenge was to create tutorials specific to USU resources and students, including distance learners, while also making them flexible so

Wendy Holliday and Britt Fagerheim are Reference Librarians; Sharolyn Ericksen is Library Assistant; Rob Morrison is Coordinator of Distance Education Library Services; and Flora Shrode is Head of Reference, all at Utah State University, 3000 Old Main Hill, Logan, UT 84322.

[Haworth co-indexing entry note]: "Instruction in a Virtual Environment: Assessing the Needs for an Online Tutorial." Holliday, Wendy et al. Co-published simultaneously in *The Reference Librarian* (The Haworth Information Press, an imprint of The Haworth Press, Inc.) No. 95/96, 2006, pp. 187-211; and: *Assessing Reference and User Services in a Digital Age* (ed: Eric Novotny) The Haworth Information Press, an imprint of The Haworth Press, Inc., 2006, pp. 187-211. Single or multiple copies of this article are available for a fee from The Haworth Document Delivery Service [1-800-HAWORTH, 9:00 a.m. - 5:00 p.m. (EST). E-mail address: docdelivery@haworthpress.com].

that other Utah colleges and universities can adapt them for their own needs. The tutorials also needed to address the information behavior of a new generation of students accustomed to using computers and the Internet. While recent studies have begun to address some gaps in our knowledge of the information behavior of the Web Generation, we conducted a needs assessment to help us create a tutorial that more accurately addresses the existing knowledge and behavior of undergraduates at USU. We used multiple methods to determine the learning needs of our audience and to provide guidance for the design process. *doi:10.1300/J120v46n95_12* *[Article copies available for a fee from The Haworth Document Delivery Service: 1-800-HAWORTH. E-mail address: <docdelivery@haworthpress.com> Website: <http://www.HaworthPress.com> © 2006 by The Haworth Press, Inc. All rights reserved.]*

KEYWORDS. Online tutorials, needs assessment, undergraduate students, information behavior

With the advent of new networked technologies, librarians have been faced with the challenge of providing services in a virtual or online environment. From complex end-user search systems to e-mail and chat reference, many of the library's core functions now take place, at least in part, online. Instruction is no exception. Over the past decade, libraries have experimented with virtual instruction. Online tutorials have been a mainstay of these efforts. While the technology has changed from static HTML pages to Flash and streaming video, the core function of the tutorial, to teach patrons how to conduct research effectively, has not.

In the summer of 2002, Utah State University Libraries received a grant to develop an online tutorial. The grant was funded by the Utah Electronic College (UEC) for curriculum/course development. The Electronic College is part of the Utah System of Higher Education's Technology and Distance Education Initiative and has a mission to ensure that all of Utah's citizens, regardless of geographic location or work and life commitments, can earn associate and baccalaureate degrees at a distance. The tutorial is meant to support a variety of courses taught in Utah institutions of higher education.

The tutorial design team, comprised of five reference librarians on the USU Libraries' Education Committee, faced several challenges regarding the online tutorial's purpose, intended audience, content, and distinguishing features. The design team wanted to create a tutorial specific to USU resources and students, including distance learners, while building a product that would be flexible so that instructors or librarians at other Utah colleges and universities could easily adapt it to meet their needs. Additionally, we did not want to duplicate excellent, existing online courses or tutorials, such as Utah's Internet Navigator or the Texas Information Literacy Tutorial (TILT). The tutorial needed to address the *Information Literacy Competency Standards for Higher Education* (http://www.ala.org/acrl/ilcomstan.html) set forth by the Association of College and Research Libraries of the American Library Association. In keeping with the UEC grant guidelines, we also wanted to build the tutorial so that it would be as easy to use for distance learners as students who are on campus.

Finally, we needed to determine just what to teach in the online tutorial. In an initial examination of other academic library tutorials, we noted that many of these tutorials are very specific and tool-based. Many teach users how to find books and articles in the online catalog and local databases, for example.[1] We were uncertain whether a tool-based approach alone could address the information behavior of a new generation of students who are accustomed to using computers and the Internet. We also thought a tool-based approach might not be flexible enough for our requirements. In order to address these design challenges, we engaged in a formal needs assessment to help us determine the actual learning needs of our users and guide the design process.

LITERATURE REVIEW

As part of the assessment, we reviewed the relevant literature on undergraduate information behavior and tutorial design. Recent literature on undergraduate information behavior tends to focus on three areas: information preferences; searching behavior; and the broader research process. Recent literature in the first area explores undergraduate use of the Web and the library. Most of these studies are quantitative in nature. A Pew Foundation study notes that all students surveyed had begun using computers by the time they were 18 years old, and nearly half began using the Internet before they entered college.[2] Not surprisingly, studies show that undergraduate students are heavy users of the Web and less frequent users of academic libraries. An OCLC survey reported that three out of four students agree that they are successful in finding school-related information on the Web.[3] Students generally find that the Web is easy to use. Even before the widespread adoption of the Web,

Valentine noted that students tend to look for the quickest and easiest way to complete an assignment.[4] The Web likely accommodates this tendency.

Several qualitative studies have explored the information-seeking behavior of students, including common search and navigation tactics and help-seeking behavior. Using a survey method, Schwartz found that academic library users search several systems, including subscription databases and the free Web, in one sitting, and that they tend to multitask, having several windows open at once. They also tend to be satisfied with their searches and think that online systems are easy to use, possibly mistaking speed with ease of use. Schwartz also noted that many patrons do not seek assistance, either from online help or from reference librarians.[5] Augustine and Greene, in an observational study, noted that students like to use familiar tools and that they had a hard time understanding library resources and how they are organized.[6]

In an exploratory study using focus groups, Young and Von Seggern found that students were frustrated by "infoglut" and had difficulty knowing where to start. They identified several instructional needs for students, including more starting points and strategies for searching information; greater skill at sifting through large quantities of information; and the ability to find good sources for their needs.[7]

The image emerging from these search behavior studies suggests that undergraduate students are quite comfortable with the Web and often go there first when seeking information. They have acknowledged or unacknowledged difficulty dealing with large amounts of information, developing effective search strategies, and evaluating information sources. While all of these studies provide intriguing glimpses of undergraduate information behavior, ranging from common search moves to preferences for electronic sources, there are still some gaps in the literature. As the Pew Study suggests, information seeking is more seamlessly integrated into college students' larger Web habits.[8] Schwartz also notes that search behavior studies tend to become outdated quickly because of rapid technological changes. Also few studies explore, in a more naturalistic way, how students approach a complex information environment in which subscription databases and free Web sources are all available from the same platform, a computer with a Web browser.[9]

What exactly are students' instruction needs in this new environment? The literature on online tutorials focuses on pedagogical issues of learning styles and technological challenges, rather than the skills that undergraduate students need to know in the current environment. Nancy Dewald, for example, has written extensively on transferring good pedagogy from the classroom to a Web-based environment. She calls for Web-based tutorials to include interactivity and the teaching of concepts rather than pure mechanics, but she says little about the concepts or material that today's students need to know.[10] Another significant body of literature on online tutorials looks at individual case studies, focusing on the technology and instructional design issues central to their creation.[11] Few of these studies address curricular content.

THE NEEDS ASSESSMENT

In order to better determine our desired learning outcomes, we engaged in a formal needs assessment to try to explore gaps in students' skills and knowledge regarding the research process. We based this assessment on Instructional Systems Design (ISD). ISD is one of the most popular instructional methods used today in the development of instruction. Simply stated, instruction is made up of systems that interact with each other. These systems consist of the learners, the instructional materials, the instructor, and the learning environment. The interactions of these systems constitute the formal teaching and learning process.[12] ADDIE (Assessment, Design, Development, Implementation, and Evaluation) is a widely used ISD model. These areas of the ADDIE model work together both linearly and concurrently. In order to adequately discern the needs of a new or existing educational system (such as the online tutorial), it is helpful to conduct an assessment of resources available, prior research done in similar situations, research of other tutorials, and the needs of the target audience.

Our assessment research included an observational study, focus groups, formal evaluations of other tutorials, and a literature review on tutorial design and undergraduate information behavior. Combined, these methods helped identify gaps and needs that we incorporated into the tutorial design.

OBSERVATIONAL STUDY

Methods

We conducted an observational study, based on a common usability methodology, in order to observe a small sample of students actually navigate and search in the library environment. We hoped to observe common behaviors and develop at least a sketchy mental model of the information environment among undergraduates.[13] Specifically, we wanted to observe students use multiple Web-based systems in one sitting.

We developed a series of typical research and library-related tasks, such as finding a full-text article on a topic. We began with a seemingly easy question, finding the library hours, to promote confidence. We also included an open-ended task, which asked students to do the first step of a 5-page paper on Internet privacy. We pilot tested the tasks with a student library worker and changed the wording and order of the initial tasks. The complete task list can be found in Appendix A.

We observed eight students attempt the tasks. Each task was written on a slip of paper. Students were asked to complete the task as naturally as possible and we asked that they give up when they might in a real situation. We discouraged students from being more persistent than normal, but there was likely some of this behavior. Students were also asked to "think aloud" as they were working on each task, so that we could record their thought processes, assumptions, and feelings. Microsoft Producer was used to capture the screen activity (such as mouse clicks) and these verbalizations. Both were transcribed for analysis. A facilitator was present to encourage the students to think aloud, while another team member took notes in the case of technology failure.

Observational tests were also conducted at a USU branch campus in eastern Utah to determine whether distance learners might have different learning needs. A librarian observed eight students using similar tasks. The distance students displayed similar behavior. The results of those tests confirmed the findings reported below.[14] The research team coded the transcriptions of the screen activity or search moves with the matching verbalizations. Open coding was applied, with only a broad schema. Team members were told to look for general categories such as barriers, common errors, common search tactics, etc. Once the transcripts were coded by each team member, the team agreed on the final codes and categories and the transcripts were re-coded an additional time.

Findings

The research team found that five major categories emerged from the observational study: barriers, behaviors, expectations, values, and feelings. Barriers included gaps in knowledge about the kinds of information sources available or the lack of effective search skills. Many students, for example, had difficulty selecting the proper tool to find a specific format of information. They searched for articles in the online catalog rather than an index, for example. Behaviors included browsing subject-based lists, experimenting or guessing, and returning to a familiar path. Many students, for example, returned to a search tool that had been previously successful, even if it was inappropriate for the current task. When asked to find a journal article, for example, one student decided to click on "Circulation" on the library home page, because "circulation worked good [sic] earlier."[15]

Common expectations included the desire to "type words in a box," regardless of the type of resource, such as a browsable list. Students also expected to find an exact match for their query or information need. For instance, students would often look for the word "women" on the subject list of databases, when suitable databases would have been found under "Social Sciences." Students valued information resources for their familiarity, such as the Web. Common feelings included uncertainty and frustration because of a lack of knowledge. Tables 1 through 4 summarize the findings.

In general, students were familiar with the Web and fairly confident in their skills in this environment. Students most often expressed uncertainty or frustration when they did not understand library terminology. Students expected to be able to type words in a box and get exactly what they needed as a result. Students had a very murky concept, however, of

TABLE 1. Common Barriers

Barriers	Number of Occurrences*
Lack of knowledge about how information is organized	n/a
Lack of knowledge about information formats	n/a
Lack of knowledge about library services	n/a
Improper tool selection (e.g., online catalog to find articles)	17 (out of 43)
Inappropriate search type (e.g., subject, keyword, alphabetical browse, etc.)	16 (out of 36)
Poor search construction or search term selection (e.g., adding stop words or dates to a journal title search)	12
Difficulty reading bibliographic records and interpreting results	10
Incorrect syntax or spelling	6

*The total *n* for each occurrence cannot be calculated. It could only be done accurately for specific and quantifiable actions, such as the search moves of selecting a tool or a search type, or typing search terms.

TABLE 2. Common Behaviors

Common Behaviors	Number of Occurrences
Scanning to get acquainted with a site	All users throughout
Browsing subject lists or directories	5
Experimenting (guessing at appropriate tool or path; random clicking)	25
Persistent unproductive behavior (e.g., changing search term or search type in an inappropriate search tool)	26
Return to familiar or previously successful path	13
Retreat from unfamiliar	5
Satisficing (choosing outcomes that might not be optimal)	1

TABLE 3. Common Expectations

Common Expectations	Number of Occurrences
Terms on website or in resource should match task exactly (e.g., looking for the terms "dictionary" on the library home page when looking for the Oxford English Dictionary online)	12
Typing words in box/search by query	6

TABLE 4. Common Information Values and Feelings

Information Values	Number of Occurrences
Familiarity (especially for the Web)	12
Feelings	
Uncertainty, confusion, or hesitation	4
Frustration	8
Confidence	1
Disappointment (in system, when something did not work)	3
Feeling incompetent	6

different types of information sources (e.g., "I'm not quite sure what a journal is"). When they made unproductive choices, such as selecting an inappropriate tool to search, they became frustrated and unable to recover from their errors because they lacked a deeper knowledge of the way information is produced and organized. This also led to persistent unproductive behavior, such as repeating similar searches in an inappropriate tool (e.g., trying a subject and then a keyword search in the Online Catalog to find articles).

FOCUS GROUPS

Method

The tutorial development team conducted focus groups to complement the findings from the observational study. Our goal for the focus groups was to understand better how students perceive the library and the research process. We also hoped that comments from these discussions would help us to understand and describe a preliminary mental model of the information-seeking process of undergraduates. We wanted to find out if undergraduate students at USU use the library and how they use it. We used the critical incident technique, asking students to begin the focus groups by recalling a recent assignment and describing how they conducted research.[16] The moderators followed up with open-ended questions designed to clarify and expand on these descriptions. (See Appendix B for the Focus Groups Questions.)

Following recommended protocol, we hired graduate students from USU's Instructional Technology department to serve as facilitators and arranged for focus group sessions to take place in a building centrally located on campus instead of in the library. The tactic of using neutral moderators in a neutral place was intended to reduce influencing focus group participants' responses.[17]

In recruiting undergraduate students to participate in the focus groups, we required volunteers to have been enrolled at the University for at least a semester. This restriction increased the chance that students would have at least some experience with the library. Recruitment channels included print advertisements posted across campus as well as in the University newspaper. Participants were paid ten dollars for their participation and offered refreshments. A total of thirty-eight students participated in four evening sessions. The participants included a range of majors. More women than men participated. A disproportionate number of seniors participated as well. This might be attributed to a higher level of motivation for volunteering for such studies among more advanced students (see Table 5-7).

Members of the online tutorial development project transcribed the focus group discussions and analyzed them for data relevant to the tuto-

TABLE 5. College of Participants

College	Number*
Agriculture	2
Business	6
Education	10
Engineering	2
Humanities, Arts and Social Science	7
Natural Resources	1
Science	3
Undeclared or no response	5
TOTAL	36

*Reflects one double major.

TABLE 6. Gender of Participants

Men	13
Women	22

TABLE 7. Academic Level of Participants

Freshmen	3
Sophomore	7
Junior	5
Senior	13
2nd Bachelor's Degree	2
No response	5

rial content. Again, research team members coded each transcript independently. Instead of open coding, we began with the categories that emerged from the observational study and then applied additional coding to the uncoded sections of the transcripts. From this set of codes, team members agreed upon a final set of codes and categories and the transcripts were coded by one team member again.

Findings

The focus groups supported and amplified the initial findings of the observational study. Students are highly motivated by convenience, speed, and familiarity. This affects how they search and the tools they select. Students preferred sources that were familiar or had worked before: "I've had a lot of success using the Online Catalog . . . that's mostly . . . where I go for most of my research." In some cases, they selected resources because of a recommendation by a teacher or, less frequently, a librarian. The most prevalent reason for selecting a resource was convenience, especially for full-text access. According to one participant, "I like to just find the articles I need right on there [EBSCO] because they're electronic, you know, already on there. And I find that easier than going to find the actual physical books."

In terms of information-searching behavior, participants generally preferred to query by keyword because it is a quick and familiar approach. One participant noted, "I rely on Google to do it for me, because . . . that's where I go . . . I just type in the word." Very few students mentioned browsing the classified shelves to find related material, applying advanced search limits, or citation chaining as a search strategy. Students also tended to "build bibliographies" rather than evaluate information and incorporate it into their own knowledge. Student comments suggest that they are highly motivated by assignment requirements, such as citing a specific number of scholarly articles, rather than selecting the most useful sources to write their papers:

> With the specific paper that I was working on, we couldn't use magazines and we can't use, we have to use more . . . in-depth research . . . journals and things like that. We couldn't use a lot of the other stuff.

Often called satisficing, some students were happy to find anything generally related to their topic, even if it was not the specific information they needed.[18] One student described the end of one research assignment:

> After those hours, I was like, "Okay [laughs] I'm done." So I just went home and wrote my paper with what I had. And then found other stuff, just off of Google or Yahoo or whatever.

A common learning barrier was the lack of knowledge of the information environment. Many students mislabeled tools they had used. One student seemed to confuse the Online Catalog with the article databases: "I usually go to the course catalog, not the course, just the online catalog, and do subject search, keywords and that'll usually pull up what journal articles they have, and then after that I'll go to the journal indexes and search some more." Some students admitted that they had no idea of what they were actually searching: "I never know which is which or how to get, find what I'm looking for."

Students expressed a high degree of confusion in determining the relevancy of their search results. In some cases, they had difficulty interpreting the bibliographic records. Some students even said they find Google results easier to assess, possibly because you can link directly to an actual document to determine relevance. According to one student, Google was easier than searching the library catalog because "the Online Catalog doesn't give me enough information to go on." In other cases, students were confused about why the system had retrieved some results:

> I think it's always hard to try to know what to put in to pull up what you want. I've done lots of searches before where it's pulling up all kinds of stuff and going, "How did you get that from that word I put in? [laughter] I don't want THAT at all."

In sum, student confusion was likely caused by a combination of factors, including:

- a lack of understanding of different types of knowledge and publishing patterns (e.g., why a book might be a better choice than an article, or vice versa)
- a lack of understanding of information formats and corresponding search tools
- a lack of knowledge of how databases are structured and searched effectively

These barriers led to the inability to evaluate the effectiveness of a search and modify search strategies as a result.

MENTAL MODEL

The focus groups and observational study suggested common elements of undergraduate information behavior, such as a desire to stick to the familiar and the high value placed on convenience and speed. The team then developed a mental model that captures some of this exploratory, qualitative data. In general, our students tended to view information as existing in an undifferentiated pool that could be searched via the computer. Students look at a computer screen, type words into a box, and then get results. Students generally do not envision any structures in the data underlying their computer searching. They consider searching to be a seamless process that should always work the same way, no matter what the computer screen (or search system) actually looks like.

As part of the assessment activities, the team members also conceptualized their model of the information universe. Librarians created a complex model reflecting ways in which users, information sources, metadata describing those sources, search systems, and librarians interact. The lines between the library, information providers, and the Internet are blurry. In some cases, the library contains the information sources and the metadata (the catalog) to describe and provide access to these sources. In other cases, the library purchases the metadata and access tools and then provides them to users via the World Wide Web. Tool selection depends on the information needed, and different tools require different search strategies.

The student model and the librarian model will obviously always be quite different in terms of complexity. The design team, however, used the discrepancies between these models as the focus for the instructional content of the tutorials.

One of the major discrepancies was the fact that the student model lacks the notion of different kinds of information sources. Further, the model implies a single tool, the computer, for discovering information sources. In both the focus groups and observational studies, students often failed or were frustrated in their searches because they selected an inappropriate information tool. Another significant missing piece in the student mental model was the notion of synthesis or process. Students often expected to find a single piece of information (such as an article or book) that would fit their need precisely. They did not seem aware of the multi-step process of finding different pieces of information from different sources. Nor did they seem aware of the need to synthesize any information with their own knowledge into a larger whole. The model was one of words in, then information out. In many cases, once students found anything that seemed generally related to their topics, they were satisfied that research was complete.

From here, we outlined several gaps that we wanted to address in our online tutorial. These shaped our learning outcomes (see Figure 1). We

FIGURE 1. Learning Outcomes

Learning Outcomes

Upon completion of the tutorial, students will be able to:

- Understand that research is a recursive process.
- Identify a specific information need and evaluate whether and how their results meet that need.
- Identify different types/formats of information and the different tools required to find them.
- Understand how databases are structured so that learning one system can transfer to another (e.g., understanding what a computer is looking for when a search is conducted).
- Synthesize information from a wide range of sources into a more meaningful whole.

wanted students to learn that research is a recursive process. Instead of looking for five citations for a bibliography, we wanted to help students learn how to figure out what they need to know, where to find it, and how to evaluate whether it answers their question or need. We also hoped to show that finding answers often leads to more questions. Instead of teaching them how to search a specific tool, we wanted to introduce how databases work more generally so that they can transfer skills from system to system. Finally, we hoped to show how information is synthesized into a larger whole, such as an argument, a thesis, or new knowledge.

EVALUATION OF OTHER TUTORIALS

The last element of the needs assessment was an evaluation of other online tutorials. We created a rubric to keep our evaluation focused on elements that would help us resolve our own design challenges. We also wanted to focus on the instructional content of these tutorials, so that we did not duplicate effort. The evaluation rubric included: target audience; language (e.g., the use of library jargon); navigation and layout; instructional load (e.g., time to complete a module); help features; instructional depth; and user accountability. We were particularly interested in the question of instructional depth because we had informally noted the tendency of online tutorials to focus on the mechanics of searching a specific tool (such as a library catalog), rather than deeper concepts. We used Bloom's taxonomy of educational objectives to structure our rubric.[19] In this taxonomy, we looked for instances of the following:

- knowledge (eliciting facts, major ideas, etc.)
- comprehension (translating or interpreting information)
- application (using skill or information in a new situation)
- analysis (breaking things down into parts or seeing patterns)
- synthesis (combining elements into a new whole; drawing conclusions)
- evaluation (judging according to criteria, assessing value of theories, etc.)

We evaluated eight tutorials in-depth from the following institutions: Colorado State University; Western Michigan University (Searchpath); University of Texas (TILT); University of Arizona (RIO); California State University (Information Competence Tutorials); University of Utah (Internet Navigator); Old Dominion University (Start Your Research Here); and the University of Sydney (Canterbury).

The results of the evaluation showed that most of the online tutorials targeted the knowledge area of Bloom's taxonomy (see Table 8). Most conveyed information about conducting research or using a particular tool without addressing the higher-level activities of analysis, synthesis, or evaluation.

DESIGN DECISIONS

The online tutorial is designed for undergraduate college students and aims to help them learn information literacy and research skills. The online tutorial can be found at http://library.usu.edu/Serv/Tutorials/ OMR-Tutorial/Index.html. Project team members intend for this approach to complement Utah's Internet Navigator, a well-established set of online instructional modules that highlights specific information tools. The tutorial emphasizes fundamental skills for information seeking and integrates steps in the research process, leading students to develop effective research strategies. We hope this approach will make the tutorial applicable to students' needs in a wide range of courses, including online classes for distance learners, and that it might convey transferable skills for lifelong learning. Unlike several of the tutorials we reviewed in our evaluation, the tutorial is designed to address higher or-

TABLE 8. Evaluation of Tutorials Using Bloom's Taxonomy

Knowledge Instances	Tutorials	Instances
Comprehension	• Cal State • Central Michigan • Old Dominion • Sydney • Texas • University of Arizona • Utah	Many
Application	• Utah	Few
Analysis	• Cal State • Colorado State • University of Arizona	Few
Synthesis	• Cal State University	Few
Evaluation	• Cal State University • Central Michigan • University of Utah	Few

der thinking skills, such as application and synthesis, in Bloom's Taxonomy.

The tutorial uses a scenario or problem-based approach in which students are introduced to a situation from a news story as a basis for identifying research questions and learning how to find information.[20] We used a real news story in which an elementary school student is punished under the zero tolerance drug policy for loaning her asthma inhaler to a friend. Tutorial users have the option to take one of two points-of-view held by characters in the story. Each path simulates steps in the process of defining research questions and conducting research, including identifying facts or advice likely to be needed for the chosen point-of-view. Within these scenarios, users answer research questions via a Web search engine, a database of scholarly journals, and a newspaper database. After we decided upon a scenario-based approach, we developed several drafts of the tutorial, using four points-of-view or scenarios. We determined that this was too cumbersome, so we scaled back to two paths.

The first point-of-view is that of the school principal who must determine what to do about the school drug policy. This path models the research process. The tutorial asks students to consider what research is needed and then identify potential information sources. To address students' lack of knowledge of the information environment, one of the learning barriers identified in the needs assessment, we included a table outlining the types of information sources available and which are most useful for different kinds of questions, under the heading "Where do you begin to look for answers?" This table is presented in the first scenario and reiterated later in the second scenario when students repeat the research process.

In order to teach a general strategy for identifying potential information sources, we provide students with a simplified model of how librarians approach reference questions in terms of academic disciplines, sources, and search tools. We asked students:

1. Who else would be interested in your topic? Who might do research on it?
2. Where might they publish or communicate their research and knowledge?
3. How do you find it?

We also ask students to explore a variety of sources to answer component questions and to document their findings and changing thinking throughout the process.

The second point-of-view, the parents of the child punished for loaning her inhaler, is less complete than the first. The first several drafts of the tutorial lacked interactivity. It was more of a "page turner," in which students read each screen without pausing to reflect. We added more interaction, using simple techniques, in the second scenario. After students have seen the research model presented in the first scenario, they are asked to pause and reflect on what they would do in the second scenario. Answers to the three framing questions (who? where? how?) are not revealed initially, giving students the opportunities to brainstorm. The answers, or suggested research strategies, are disclosed as pop-up windows, which increases the interactivity of the tutorial. The tutorial was created using Macromedia Dreamweaver, allowing us take advantage of several built-in features to easily add interactivity and provide opportunities for students to reflect on the research process. The pop-up windows use a pre-set action to open a browser window of a specified size. The integration of Dreamweaver with Macromedia's graphics program, Fireworks, provided a method to create labeled buttons which trigger the pop-up windows. In addition, Flash videos lead students through a sample database search and dramatize the scenario at the beginning of the tutorial. We are currently exploring ways to use a database residing on our server to record student responses in the worksheet. This would enable students to keep track of their research process online and then send results to a librarian or instructor in an easily readable format.

Users also have the option to work on their own research project, following the research steps outlined in the scenarios and using a worksheet provided in the tutorial. Students are encouraged to keep notes on their work, which they may print or e-mail to themselves, their instructors, or a librarian, as a research log. The tutorial can serve as an assignment in English or other introductory classes, possibly giving students credit toward their grade as an incentive to complete it. The tutorial has been incorporated into a menu of learning options for sophomore English courses. A brief lesson plan was developed around the tutorial, and instructors have the option to include all or specific sections of the tutorial as part of the students' information literacy goals. We plan to incorporate two additional scenarios into the tutorial, including a scenario in which one character takes the opposite point-of-view from the other characters. This scenario mimics a common sophomore English assignment in which students take stands on specific topics and then research the opposing arguments or points-of-view. The lesson plans can be found at http://library.usu.edu/instruct/eng2010/index.php.

IMPLICATIONS FOR FURTHER RESEARCH AND PRACTICE

The ADDIE process has not ended for the USU online tutorial project. The tutorial must now be evaluated with our learning outcomes in mind (see Figure 1). These clear learning outcomes highlight one of the values of the needs assessment process. We have clear goals for student learning that we can measure and use to refine both our online and in-person instruction. With the time and technical expertise required to develop a robust online tutorial, we felt we had to get it right not only technically, but pedagogically as well.

One interesting result of the online tutorial project was that it made us question and revamp some of our face-to-face instruction. For example, several librarians incorporated the "who, where, how" questions from the tutorial into instruction sessions. Informal in-class assessments suggest this is a fruitful exercise for teaching students to begin their information seeking in the most appropriate disciplinary tools.

Needs assessment techniques can be applied to the design of electronic reference services more generally. The time, resources, and steep technological learning curve for many e-reference projects (such as chat reference) require librarians to examine their goals, audience, and available resources very carefully. We must also remember to apply this knowledge to all of our services, whether they occur online or in-person. During an in-person reference encounter, for example, we can model how to break a large research question into component parts that might require multiple sources, rather than providing a laundry list of suggestions.

Needs assessment is a time-consuming process. The design team spent the better part of a year on the observational study and focus groups alone. While there were significant benefits in, we think, a better tutorial product and improved classroom teaching, a needs assessment of this type is not realistic for many library projects. Librarians need to keep the scope of their project in mind. However, there are some simple steps that librarians can take before embarking on any design project, whether it be developing online tutorials, virtual chat reference services, or complex Web-based subject guides and recommender systems.

First, review the relevant literature, not only on the technical requirements for the project, but also on your primary user group. While there is still much to be learned about user information behavior, for example, several bodies of literature can provide important clues for designing in an increasingly networked world. Human-computer interaction studies, for example, can provide important information for how people navigate information spaces and use common Web features.[21] A growing body of information science literature is beginning to develop a better idea of how people search for information on the Web, determine relevance, and navigate electronic information environments.[22] The education literature, especially as related to distance learners, can provide clues for how students learn in an online environment. More synthesis of this literature is required, and it should be noted that information behavior often seems to change as quickly as the systems themselves. Nevertheless, the literature is often the best and simplest place to begin assessing the needs of your particular audience.

Another cost effective needs assessment method is competitor evaluation. Look at similar products and tools developed by other libraries. Evaluate these products with a clear set of heuristics or principles in mind. For example, we focused our evaluation of online tutorials on what types of skills and knowledge they taught. Bloom's taxonomy provided a framework to assess where these skills fell along a defined spectrum. The evaluation suggested a gap that we might fill by focusing on knowledge synthesis, for example.

Finally, learn as much as you can firsthand about your specific group of users. The design team was influenced significantly by the field of usability. We knew that we could not learn everything about our diverse group of users (Utah undergraduates and distance learners from across the state). Nevertheless, we borrowed Jakob Nielsen's insight that testing only one user provides more information for your design than testing none.[23] We tried to triangulate our data collection methods in order to get a general, if preliminary, understanding of undergraduate information behavior and learning needs. We used both retrospective (focus groups) and observational methods. We informally polled our fellow reference librarians to see if our identified gaps in student knowledge matched their perceptions of student behavior.

We admittedly based our tutorial design on a limited sample that is in no way generalizable to a larger population. Nevertheless, using even a single method can provide a focus for designing online reference services and products. Needs assessment has a different goal than more general research studies, which attempt to find verifiable and replicable results and truths. In our case, needs assessment was part of a design process in which there were no perfect solutions. Again, borrowing from usability research, we tried to determine the best possible solutions among a series of trade-offs. In order to do this, we had to have a basic, if not completely generalizable picture, of our intended audience. We built our tutorial around a model of student behavior that emerged from a variety of sources and research methods. When designing and evaluating e-reference services, this same design philosophy can guide assessment methods that are cost-effective and appropriate for the scope of the project, resulting in products and services that better meet the needs of our users.

NOTES

1. See, for example, Research Instruction Online (RIO), University of Arizona, http://dizzy.library.arizona.edu/rio/; Start Your Research Here!, Old Dominion University, http://www.lib.odu.edu/libassist/tutorials/start/index.htm; Colorado State University Tutorials, http://lib.colostate.edu/tutorials/.

2. Steve Jones, *The Internet Goes to College* (Pew Internet and American Life Project, 2002 [cited November 21, 2003]): 2; available from http://www.pewinternet.org/reports/pdfs/PIP_College_Report.pdf.

3. OCLC, *White Paper on the Information Habits of College Students: How Academic Librarians Can Influence Student's Web-Based Information Choices* (2002

[cited November 21, 2003]): 3; available from http://www5.oclc.org/downloads/community/informationhabits.pdf.

4. Barbara Valentine, "Undergraduate Research Behavior: Using Focus Groups to Generate Theory," *Journal of Academic Librarianship* 19, no. 5 (1993): 300-304.

5. Jennifer Schwartz, "Internet Access and End-User Needs: Computer Use in an Academic Library," *Reference and User Services Quarterly* 41, no. 3 (2002): 253-62.

6. Susan Augustine and Courtney Greene, "Discovering How Students Search a Library Web Site: A Usability Case Study," *College & Research Libraries* 63, no. 4 (2002): 354-65.

7. Nancy J. Young and Marilyn Von Seggern, "General Information Seeking in Changing Times," *Reference and User Services Quarterly* 41, no. 2 (2001):159-169.

8. Jones, 2.

9. Schwartz, 260.

10. Nancy Dewald, "Transporting Good Library Instruction Practice into the Web Environment: An Analysis of Online Tutorials," *Journal of Academic Librarianship* 25, no. 1 (1999): 26-32; Nancy Dewald, "Web-Based Library Instruction: What Is Good Pedagogy?" *Information Technology and Libraries* 18, no. 1 (1999): 26-31; Nancy Dewald et al., "Information Literacy at a Distance: Instructional Design Issues," *Journal of Academic Librarianship* 26, no. 1 (2000): 33-44.

11. See, for example, Ann Marie Johnson and Phil Sager, "Too Many Students, Too Little Time: Creating and Implementing a Self-Paced, Interactive Computer Tutorial for the Libraries' Online Catalog," *Research Strategies* 16, no. 4 (2000): 271-84.

12. Walter Dick and Lou Carey, *The Systematic Design of Instruction* (New York: Harper Collins, 1996).

13. For an example of applying a usability methodology to investigate larger issues of information behavior, see Augustine and Greene. For more on observational usability testing in libraries, see Ruth Dickstein and Vicki Mills, "Usability Testing at the University of Arizona Library: How to Let the Users in on the Design," *Information Technology and Libraries* 19, no. 3 (2000): 144-151.

14. The protocol was slightly different, as the purpose of the branch campus study was to learn more about distance learners and their needs more specifically. The results reported in this article reflect the coding of the on-campus transcripts only, for reasons of consistency in data collection and analysis.

15. All quotations are taken directly from the transcripts.

16. For more information on the critical incident technique, see Christine Urquhart et al., "Critical Incident Technique and Explication Interviewing in Studies of Information Behavior," *Library and Information Science Research* 25, no. 1 (2003): 63-88.

17. Richard A. Krueger, *Focus Groups: A Practical Guide for Applied Research* (Thousand Oaks, CA: Sage, 1994).

18. For an explanation of satisficing in information behavior, see Denise E. Agosto, "Bounded Rationality and Satisficing in Young People's Web-Based Decision Making," *Journal of the American Society for Information Science and Technology* 53, no. 1 (2002):16-27.

19. Benjamin Bloom, *Taxonomy of Educational Objectives: The Classification of Educational Goals* (New York: D. McKay Co., 1956).

20. For a discussion of problem-based learning and information literacy, see Alexius Smith Macklin, "Integrating information literacy using problem-based learning." *Reference Services Review* 29, no. 4 (2001): 306-314.

21. See, for example, Ben Schneiderman et al., "Clarifying Search: A User-Interface Framework for Text Searches," *D-Lib Magazine* 3, no. 1 (1997): 1-18.

22. Harry Bruce, "User Satisfaction with Information Seeking on the Internet," *Journal of the American Society for Information Science* 49, no. 6 (1998): 541-56; Chun Wei Choo et al., "Information Seeking on the Web: An Integrated Model of Browsing and Searching," *First Monday* 5, no. 2 (2000); Eszter Hargittai, "Beyond Logs and Surveys: In-Depth Measures of People's Web Use Skills," *Journal of the American Society for Information Science and Technology* 53, no. 14 (2002): 1239-44; Bernard Jansen and Udo Pooch, "A Review of Web Searching Studies and a Framework for Future Research," *Journal of the American Society for Information Science and Technology* 52, no. 3 (2001): 235-46; Gary Marchionini, *Information Seeking in Electronic Environments* (Cambridge: Cambridge University Press, 1995); Peiling Wang et al., "Users' Interactions with World Wide Web Resources: An Exploratory Study Using a Holistic Approach," *Information Processing and Management* 36, no. 2 (2000): 229-251.

23. Jakob Nielsen, *Usability Engineering* (San Diego: Academic Press, 1994).

REFERENCES

Agosto, Denise E. "Bounded Rationality and Satisficing in Young People's Web-Based Decision Making." *Journal of the American Society for Information Science and Technology* 53, no. 1 (2002): 16-27.

Augustine, Susan and Courtney Greene. "Discovering How Students Search a Library Web Site: A Usability Case Study." *College & Research Libraries* 63, no. 4 (2002): 354-65.

Bloom, Benjamin. *Taxonomy of Educational Objectives: The Classification of Educational Goals.* New York: D. McKay Co., 1956.

Bruce, Harry. "User Satisfaction with Information Seeking on the Internet." *Journal of the American Society for Information Science* 49, no. 6 (1998): 541.

Choo, Chun Wei. "Information Seeking on the Web: An Integrated Model of Browsing and Searching." *First Monday* 5, no. 2 (2000).

Dewald, Nancy. "Transporting Good Library Instruction Practice into the Web Environment: An Analysis of Online Tutorials." *Journal of Academic Librarianship* 25, no. 1 (1999): 26-32.

_____. "Web-Based Library Instruction: What Is Good Pedagogy?" *Information Technology and Libraries* 18, no. 1 (1999): 26-31.

Dewald, Nancy et al. "Information Literacy at a Distance: Instructional Design Issues." *Journal of Academic Librarianship* 26, no. 1 (2000): 33-44.

Dick, Walter and Lou Carey. *The Systematic Design of Instruction.* New York: Harper Collins, 1996.

Dickstein, Ruth and Vicki Mills. "Usability Testing at the University of Arizona Library: How to Let the Users in on the Design." *Information Technology and Libraries* 19, no. 3 (2000): 144-51.

Hargittai, Eszter. "Beyond Logs and Surveys: In-Depth Measures of People's Web Use Skills." *Journal of the American Society for Information Science and Technology* 53, no. 14 (2002): 1239-44.

Jansen, Bernard J. and Udo Pooch. "A Review of Web Searching Studies and a Framework for Future Research." *Journal of the American Society for Information Science and Technology* 52, no. 3 (2001): 235-46.

Johnson, Ann Marie and Phil Sager. "Too Many Students, Too Little Time: Creating and Implementing a Self-Paced, Interactive Computer Tutorial for the Libraries' Online Catalog." *Research Strategies* 16, no. 4 (2000): 271-84.

Jones, Steve. *The Internet Goes to College* Pew Internet and American Life Project, 2002 [cited November 21, 2003]. Available from http://www.pewinternet.org/reports/pdfs/PIP_College_Report.pdf.

Krueger, Richard A. *Focus Groups: A Practical Guide for Applied Research.* Thousand Oaks, CA: Sage, 1994.

Marchionini, Gary. *Information Seeking in Electronic Environments.* Cambridge: Cambridge University Press, 1995.

Nielsen, Jakob. *Usability Engineering.* San Diego: Academic Press, 1994.

OCLC. *White Paper on the Information Habits of College Students: How Academic Librarians Can Influence Student's Web-Based Information Choices* 2002 [cited November 21, 2003]. Available from http://www5.oclc.org/downloads/community/informationhabits.pdf.

Schneiderman, Ben et al. "Clarifying Search: A User-Interface Framework for Text Searches." *D-Lib Magazine* 3, no. 1 (1997): 1-18.

Schwartz, Jennifer. "Internet Access and End-User Needs: Computer Use in an Academic Library." *Reference and User Services Quarterly* 41, no. 3 (2002): 253-62.

Valentine, Barbara. "Undergraduate Research Behavior: Using Focus Groups to Generate Theory." *Journal of Academic Librarianship* 19, no. 5 (1993): 300-04.

Urquhart Christine et al. "Critical Incident Technique and Explication Interviewing in Studies of Information Behavior." *Library and Information Science Research* 25, no. 1 (2003): 63-88.

Wang, Peiling et al. "Users' Interactions with World Wide Web Resources: An Exploratory Study Using a Holistic Approach." *Information Processing and Management* 36, no. 2 (2000): 229-51.

Young, Nancy J. and Marilyn Von Seggern. "General Information Seeking in Changing Times." *Reference and User Services Quarterly* 41, no. 2 (2001): 159-69.

doi:10.1300/J120v46n95_12

APPENDIX A

OBSERVATIONAL TESTING TASKS

1. What hours are the University Libraries open Fall semester?
2. If you are an undergraduate student, how long may you keep a book that you check out the library?
3. You need to get a copy of the book, *Women of China: Economic and Social Transformation* by Jackie West. But the USU libraries do not own it. How can you get a copy?
4. You have been asked to write a five-page paper in Internet privacy. What is your first step?
5. Find out if the library has any books on native plants in Utah.
6. Does the library own a copy of *Complete Book of Electronic Vehicles* by Sheldon R. Shacket?
7. Find out if the library has a copy of the *Journal of American History* from 1999.
   - If so, can you read an article from the journal on your computer?
8. Find a full-text article on the topic of pay equity for women.
9. Find the electronic version of the *Oxford English Dictionary*.

APPENDIX B

FOCUS GROUP QUESTIONS

1. Briefly describe a recent research assignment. How did you begin?
   Prompts/follow-up:
   --How did you hope that this might help?
   --What did you do next?
   --Can you give me an example?
   --What was most useful during the process?

2. Were there times during the research process when you got stuck or didn't know what to do next? What did you do?
   Prompts/follow-up:
   --What questions/confusions did you have?
   --How did you get going again?
   --Did you talk to anyone?
   --How did you hope this might help?
   --Can you give me an example?

3. Once you completed your research, what kinds of information sources did you use for your assignment?
   --Why did you choose these sources?
   --Which resources gave you the most useful information? Why?

4 Information Sources:
   a. Did you use the library web page? Did you find it useful? Why or why not?
   b. Did you use books . . .
   c. Did you use the Internet or World Wide Web . . .
   d. Did you use newspapers or magazines . . .
   e. Did you use people as information sources . . .

Virtual Reference Services and Instruction: An Assessment

Lesley M. Moyo

SUMMARY. This paper assesses the incorporation of instruction in library virtual reference services (VRS), and explores whether the rate, and nature of instruction provided to patrons during VRS sessions is different than that provided during face-to-face reference. The Penn State VRS was used as a case study in this assessment. An analysis of a sample of archived Penn State VRS transcripts was conducted to assess the nature and quantity of instruction provided based on the presence of defined instructional elements incorporated in the sessions. The paper discusses the similarities and differences in approach to instruction during VRS and face-to-face reference, and how these relate to overall instructional services in academic libraries. The paper also reviews findings of some similar studies cited in the literature. The findings of this study indicate that there is a significant amount of instruction taking place during both face-to-face reference and VRS. Furthermore, the approach to instruction in both reference environments is very similar. However, the VRS system in use at Penn State (LSSI Virtual Reference Toolkit), because of its technological features and capability, has facil-

Lesley M. Moyo is Head, Gateway Libraries (i.e., the *Gateway Commons*, an electronic reference center and the *Pollock Laptop Library*), Penn State University, University Park, PA (E-mail: lmm26@psu.edu).

[Haworth co-indexing entry note]: "Virtual Reference Services and Instruction: An Assessment." Moyo, Lesley M. Co-published simultaneously in *The Reference Librarian* (The Haworth Information Press, an imprint of The Haworth Press, Inc.) No. 95/96, 2006, pp. 213-230; and: *Assessing Reference and User Services in a Digital Age* (ed: Eric Novotny) The Haworth Information Press, an imprint of The Haworth Press, Inc., 2006, pp. 213-230. Single or multiple copies of this article are available for a fee from The Haworth Document Delivery Service [1-800-HAWORTH, 9:00 a.m. - 5:00 p.m. (EST). E-mail address: docdelivery@haworthpress.com].

itated new and unique enhancements to instructive reference that are not available in face-to-face reference. doi:10.1300/J120v46n95_13 *[Article copies available for a fee from The Haworth Document Delivery Service: 1-800-HAWORTH. E-mail address: <docdelivery@haworthpress.com> Website: <http:// www.HaworthPress.com> © 2006 by The Haworth Press, Inc. All rights reserved.]*

KEYWORDS. Virtual reference service–assessment, digital reference service–assessment, VRS–instruction, reference services–instruction, reference services–pedagogy, e-reference

INTRODUCTION

In most academic library reference situations nowadays, librarians are increasingly providing both reference and instructional support to patrons. This increasing rate of 'instructive reference,' particularly in electronic library settings, points to a convergence of the reference and instructional roles of librarians in facilitating patrons' access to electronic information. Reference situations in hi-tech libraries often require the librarian to teach patrons how to use a myriad of technology tools and resources that enable access to electronic/Web-based information. It is becoming more and more difficult to divorce the information being sought by library patrons from the media and technology that facilitates its storage, access, and transmission. Therefore, information literacy in an electronic environment also implies a level of technology literacy or competence that permits the information seeker to utilize various technology tools and resources in their quest for information. The convergence of instruction and reference roles of librarians in academic library environments is further perpetuated by the fact that in many academic libraries, including Penn State, the librarians who provide formal information literacy instruction are the same librarians who also provide reference support to patrons. Therefore, it is easy for the librarians to cross over from reference to instruction when assisting patrons during the reference process. Depending on the nature of the reference question at hand, it is often necessary for reference librarians to provide one-on-one instruction to the patron as part of the response to their question. Typically, such instruction tends to be provided when answering reference questions of an instructional nature that include 'how to' components, such as, how to search a particular database, how to configure a Boolean search, how to request interlibrary loan items online, etc. Moreover, librarians working in electronic environments are seizing more opportunities to create 'teachable moments' when answering questions that are not necessarily classified as being of an instructional nature, in order to assist library patrons working in these environments to become more effective independent researchers.

The proliferation of electronic collections and other Web resources in many libraries is, undoubtedly, generating a greater need for instructional support to patrons. In addition to formal library instruction, there is a growing need to integrate instruction in many other public services, including reference, to help patrons learn how to use various electronic resources such as databases, e-journals, e-books, etc., as well as the technology that facilitates their use. Although many library patrons may feel confident about their online/Web research skills, professional literature indicates that the majority of library users in academic settings have only basic to moderate research skills and are often unable to use advanced features of many electronic resources. In response to this trend, librarians are reaching out to patrons in the online environment and assisting them to improve their information literacy skills and competencies through various forms of instruction and mediation. Virtual reference service (VRS) is one way in which librarians have been able to reach out and continue to provide assistance to patrons in the online environment. However, being a relatively new service mode that is still rapidly evolving, VRS is being adopted mostly on an exploratory basis by many institutions. Librarians and other information professionals are still investigating its effectiveness in meeting the peculiar needs of patrons working online, and exploring its equivalency to face-to-face reference. In addressing various reference service issues, professionals have begun to assess aspects of VRS such as question types, duration of transactions, resources used in answering questions, and reference interview capabilities, to mention a few. Results of these and similar assessments will not only address immediate challenges of providing reference at a distance, but also illuminate the future role of VRS in overall reference and instruction services in libraries.

Although it is evident that the need for instructional support to patrons does not diminish as one moves from the face-to-face reference environment to the VRS environment, attempting to meet this need using similar methods used in face-to-face reference may be a challenge as the attributes of a face-to-face reference situation cannot be fully replicated in the virtual environment. There are some fundamental differences between the virtual and the face-to-face reference situations. For instance, the reference interview that helps clarify what a patron really needs may be hindered by the absence of visual cues when one is assisting a patron online. Moreover, the dialog between the librarian and the patron is highly dependent on the features and capabilities of the VRS system in use. As Ronan (2003) says, "Chat is a wonderful tool for teaching searching techniques. Depending upon the software being used, at the very least, the librarian can search in tandem with the user in the same databases in real-time, messaging while they search and sharing insights on effective keywords or ways to apply truncation and proximity operators to improve the search." Libraries employing more advanced VRS systems such as the LSSI Virtual Reference Toolkit are able to achieve more because of the superior system capabilities such as collaborative browsing, pushing pages, archiving of transcripts, creation of knowledge bases, etc., whereas those using simple chat systems, such as AOL instant messaging, are restricted to mostly text messaging. Therefore, it is ultimately the VRS system capability that defines the extent to which effective instruction can be incorporated into a VRS session. A VRS system that uses only the chat capability to provide reference services would have to depend on text messaging to assist/guide patrons. This may not be very effective when instructing a patron on how to construct a search. On the other hand, a VRS system that has co-browsing capability enables the librarian and patron to work collaboratively while constructing the search, and accompany text messaging with actual demonstrations in the appropriate databases and other e-resources where possible. Moreover, the co-browsing capability facilitates better engagement and active participation of the patron in configuring and executing a search.

The Penn State University Libraries began offering VRS in the fall of 2001. Starting with a pilot service that was offered to a limited population through the summer of 2002, the full service was later launched in fall 2002. At this time the service was expanded to the entire Penn State community comprising 24 campus locations. Currently 13 librarians provide VRS to the entire Penn State Community. The service currently employs the LSSI Virtual Reference Service Toolkit (version 2.5). This system not only incorporates co-browsing capabilities, but also has a host of other features that make it possible for librarians to provide detailed instruction to patrons, as evidenced in the archived transcripts.

From the fall of 2002 when the full service was launched, through spring 2003, 802 questions were answered. The summer of 2003, with reduced hours, saw a total of only 43 questions. In fall 2003, 775 questions were answered, bringing the total number of questions answered from the start of the full service to 1,620 by the end of the fall 2003 semester. Additional information and statistics of the Penn State Virtual Reference Service is available on the Web at: http://www.de2.psu.edu/faculty/saw4/vrs/stats/; Penn State Virtual Reference Service: Annual Statistics (2004).

Of the 1,620 questions answered by the end of fall 2003, 405 questions (25%) were sampled for analysis to determine the nature and rate of instruction inherent in the transactions. The results of this analysis were compared with typical reference transactions in the face-to-face reference environment, as reported in professional/research literature. Furthermore, the results were compared with the findings of a short survey of Penn State's VRS librarians conducted in March 2003, which incorporated questions requiring VRS librarians to compare their reference tactics in VRS situations to those in the face-to-face situations. Although there are some features of reference instruction that are peculiar to VRS, the overall results of this assessment indicate that the nature of reference instruction provided during VRS is not significantly different than that provided in face-to-face reference. However, instruction offered via VRS incorporates advantageous features that are not available in face-to-face instruction at a reference desk or in formal course-related instruction in a classroom-based session. This is particularly true when software used for VRS has features that facilitate enhancements to reference instruction.

Some instructional benefits of using the LSSI Virtual Reference Service Toolkit include:

- Ability to jointly construct a search with the user typing in the search terms, setting the search parameters, etc., under the guidance of the librarian. This allows more *active patron participation* than when a patron is sitting across the reference desk, with the librarian constructing the searches while the patron watches.
- Availability of the session transcript at the end of the session for the patron to review the *process* used to locate required information, and the *instruction* provided by the librarian.
- Incorporation of all visited links in the session transcript to review *tools and resources used* in locating the desired information.
- Ability for the librarian to review the session transcript and provide *follow-up instruction* via e-mail where necessary, using patron e-mail address and information provided at log-in time.

- Capability to create searchable knowledge-bases from previous reference sessions. Librarians can use the knowledge base as an *instruction resource* for answering previously asked questions. Patrons can use the knowledge base as an FAQ.

VRS as an instruction tool holds a lot of promise in addressing one-on-one instruction needs, as well as instruction needs of students at a distance. Through the chat transcripts and other logs, VRS also provides raw data such as user statistics, frequently asked questions, peak service times, frequently used databases, average session duration, patron satisfaction rate (from pop-up survey at the end of each session), etc. This information is invaluable for planning purposes.

INTEGRATION OF INSTRUCTION IN VRS AT PENN STATE: LIBRARIANS' PERSPECTIVES

In April 2003 a short survey of Penn State VRS librarians was conducted to assess their experiences on various aspects of the service, including their motivation to participate in VRS, workload issues, challenges and rewards of participating in VRS, etc. At that time, a total of eleven librarians were participating in providing reference to the entire Penn State Community. Among the questions asked in the survey, the following three questions related, directly or indirectly, to instruction during VRS:

1. During VRS, I tend to offer instruction

   a. Less often than face-to-face
   b. As often as during face-to-face
   c. More often than during face-to-face

2. During VRS my reference interviews tend to be

   a. Less in-depth than face-to-face
   b. No different from face-to-face
   c. More in-depth than face-to-face

3. Do you answer questions received through VRS differently than you would if received face-to-face or by phone? Please elaborate.

In response to the first question, 3 (27.3%) librarians said they tend to offer instruction less often in VRS than in face-to-face, while 8 (73%) librarians said they offered instruction in VRS as often as during face-to-face reference. None of the librarians responded that they offered instruction more often than during face-to-face reference.

In response to the second question, 5 librarians (45.4%) said they had less in-depth reference interviews than in face-to-face, 3 (27.3%) librarians responded that they had the same depth of reference interviews in VRS as in face-to-face reference, and 3 (27.3%) had more in-depth reference interviews than in face-to-face.

The third question drew a variety of comments and explanations on how the VRS librarians perceive and handle VRS questions as compared to questions in the face-to-face environment. Below is a sample of their responses, verbatim:

- I don't answer VRS questions differently, but I communicate differently.
- There is somewhat less verbal negotiation but a greater opportunity for visual guidance–actually showing users the process of finding information and the results–but still try to provide the same level of service.
- I tend to probe more because I cannot see or hear their [the students] reactions to my guidance. I also have time to perform side searches about their questions while they search a resource I've suggested. This action increases the number of fruitful searches since I can offer resources that I know will have the information they seek. In addition, I bide time while I call or browse the Website of other units for further recommendation.
- I usually do more of the work for the patron than normal. I show them different words or phrases to use, and tend to direct them to online resources more often.
- It seems like I need to go more in depth in VRS because I need to "draw out" the question more.

A review of the responses above reflects how Penn State VRS librarians handle instruction during VRS sessions, and shows a similar approach in instructive reference in both VRS and face-to-face reference. More detailed information on this survey and the Penn State VRS service in general are outlined by Ware et al. (2003).

ASSESSING INSTRUCTION IN PENN STATE'S VRS TRANSCRIPTS

While the previous short survey focused on getting Penn State VRS librarian feedback about how they handle instruction and other issues during VRS, the current study sought to review and assess the level of integration of instruction in VRS by defining and measuring instructional content in archived VRS chat transcripts starting from fall 2002, through fall 2003.

For purposes of this study, an instructional session is assessed as containing one or more of the following instructional elements:

1. Guiding patrons in navigating the library's Web resources
2. Recommending specific databases to be used, and explaining the reason for the selection
3. Helping the patron formulate a search strategy (e.g., Boolean searching)
4. Explaining the features of a particular database and showing how to use them
5. Providing search tips and tricks
6. Helping patrons understand the components of bibliographic citations/records
7. Showing (demonstrating) how to conduct online transactions such as ILL requests, placing personal holds, etc.
8. Helping patrons understand search results

The above instructional elements are adapted from those used by Johnston, Patricia E. (2003) in a similar study.

LITERATURE REVIEW

Johnston (2003) argues that although reference and instruction usually fall into different departments in libraries, they are closely related and librarians who offer reference and instruction must work collaboratively. In many situations the librarians who provide reference services also provide instruction. Indeed many reference librarians helping patrons at reference desks use instruction tactics. Johnston discusses the advantages of reference instruction in meeting individual needs of patrons. She highlights the use of digital reference as an instruction tool that provides individualized instruction at the time of need and in small quantities that address a specific need. Providing an analysis of 50 chat transcripts from LIVE, a virtual reference service offered by The University of New Brunswick, Johnston reports that 60% of the transcripts included some instructional elements (instances of instruction were identified based on a set of attributes describing various instructional possibilities, similar to the adapted list above), 30% required no instruction and 10% consisted of referrals to other departments or libraries. Of the questions that incorporated instruction, 43% included one instance of instruction, and 57% included two or more instances of instruction. Johnston concludes that instruction is happening in digital reference, but that this instruction is not a substitute for more formalized information literacy, but complements it by focusing on the needs of an individual patron.

McCutcheon and Lambert (2001), in an exploration of the relationship between reference and instruction, cite literature that discuss various connections between instruction and reference. Some of the literature suggests that both reference and instruction serve the same purpose and they are "intrinsically linked, complementary, and intertwined services." In some institutions, including Penn State, the librarians who participate in providing VRS also provide formal library instruction, both course-related and credit instruction. There is, therefore, an even greater possibility that these librarians approach VRS service from an instructive perspective.

The reference interview is one of the key elements that determine the success of an instructive reference session, and the quality of the one-on-one interaction between the librarian and the patron. Therefore, the ability to conduct a fruitful reference interview in the VRS environment will continue to be a key success factor in integrating quality instruction in VRS. Janes and Hill (2002) surveyed librarians to determine how they are adapting reference practice to the digital environment. One of the issues explored in their survey was the reference interview. Some of the responses by librarians in this survey indicated some concern and discomfort that because there are some constraints to conducting a good reference interview in the digital environment, this would adversely affect the ability to provide instruction as part of the virtual reference process, and that instruction provided would be limited.

Tenopir's review of electronic reference through the 1990s outlines changes reported by librarians. Some of the key changes reported are in library instruction, both formal instruction classes and point-of-use instruction. With regard to point-of-use instruction, she reports that the widespread availability of electronic resources requires more time spent helping users; moreover, in providing one-on-one instruction more time is being spent with each individual person. In some cases, overall reference statistics were reported to have declined as a result of more time being spent with individuals. One librarian responding to the survey reports that "our statistics are down and our workload is up. We can do more so each question takes longer as we explore and teach varied resources. The technologies allow us to do more and provide more information to patrons." Tenopir also suggests that point-of-use instruction is necessary because often patrons do not think that they need to attend formal instruction classes or use online instructional guides until they are ready to search. Although librarians see the increased need for instruction, patrons may not necessarily recognize that need. Tenopir concludes "The instructional role of reference librarians will become even more important in the future, with an increased need for formal information literacy instruction, more time required for detailed one-on- one point-of-use instruction, and the challenges of taking high quality instruction to remote users."

Campbell and Fyfe (2002) provide practices for successful one-on-one reference instruction in the face-to-face environment based on the model of the 'roving reference' in which reference librarians move among terminals in the reference area assisting patrons with their research needs. The practices outlined in their survey report indicate that librarians in this particular face-to-face setting were spending a significant amount of time assisting users, providing one-on-one instruction and helping them through entire search processes.

According to Beck and Turner (2001), students are most receptive to learning research techniques at the point of need. This may occur at the reference desk. One way suggested for librarians to provide instruction on the reference desk is to talk aloud as they conduct a search for the user to ensure that the user is following along. In the VRS environment, instead of 'talking aloud' the librarian can let the patron do the actual searching while he/she provides direction/guidance via text messaging. This way, the librarian engages the patron to actively participate in the search.

In another assessment of reference at the University of Illinois at Springfield, Green and Peach (2003) set out to document reference as a teaching and learning activity. A survey questionnaire similar to evaluation instruments used in assessing classroom teaching was given to patrons who had complex reference questions. Afterwards, patrons completed and submitted their feedback on the reference experience. Results of this assessment validate reference instruction as a teaching and learning activity. The results indicate that the majority (92%) of the respondents who participated in the survey agreed that by the end of their reference experience they had learnt something new about how to do research.

Mercado (1999) outlines technological developments in online database searching, and how these have impacted library instruction over the years. Among her topics of discussion is what she refers to as '*Electronic Information Literacy*,' information literacy in an electronic context. She states that the "new technological developments in libraries have increased the need for help from librarians, and have had a powerful influence on library instruction." Mercado goes on to say that "one result of the proliferation of electronic databases is that reference librarians spend less time behind the desk and more on instructional tasks, often one-on-one with a library user." However, Mercado points out that for the remote library user, information literacy instruction would have to be achieved via the Internet, and that currently training offered through online tutorials, one-on-one instruction; research consultation, class instruction, library credit classes, etc., all do not fully address the instruction needs of remote users. VRS appears to be a key solution to this dilemma. Coffman (2001) outlines how VRS can help libraries "Go the distance" in meeting the instruction needs of remote learners. He profiles the features of VRS systems that make it possible to use them for assisting patrons virtually.

METHODOLOGY

This study began with a general definition of what constitutes an instructive reference session: "*A reference session that incorporates activities that impart knowledge or skill.*" Following this definition, the study adapted and adopted a list of the attributes of an instructive reference session developed by Johnston (2003). These attributes were used to evaluate the presence, nature, and quantity of instruction in the sampled transcripts.

Penn State VRS chat transcripts were reviewed from the start of the service in fall 2002 (excluding the pilot phase) to the end of the 2003 fall semester. Out of a total of 1,620 transcripts, 405 (25%) were drawn from the archives. The sample transcripts were analyzed for instructional content based on the list of instructional attributes, and coded accordingly.

After the selection and coding, the transcripts were also reviewed and classified into categories based on the McClure et al. (2002) question typology. However, the focus of the analysis was on determining the type and frequency of instructive elements in the session, rather than on the question type.

Correlations were explored to determine whether there was a relationship between question typology and presence/quantity of instructive elements.

This study also involved a review of the literature addressing instruction in face-to-face reference to compare issues and descriptions of this type of reference with those in VRS as found in this study. However, due to the fact that face-to-face reference transactions have no transcripts that allow detailed review, the comparison of VRS reference with face-to-face reference is not based on common attributes/criteria. While on the one hand, observations about instruction during VRS is based on transcript analysis, on the other hand, observations about instruction during face-to-face reference is based on case studies and surveys reported in the literature, as well as the librarian perspectives reported in the short survey of Penn State VRS librarians.

FINDINGS

Instruction in Penn State VRS Sessions

Types of Questions

Although the McClure et al. (2002) reference question typology was not applied when sampling questions for inclusion in the survey, it was clear in the end that questions that incorporated the highest rate of instruction fell largely into two categories, the *instructional* and *research and subject* categories as described by McClure et al.:

1. *An instructional question is one in which the user asks for assistance in using electronic resources that may be available to them, and that may provide the answer to another reference question. Examples of instructional questions include requests for information on how to construct a search statement in an online periodical database, how to search the online catalog (OPAC), how to request books and other materials from the catalog, how to limit*

searches by domain in a particular search engine, and how to use Boolean Logic.

2. *A research [or Subject Request] question is one that requests a variety of information on a particular topic. The research [or Subject Request] question will most likely have many components to the answer (i.e., articles from journals, book citations, essays, statistics, raw data) and the answer may consist of responses sent in many formats (e-mailing of full-text articles or citations, pushing websites, documents or spreadsheets, image files, video clips, etc.).*

Even though questions that incorporated the highest rate of instructive elements fell in the above two categories, other questions outside these two categories drew responses that incorporated instruction. For instance, a patron who asked a bibliographic question to verify a citation, not only received the information they requested, but was also taught how to conduct a search that yields the information they required in order to verify the citation.

Instruction Integration Rate

Of the 405 transcripts analyzed in this study, 349 (86%) contained at least one instructional element; 267 (66%) contained more than one instructional element; and 32 (8%) questions contained as many as five instructional elements. This was the highest rate of incorporation of instruction in the VRS transactions reviewed.

The most prevalent instructional element was *"Guiding patrons in navigating the library's web resources"* and was present in 316 (78%) of the transcripts. *"Providing search tips and tricks"* was the next most prevalent, occurring in 267 (66%) of the transcripts, and *"Recommending specific databases to be used, and explaining the reason for the selection"* occurring in 109 (27%) of the transcripts. *"Helping patrons understand the components of bibliographic citations/records"* was the least prevalent element in the instructive sessions, followed by *"Helping patrons understand search results."*

Question Typology and Instruction Integration

Based on the McClure et al. question typology, out of the 349 questions that contained at least one instructional element, 183 fell into the *Instructional* category, and 122 into the *Research or Subject Request* category. Forty-four questions fell into other categories, but the patron still received instruction as part of the response.

INSTRUCTION IN FACE-TO-FACE REFERENCE

Although there's not much published in the literature to provide detailed analyses of instructional content based on specific instructional elements in individual face-to-face reference transactions, there is, nevertheless, some research that shows the nature and extent of instruction taking place in face-to-face reference.

Mercado (1999), Campbell and Fyfe (2002) describe scenarios that illustrate an increase of personalized one-on-one instruction during face-to-face reference, as a result of the proliferation of electronic resources in libraries, and the increased capabilities of technology systems, allowing librarians to do more for patrons. Librarians are spending more time with individuals on a one-on-one basis. Furthermore, Green and Peach (2003) also conclude in their study that reference instruction is taking place in the face-to-face setting and is indeed an effective teaching and learning activity.

DISCUSSION

A review of different reference situations with both in-person and virtual patrons indicates that librarians provide a significant amount of instruction during both VRS and face-to-face reference. Instruction in both types of environment is comparable; however, it is evident that there are additional technological factors that influence not only the ability to offer instruction during VRS, but also the nature of instruction that can be offered.

Some Factors That Affect the Ability and Desire to Offer Instruction During VRS

One of the key factors is the capability of the software in use. As Coffman (2001) states, to be truly effective, virtual reference systems must provide the capability to escort the patron anywhere on the Web, including in proprietary databases, therefore it is important for the VRS system to facilitate proxy-server-based co-browsing. Technology inadequacies may be a barrier to instruction during VRS. Moreover, technological malfunctions are also an impediment to successful instructive reference. As seen from the transcripts that were analyzed, 7 instructional transactions out of 405 ended abruptly due to technical glitches.

Access to online resources such as online databases, Web sites, etc., is necessary for librarians to offer effective instructive reference. In situations where the reference question requires the use of online databases or other Web resources that are readily accessible, librarians can offer comprehensive instruction incorporating demonstrations of how to configure and execute a search in a particular database, and explanation of some database features, limitations, etc. In cases where the questions required the use of offline material, referrals were made to other units for the patrons to receive assistance by visiting the library in person. Alternatively, the patron was offered a delayed response via e-mail, to allow the librarian time to consult offline resources.

The decision whether or not to incorporate instruction in a reference session is also influenced by the way the question is articulated. Some patrons' questions may indicate that they already understand what they are looking for, and how to search, they just need direction on where to find the database or Website that has the information. However, even when questions seem to indicate that the patron just needs assistance to locate a resource that they wish to search, there are opportunities for the VRS librarian to provide instruction, by proactively offering further help to the patron. For example, the two following questions from the Penn State VRS archives seem to indicate that the patron just needed help in locating the resources:

1. In my course materials for IST 110 there are several books listed in the resources page that say they are available full text on LIAS [library information access system] however I cannot locate them.
2. I am to use the ABI/INFORM Database available in the PSU Library "E-Journal" to answer some questions. Where can I find this?

On the other hand, some patrons' questions, such as the examples below, also from the Penn State VRS archives, indicate that they require more instructive assistance:

1. I was wondering what would be the best way to search for books pertaining to my Chemistry project, more importantly dealing with water hardness, softeners, EDTA, etc.?

2. I am doing an assignment for my first year seminar and I need to know how I would find the differences between popular and scholarly resources when doing research.

The second set of questions renders itself more to instruction because of the way the questions are articulated. However, even in answering the first set of questions, a librarian can still offer instruction by probing more, and determining whether the patron requires any help in searching once they have located the resource that they asked for. Therefore, the decision to incorporate instruction in a VRS session is not only based on the question typology, but also on the librarian's willingness to probe and offer further assistance even when the need for instruction is not apparent in the way the question is articulated.

One of the results of incorporating instruction in VRS is that sessions are prolonged. Sessions incorporating instruction are much longer than those without. Given that Penn State uses the LSSI VRT (Virtual reference Toolkit), which provides a multiple in-box feature allowing librarians to help up to about four patrons simultaneously (system capability is 16 simultaneous users), there's a possibility that a librarian helping several patrons at the same time might be less likely to go into lengthy instruction, especially in a situation where additional patrons are queuing for assistance. Therefore, overall traffic pattern during VRS service is another factor that might impact the nature and rate of incorporation of instruction in VRS. Similarly, in the face-to-face environment, a reference librarian may decide against offering extensive instruction to a patron at the desk if there are other patrons waiting to be served.

CONCLUSION

Reference service is one of the most variable and most personalized services in the library setting. Both face-to-face reference and VRS are increasingly incorporating instruction because of the growing need to teach patrons how to use the exploding electronic resources in libraries. The findings of this study indicate that there is a significant amount of instruction taking place during both face-to-face reference and VRS. Moreover, the approach to instruction in both VRS and face-to-face environments is very similar, and the technological features and capabilities of advanced VRS systems have facilitated new and unique enhancements to instructive reference that are not available in face-to-face reference.

The fundamental precepts of instructive reference are the same in both face-to-face reference and VRS. However, as a result of system features, instruction offered during VRS can be tracked more systematically. Depending on the features of the system in use, libraries can track the types of questions, nature and extent of instruction provided, resources used to answer the questions, etc. The instruction taking place during VRS can be assessed and measured more easily because of the ability to archive transcripts. On the other hand, instruction taking place during face-to-face reference is more difficult to assess and measure. However, librarians' experiences and various surveys indicate similar trends in instructive reference, regardless of whether it is virtual or face-to-face.

The conclusion of this assessment is that whereas VRS practice incorporates a significant amount of instruction to patrons, the instruction is not significantly different from the instruction inherent in face-to-face instruction. This study suggests that the main differences between the two instruction scenarios stems from technological factors. It was feared by some librarians that instruction via VRS to remote patrons would be very limited because of the absence of visual cues, voice, etc. On the contrary, technology systems that facilitate VRS offer some advantages to the reference process which are not available in the face-to-face environment, such as sharing of transcripts with patrons, archiving of transcripts, creation of knowledge bases, session logs and statistics, immediate feedback from the pop-up survey at the end of the session, and so on.

The instruction incorporated in VRS should be viewed as complementary to course-related instruction and should not be perceived as a replacement for standard library instruction sessions. As pointed out by Johnston (2003), VRS instruction provides just in time and just enough instruction for a specific need. Although patrons may apply the skills gained during VRS instruction to other research situations, that instruction tends to be very focused and may not address the broad information literacy issues covered during standard library instruction sessions. Similarly, patrons seeking assistance at reference desks in a face-to-face reference situation may receive one-on-one instruction focusing on their immediate need. However, they would still need to address their broad information literacy skills through formal library instruction sessions.

VRS will continue impacting library instruction programs in many ways. It is one of the ways libraries provide one-on-one instruction to individual patrons at their points of need, and it is also one of the few ways in which libraries can provide instruction at a distance to remote patrons. Furthermore, VRS allows the librarian to provide instruction within the same online environment that e-resources are located, so it is easy to incorporate Web searches and database searches within the reference session. Most pedagogic principles and precepts inherent in instructive reference will remain constant regardless of the new reference environment, while others will continue to evolve and change as a consequence of the new electronic environment.

REFERENCES

Beck, Susan E. and Turner, Nancy B. (2001) 'On the fly BI: Reaching and teaching from the reference desk' *Reference Librarian* 72 (1): 83-96.

Campbell, Sandy and Fyfe, Debbie (2002) 'Teaching at the computer: Best practices for one-on-one instruction in reference' *Feliciter* 48(1): 26-28.

Coffman, Steve (2001) 'Distance education and virtual reference: Where are we headed?' *Computers in Libraries* 21(4): 20-24.

Green, Denise D. and Peach, Janice K. (2003) 'Assessment of reference instruction as a teaching and learning activity: An experiment at the University of Illinois-Springfield' *College and Research Libraries News* 64(4): 256-258.

Janes, Joseph and Hill, Chrystie (2002) 'Finger on the pulse: Librarians describe evolving reference practice in an increasingly digital world' *Reference and User Services Quarterly* 42 (1): 54-65.

Johnston, Patricia E. (2003) 'Digital reference as an instruction tool: Just in time and just enough' *Searcher* 11 (3): 31-33.

McCutcheon, Camille and Lambert, Nancy M. (2001) 'Tales untold: The connection between instruction and reference services.' *Research Strategies.* 18:203-214.

McClure, Charles R.; Lankes, R. David; Gross, Melissa; and Choltco-Devlin, B. (2002) Statistics, Measures and Quality Standards for Assessing Digital Reference Library Services: Guidelines and Procedures. Syracuse, New York: Information Institute of Syracuse, School of Information Studies, Syracuse University.

Mercado, Heidi (1999) 'Library instruction and online database searching' *Reference Services Review* 27 (3): 259-265.

Penn State Virtual Reference Service: Annual Statistics. Penn State University Libraries. http://www.de2.psu.edu/faculty/saw4/vrs/stats/ (accessed 3/24/2004).

Ronan, Jana (2003) 'The reference interview online' *Reference and User Services Quarterly* 43 (1): 43-47.

Smyth, Joanne (2003) 'Virtual reference transcript analysis: A few models' *Searcher* 11 (3): 2-30.

Tenopir, Carol (1999) 'Electronic reference and reference librarians: a look through the 1990s' *Reference Services Review* 27 (3): 276-279.

Ware, Susan, Joseph Fennewald, Lesley Moyo, and Laura Probst (2003) 'Ask a Penn State librarian, live: Virtual reference service at Penn state' *The Reference Librarian* 79/80(2002/2003): 281-95.

doi:10.1300/J120v46n95_13

Index

Page numbers in *italic* indicate figures; page numbers followed by "t" indicate charts or tables; *See also* indicates related topics or more detailed lists of subtopics.

BOOK ORDER FORM!

Order a copy of this book with this form or online at:
http://www.HaworthPress.com/store/product.asp?sku= 5874

Assessing Reference and User Services in a Digital Age

— in softbound at $24.95 ISBN-13: 978-0-7890-3350-5 / ISBN-10: 0-7890-3350-X.
— in hardbound at $39.95 ISBN-13: 978-0-7890-3349-9 / ISBN-10: 0-7890-3349-6.

COST OF BOOKS _____

POSTAGE & HANDLING _____
US: $4.00 for first book & $1.50
for each additional book
Outside US: $5.00 for first book
& $2.00 for each additional book.

SUBTOTAL _____
In Canada: add 6% GST. _____

STATE TAX _____
CA, IL, IN, MN, NJ, NY, OH, PA & SD residents
please add appropriate local sales tax.

FINAL TOTAL _____
If paying in Canadian funds, convert
using the current exchange rate,
UNESCO coupons welcome.

❑ BILL ME LATER:
Bill-me option is good on US/Canada/
Mexico orders only; not good to jobbers,
wholesalers, or subscription agencies.

❑ Signature _____

❑ Payment Enclosed: $_____

❑ PLEASE CHARGE TO MY CREDIT CARD:
❑ Visa ❑ MasterCard ❑ AmEx ❑ Discover
❑ Diner's Club ❑ Eurocard ❑ JCB

Account #_____

Exp Date_____

Signature_____
(Prices in US dollars and subject to change without notice.)

PLEASE PRINT ALL INFORMATION OR ATTACH YOUR BUSINESS CARD

Name _____

Address _____

City _____ State/Province _____ Zip/Postal Code _____

Country _____

Tel _____ Fax _____

E-Mail _____

May we use your e-mail address for confirmations and other types of information? ❑Yes ❑No We appreciate receiving your e-mail address. Haworth would like to e-mail special discount offers to you, as a preferred customer.
We will never share, rent, or exchange your e-mail address. We regard such actions as an invasion of your privacy.

Order from your **local bookstore** or directly from
The Haworth Press, Inc. 10 Alice Street, Binghamton, New York 13904-1580 • USA
Call our toll-free number (1-800-429-6784) / Outside US/Canada: (607) 722-5857
Fax: 1-800-895-0582 / Outside US/Canada: (607) 771-0012
E-mail your order to us: orders@HaworthPress.com

For orders outside US and Canada, you may wish to order through your local
sales representative, distributor, or bookseller.
For information, see http://HaworthPress.com/distributors

(Discounts are available for individual orders in US and Canada only, not booksellers/distributors.)

Please photocopy this form for your personal use.
www.HaworthPress.com

BOF07